Touring East Coast Wine Country

A Guide to the Finest Wineries

The tasting room and winery at Lamoreaux Landing Wine Cellars in the Finger Lakes, New York.

TOURING EAST COAST WINE COUNTRY

A Guide to the Finest Wineries

Marguerite Thomas

Berkshire House Publishers
Lee, Massachusetts

Touring East Coast Wine Country: A Guide to the Finest Wineries
Copyright © 1996, 1997, 1999, 2002 by Berkshire House Publishers
Cover and interior photographs © 1996, 1997, 1999, 2002 by Marguerite Thomas and other credited sources.

ISBN 1-58157-057-0
ISSN 1056-7968 (series)

Editor: Constance Lee Oxley. Managing Editor: Philip Rich. Design and page layout: Dianne Pinkowitz. Cover design: Jane McWhorter. Index: Diane Brenner. Maps: Maps.com.

Berkshire House books are available at substantial discounts for bulk purchases by corporations and other organizations for promotions and premiums. Special personalized editions can also be produced in large quantities. For more information, contact:

Berkshire House Publishers
480 Pleasant St., Lee, MA 01238
800-321-8526
www.berkshirehouse.com
info@berkshirehouse.com

Manufactured in the United States of America

10 9 8 7 6 5 4 3 2 1

Berkshire House Publishers'
Great Destinations™ travel guidebook series

Recommended by NATIONAL GEOGRAPHIC TRAVELER and TRAVEL & LEISURE magazines.

. . . a crisp and critical approach, for travelers who want to live like locals.

USA TODAY

Great Destinations™ guidebooks are known for their comprehensive, critical coverage of regions of extraordinary cultural interest and natural beauty. The authors in this series are professional travel writers who have lived for many years in the regions they describe. Each title in this series is continuously updated with each printing, in order to insure accurate and timely information. All of the books contain over 100 photographs and maps.

Neither the publisher, the authors, the reviewers, nor other contributors accept complimentary lodgings, meals, or any other consideration (such as advertising) while gathering information for any book in this series.

Current titles available:
The Adirondack Book
The Berkshire Book
The Charleston, Savannah & Coastal Islands Book
The Chesapeake Bay Book
The Coast of Maine Book
The Finger Lakes Book
The Hamptons Book
The Hudson Valley Book (Spring 2003)
The Monterey Bay, Big Sur & Gold Coast Wine Country Book
The Nantucket Book
The Napa & Sonoma Book
The Santa Fe & Taos Book
The Sarasota, Sanibel Island & Naples Book
The Shenandoah Valley Book (Spring 2003)
The Texas Hill Country Book
Touring East Coast Wine Country

If you are traveling to, moving to, residing in, or just interested in any (or all!) of these enchanting regions, a **Great Destinations**™ guidebook is a superior companion. Honest and painstakingly critical, full of information only a local can provide, **Great Destinations**™ guidebooks provide you with all the practical knowledge you need to enjoy the best of each region. Why not own them all?

To David and Adam

Contents

CHAPTER ONE
History, Grapes & Marketing
1

CHAPTER TWO
New England
**CONNECTICUT, MASSACHUSETTS,
& RHODE ISLAND**
12

CHAPTER THREE
New York State
**LONG ISLAND, THE FINGER LAKES,
& THE HUDSON RIVER VALLEY**
26

CHAPTER FOUR
Mid-Atlantic States
**NEW JERSEY, PENNSYLVANIA,
& MARYLAND**
95

CHAPTER FIVE
Virginia
**COASTAL VIRGINIA,
NORTHERN & CENTRAL VIRGINIA,
& THE VIRGINIA MOUNTAINS**
117

CHAPTER SIX
Winery Restaurants & Lodging
153

CHAPTER SEVEN
Wine Information
167

Acknowledgments

With deepest thanks to the many people who encouraged, advised, and shared their knowledge and time with me. First, to the vintners whose expertise and enthusiasms for this project helped to steer me in the right directions. To Marsha Palanci, Lila Gault, Lynn O'Hare Berkson, and the many others who guided and inspired me with their common sense and creative ideas. To my family, friends, and colleagues who helped me taste and evaluate the wines. And special thanks to Jean Rousseau, publisher of Berkshire House, to managing editor Philip Rich for his unfailing patience and thoroughness, to my editor Constance Oxley for all her good work, and to sales and marketing director Carol Bosco Baumann for her thoughtful and energetic promotion of the book.

Introduction

The realization of a competitive wine industry in the East has taken 350 years to achieve. When Peter Stuyvesant was governor of New Netherland more than three centuries ago, he planted grapes on Manhattan Island in an attempt to develop a wine industry. In 1662, Lord Baltimore called his land grant in Maryland "The Vineyard" and, in his enthusiasm for wine, planted his own 300-acre plot of vines. Connecticut's official seal depicts three grape vines bearing fruit, a symbol of that state's early viticultural aspirations. George Washington grew grapes at Mount Vernon, but it was Thomas Jefferson who proved to be the most zealous early proponent of wine. Jefferson yearned to see serious wine produced in America. "It is desirable that it should be made here," he wrote, "and we have every soil, aspect, and climate of the best wine countries." For 30 years, Jefferson tried unsuccessfully to grow European grapes at Monticello.

What went wrong? Until recently, wine produced in the Eastern United States failed to attract the praise West Coast wines had been garnering for almost half a century. It wasn't just that California was better at promoting its product. The reason Eastern wineries failed to receive unconditional thumbs up from critics and consumers is because their wine simply wasn't good enough.

California, with its temperate climate and hospitable agricultural environment, has been turning out rivers of premium wine for many decades, while most of the rest of the country — where temperatures regularly range from root-splitting sub-zero to wilting stretches of high humidity in the upper nineties — lagged behind. Now, thanks to a host of factors coming together at the same time, including technological advances, agricultural improvements, and more progressive winery licensing regulations, we are at the dawn of a new era in American winemaking. In the Pacific Northwest, in New Mexico, Arizona, Texas, and other parts of the Southwest, in Missouri, Michigan, and most other Midwestern states, and certainly in the Eastern section of the United States, the wine industry is surging forward.

The radical alterations in both the content and format of the fourth edition of this book reflect the dramatic changes that have taken place over the past handful of years in the Eastern winemaking industry. A decade ago, when I began visiting wineries in the Eastern states and gathering information for the first edition of this book, the majority of the wines I tasted were, at best, run-of-the-mill (and to be frank, a lot of them were simply awful). Much of the wine in the East was still being made from hybrid and/or native American grapes, which impart a flavor that appeals mostly to local devotees but fails to attract a wider following. The revolutionary switch to the vinifera grapes from which the great wines of Europe and California are made was just beginning to sweep the East, but very few of the wines emerging then were in any sense competitive. And yet, there certainly were notable exceptions to the generally mundane quality — and it was these exceptions that inspired me to write the book in the first place, for they proved that the East was capable of producing great wine. The potential was clearly there, but several things stood between the promise and its fulfillment.

One of the first things the East lacked was winemakers who had considerable knowledge not only about the art and science of turning grapes into wine, but even more importantly perhaps, who had the experience of having tasted a broad range of the world's wine. There is no doubt that to succeed on a scale beyond local expectations, a winemaker must be familiar with the taste and traditions of the world's best wines. Indeed, the first wave of contemporary vintners to lead the Eastern states forward had trained their palates on European and California vintages — Luca Paschina (Barboursville), Eric Miller (Chaddsford), Konstantin Frank (Dr. Frank's), Peter Bell and Scott Osborne (Fox Run), Louisa and Alex Hargrave (Hargrave), and Susan and Earl Samson (Sakonnet) are among the pioneering producers of quality wine who come to mind.

Also lacking in the East were mature vinifera vineyards. While delicious wine is sometimes made from very young vines, the general wisdom holds that older vines contribute character, structure, and complexity to a wine. Since the evolution from hybrid grapes to European vinifera species occurred gradually in the East during the last couple of decades in the 20th century, only in the past few years has the region had a significant acreage of mature vinifera vines. A problem related to immature vineyards is that the composition of soil seems to be altered by decades of vines growing in it, and these changes will, in turn, affect the flavor of the grapes. So far as I know this notion has not been substantiated by scientific inquiry, but think of the great vineyards of Burgundy, for example, which have known no other crop for eons — surely the chemistry and textures of the soil there have been affected by the roots of vines burrowing deep into the earth for countless generations. If there is any truth to this hypothesis, Eastern vines will continue to produce increasingly superior grapes as the soils adapt.

Bringing vineyards up to speed is one of the most important things that has happened to the Eastern wine industry in the past few years. For that matter, modern vineyard practices have had an impact on quality everywhere in the world, but in regions such as the eastern United States where the weather is marginal, these viticultural advances have proven singularly crucial. New trellising techniques that open the vines to better sun and heat exposure, for example, have led to more complete ripening of the grapes. Viticulturalists are also learning that reducing the size of the grape crop usually results in richer flavors. Selecting clones most suitable for the conditions of specific vineyard sites has also greatly influenced the overall quality of grapes in the East. Other techniques in the vineyard — proper spacing between the rows, planting cover-crops, selecting sites with well-drained soils — all affect the ultimate outcome.

Stylistic focus was long missing in the East as winemakers tried to force their product to replicate the image of big, fruit-driven, heavily oaked wines of California. Only in recent years have vintners come to understand and appreciate the comparative delicacy of Eastern grapes and to recognize that too much time spent in new barrels masks the wine's fruit flavors, leaving nothing more than something resembling oak tea (to be fair, even California winemakers are lightening up on the oak these days).

One of the most heartening symptoms of Eastern viticultural success has been the wine's recent acceptance beyond its own immediate backyard. While the majority of Eastern wines are still sold directly at the wineries, an astonishing number of good wines are making their way into Boston, Washington, D.C., Manhattan, and other major markets. Even five years ago it was rare to spot a single New York vintage on a restaurant wine list, but today, a number of the Big Apple's top eateries offer a generous range of local wines.

It is an exciting time for writers such as myself, who specialize in wine. It is also an exciting time for winemakers, who suddenly have a whole new universe of possibilities open to them. Above all, it is an exciting time for consumers who love good wine and who love discovering new wineries.

For those of us with a passion for travel, the birth of scores of new wineries gives us new reasons to visit the American countryside. The Eastern segment of the nation, where the concentration of wineries is greater than anywhere, except California, is a particularly rewarding travel destination. Fortuitously, vines seem to grow best in places where the landscape is spectacular. From the comely beauty of New York's Finger Lakes to the maritime attraction of New England's coast to the lush and fertile plateau of the Shenandoah Valley, there's plenty of dramatic scenery to explore. A sojourn in the Eastern wine regions is also an opportunity to become reacquainted with the history of our country.

In addition, as wine is meant to accompany food, visits to the wine country should also include samplings of the best regional foods. As the public's palate has become more refined, gastronomic entrepreneurs and small-scale farmers, like the wine producers themselves, are responding by growing, producing, and preparing more sophisticated ingredients and dishes.

The unpredictable climate and weather and the variety of plant pests and diseases will always make winemaking in the Eastern states a challenge. But it is now undeniable that the supreme effort will pay off for both the winemaker and the wine drinker, especially in the best viticultural regions. With a greater number of wineries producing better and better wines, today's wine enthusiast can visit more cellars and sample the product in more tasting rooms than ever before. In fact, as most wineries in the East are small, producing anywhere from a few hundred to several thousand cases a year, the only way most of us will ever have a chance to taste some of these wines is by visiting the wineries. If we come home with an extra case of wine in the trunk, it will be a vacation to remember every time we pour a glass for ourselves and our friends.

Happy travels, and *santé!*

THE WAY THIS BOOK WORKS

THE WINE REGIONS

Previous editions of this book were organized around three different wine regions (the Benchlands, the Atlantic Uplands, the Mountains) rather than state by state. Part of the reason for this was that during the earliest stages of the emergence of the Eastern wine industry, there was little cohesiveness among vintners in any given state. The impression one got in those early days was of individual wineries — a few good, some bad, many mediocre — scattered around the Eastern states with little connection or communication between them. They had more in common with the terrain that their vineyards were planted on than anything else.

Today, the picture is very different as the wine industry in most Eastern states is reaching maturity. Indeed, one sure sign that a wine region has come of age is when its vintners present themselves to the outside world as a unified group of colleagues rather than competitors. Of course, they are rivals in that each wants to make better wine than the others — winemaking is after all a business, with a product that needs to be sold in the marketplace. It is furthermore a business in which individual egos loom large, which is often a deterrent in cooperative ventures. But no winery can truly succeed in a vacuum, and until the entire region gains a reputation for excellence, any single winery that happens to make superior wine can only be considered an anomaly, a freak of nature along the lines of a two-headed calf.

As the wine industry in the East grows stronger, the influence of individual state regulations and the degree of organization of wineries within the state become more apparent. New York and Virginia are light-years ahead of other Eastern states in developing a strong image for their wines. In addition to their liberal laws that promote rather than discourage winegrowing, these states actively encourage, support, and educate vintners through the efforts of advisors from their major universities, especially Virginia Tech and New York's Cornell. Their effectiveness in boosting the wine industry in their states is very apparent. Virginia and the Long Island and Finger Lakes regions in New York, especially, are also feeling the impact of increasingly active grape growers' associations, winery unions, and regional marketing organizations, all of which is proof of a healthy and forward-moving industry.

New Jersey seems on the cusp of becoming a visible wine-producing state as various statewide competitions and fairs in recent years have focused attention on the industry. A new statewide winery association is having a beneficial impact on a wine region that until now has been struggling for its identity. State support is growing, and a few new serious vintners are stepping onto the stage who are bound to raise the overall quality of New Jersey wines.

Pennsylvania, with scores of wineries scattered all across the state, producing an enormous range of wines — from quality to barely quaffable — is a challenging region to synthesize into a cohesive whole. But as cream rises to the top, the industry leaders will inspire and encourage more ambitious winemaking and courageous viticulture. Like neighboring Maryland, Pennsylvania is beginning to benefit from recently enacted laws that lift, or at least lighten, certain restrictive regulations that have hindered progress since Prohibition.

Maryland has had one of the most dismal records of all the Eastern states in terms of political support and local recognition, but this state seems finally to be catching up to the modern world. As in most other states, the last bastion of serious restrictions in Maryland is the web of laws concerning direct shipping. Other cumbersome issues also remain on the books (for example, if you own a winery, you can't branch out and start a microbrewery or open a restaurant that serves wine on your premises. But in 2000, a series of bylaws were passed to liberalize the contact between wineries and consumers. The right to sell wine by the glass on winery premises, to conduct wine tastings in stores, to participate in fairs and farmers' markets, and to purchase grapes from other states are some of the issues that the new regulations have opened up to wineries. Another milepost that bodes well for the state's vinous future is the arrival in 2001 of Joe Fiola, a viticultural specialist who has come to Maryland from Rutgers University. At last the state will have its own viticulturist dedicated to coordinating, evaluating, educating, and advising Maryland's wineries. For anyone who thinks that I am exaggerating the importance of active statewide support on a wine region, consider this: Two decades ago, Virginia and Maryland, which share similar *terroirs,* each had seven commercial wineries. Today, Virginia, with its strong track record of vigorous viticultural support and liberal state laws, has 75 wineries, while Maryland has 10.

One final note of progress regarding archaic alcohol regulations: A Chicago law that banned giving wine to a dog has at long last been repealed. "There is no way of telling how dogs feel about this," remarked Frank Prial in his *New York Times* column, "but among connoisseurs of ludicrous wine legislation, the dog law will be missed."

Connecticut, Massachusetts, and Rhode Island, meanwhile, are in the earliest stages of organization. Since there are too few competitive wineries in any one of these states, they have wisely united for the common cause under the Southeastern New England appellation.

THE WINE, WINERIES & WINE REGIONS

The intent of this book is to identify the best wine made from grapes in the Eastern states rather than to provide a definitive guide to every single winery in the East. A few of the places described in these pages produce wine that is as good as any in the world. Others may not be quite up to that standard, but I have included them when the wines seemed to me to be at least average. I have not included wineries whose goal appears to be more of attracting tour busses than on making wine. Although I have included some wineries that produce wine made from fruit in addition to grape wine, I do not list those that make only fruit wine; I have nothing against fruit wine — it simply isn't the focus of this book.

Many new wineries have been added to this book, while several others have been dropped either because I did not feel that the quality of the wines was up to the standard of the others, or because they were so new at the time I was doing the research for the book that they did not yet have a tasting room (or enough of a track record) to be included. Other wineries have not been included because they are in an obvious state of transition — some are searching for new owners, others have been recently purchased by new owners who are in the process of upgrading. Only a couple of wineries have actually folded during the last few years, but a handful of others seem to have simply run out of steam. One can only hope that these last will be reinvigorated by more up-to-date winemaking, new ownership, more capital investment, or more modernized vineyard management — or possibly all of the above.

Previous editions of this book included wine regions that have been dropped from this new edition, both for the purpose of narrowing the geographic focus and for concentrating on the highest quality wines in the East. Lake Erie, Western and Central Pennsylvania, and Western Connecticut all fall outside the wine-producing area that the book is now emphasizing. Because the number of producers of truly fine wine has increased so dramatically in the East, the current goal of this book is to limit the overall geographic span, while giving more emphasis to quality. The decision to delete these regions does not, by any means, imply that they are incapable of producing excellent wine. On the contrary, many fine wines are emerging from these places. Harpersfield Vineyard in Geneva, Ohio, for example, makes exquisite Chardonnay, Gewürztraminer, and a host of other world-class wines. Nearby Presque Isle Wine Cellars (North East, Pennsylvania) was one of the pioneering Eastern vintners, whose admirable Cabernet Franc, Cabernet Sauvignon, Chardonnay, and other varietals continue to inspire and encourage winemakers across the region. Hopkins Vineyard in Preston (Western Connecticut) continues to make rapid progress, especially with Cabernet Franc, and furthermore is located in one of the most bucolic sites in the East. Of course, if these regions continue to grow in quality, and if they attract good new wineries, they may be reintroduced in future editions of this book.

THE *TERROIR* OF EASTERN WINE REGIONS

One of the characteristics of wine that attracts discerning consumers is the element the French call *terroir* — the individual characteristics imparted to wine by specific types of climate, soil, and other geologic factors. For example, the crisp, mineral-scented wines from the cool Burgundy region of Chablis are typically very different from the richer, flowery white wines from the Côte de Nuits section of Burgundy, although both are made from the same Chardonnay grape. A robust, intensely colored Cabernet from Long Island is unlike the usually lighter, more delicate Cabernet produced in the Finger Lakes. Some of these differences are a result of the deliberate stylistic imprint and philosophy of individual winemakers, but much of the character of wine is a consequence of the locale where the vines grow.

In the Eastern United States, as in much of Europe, *terroir* is more important than in California, where variations in climate are less pronounced. Here, individual microclimates have a profound effect on the grapes, which means that wine made from fruit grown in a specific region is more apt to possess a personality of place. The reflection of locale in wine contributes some of the subtle charm and mystery, as well as the individual character that we look for in the best wines. And so, while some vintners purchase grapes or juice from California or even, in some cases, Chile, Argentina, or France, the wineries included in this book grow at least a portion of their grapes on their own property or purchase them from vineyards in their own viticultural region.

Every state featured in this book can be seen as a separate unit, but each of them includes at least a couple of different *terroirs,* whose growing conditions transcend state lines and ultimately affect the character of the wine. The East is divided into three distinct geologic regions: the Benchlands, the Atlantic Uplands, and the Mountains. Each of these regions has its own characteristic climate and soil type. In each, vines perform in a relatively similar fashion, and the wines in turn reflect the individuality of the land. While this edition of the book is organized for greater convenience to the reader by separate states, it may be helpful to some wine country visitors to have an overview of the three principle viticultural conditions in the East.

The Benchlands, composed of sand, sediment, and stony glacial debris, includes Southeastern Massachusetts and the coastal sections of Rhode Island, Connecticut, New Jersey, and Virginia. Benchlands weather is affected along the coast by the moderating influence of the Atlantic Ocean and Long Island Sound and tends, therefore, to be relatively mild. Like most grapes grown in temperate climates, these grapes tend to have more pronounced color and flavor. Wine made from these grapes may also be softer and slightly lower in acidity.

The Atlantic Uplands lie between the coastal zones, bordering the Atlantic Ocean and the Eastern mountain ranges. This vast plateau runs north to south, and it is also sometimes called the Piedmont, or "Up-Country." Higher above sea level than the Benchlands, the Uplands are characterized by gently rolling hills easing up toward the Allegheny, Blue Ridge, and Appalachian Mountains. The Uplands of Eastern viticulture include Northern New Jersey, the Delaware River Valley, Pennsylvania (except the Central and Western mountainous sections), Maryland, Northern and Central Virginia, Western Connecticut, the Hudson River Valley, and the Finger Lakes region of New York. The Uplands feature mineral-laden soils and a long growing season. Good Uplands wines therefore will show a beautiful balance between sweetness, acidity, and alcohol, and the best ones will also have rich and intense flavors.

In most mountainous regions in the East, the weather is too extreme for grapes to grow. In a few places, however, specific microclimates offer a hospitable environment. These small viticultural regions can be at relatively high altitudes, but grapes will do well with proper care in the good soils, ample sunlight, and appropriate temperatures (warm days, cool nights) of the mountains. Additionally, dry mountain air keeps fungus, molds, and other damp-loving diseases at bay.

VITICULTURAL AREAS OF THE EASTERN UNITED STATES

In addition to being divided into separate states, the East, like all wine regions, is further broken up into smaller subsections known as American Viticultural Areas (AVAs). Like the *appellation contrôlée* that designates and controls France's geographically based names, the notation of an official AVA on a wine label is meant to imply a certain quality related to a geographical region. AVAs come under the jurisdiction of the BATF (Bureau of Alcohol, Tobacco, and Firearms). As of 2001, there are 145 AVAs in the United States.

In the East, they are the following:

Connecticut: Southeastern New England and Western Connecticut Highlands.

Maryland: Catoctin, Cumberland Valley, Lingamore, and Northern Neck.

Massachusetts: Martha's Vineyard and Southeastern New England.

New Jersey: Central Delaware Valley and Warren Hills.

New York: Cayuga Lake, Finger Lakes, Hudson River Valley, Lake Erie Region, Long Island (the newest in the East, granted 5/15/01), North Fork of Long Island, and The Hamptons.

Pennsylvania: Central Delaware Valley, Cumberland Valley, Lake Erie, and Lancaster Valley.

Rhode Island: Southeastern New England.

Virginia: Monticello, North Fork of Roanoke, Rocky Knob, Shenandoah Valley, and Virginia's Eastern Shore.

TASTING WINE: A SUBJECTIVE EXPERIENCE

Although much of the wine evaluated for this book was sampled by various tasting panels whose judgment I value and have taken into account, when all is said and done the final decision about which wines and wineries to include was based entirely on my own reactions. If I liked the wine, if I thought it would in some way enhance one's dining experience, and if I believed that a majority of wine drinkers would also have a favorable impression of it, then that winery was included in this book. If I didn't think the wines tasted up to par overall, then I didn't include that winery.

Taste — whether figuratively as in art or fashion, or literally, as in gastronomy — is, of course, a subjective experience. Nevertheless, there are certain universal standards based on generally accepted group cultural experiences that define taste. Because I have spent many years sampling wines from all over the world and writing about them for both American and international audiences, I think I have acquired a reasonably broad sense of the type of wine that the majority of wine consumers prefer. This does not mean, of course, that I like what *you* will like, or that my preferences are intrinsically better than yours. I can think of at least one winery that has not been included in this book despite having heard people rave about their wines. I will certainly revisit this place within the next couple of years; for now, however, I could not in good conscience recommend wines that I myself found abysmal. But the bottom line is that we should always drink the wine that tastes best to us, and the heck with what any critic says!

WINERY RESTAURANTS & LODGING

When the first edition of this book came out in 1996, it included suggestions for dining in restaurants where local wines were served. At that time, such restaurants were few and far between (as one of the subjects I interviewed put it, a few years ago it would have taken an Act of Congress to make a restaurant serve local wines). In a very short time, that picture has changed dramatically as wineries improved both their product and their marketing skills. Although there is still plenty of room for improvement in restaurant support, today, it is the rule, rather than the exception, that local wines will be featured on the wine list. Since there are now so many eateries pouring the local stuff, I decided to drop this category altogether rather than attempt to evaluate such a great number of restaurants. So the bad news is that readers who found this guidance helpful in past editions of the book will no longer be able to rely on it for dining out. The good news is that Eastern wines are now fine enough to demand a place on restaurant wine lists side by side with wines from Europe and California.

A developing trend in wine country is the number of wineries that feature their own dining opportunities, ranging from small snack bars to full-blown gourmet restaurants. A growing number of wineries also own inns or B&Bs that provide cozy and sometimes very elegant accommodations. Local ordinances in some areas prohibit wineries from operating restaurants or offering overnight accommodations on winery property. Dining out in a winery, and even spending the night right in the middle of the vineyards, can greatly add to the pleasures of wine country travels. Chapter Six, *Winery Restaurants & Lodging* (see page 153) lists these wineries.

THE WINERY LISTINGS

We have included (in small type alongside each winery's entry) such practical information as we believe is helpful. While we have made every effort to ensure that these facts are true as of publication, they are of course subject to change. It's a good idea to call ahead if you're planning a trip to a winery.

New in this edition are the Web and E-mail addresses for wineries that have them. These, too, are subject to change, as wineries take advantage of the Internet to reach an ever-wider audience. Many wineries that do not now have Web addresses will very likely have them in the future.

ABOUT THE RATINGS

Earlier editions of this book rated the overall quality of individual wineries as an attempt to help those visitors sort out the great from the mediocre wines in what was then a veritable minefield of uneven quality. Today, the quality of Eastern wine has progressed to the point where truly inferior wines are rare. Oh yes, you can still find them. But most of the wineries listed in this book now turn out wines that will seldom disappoint. A few wineries have the magic touch with everything they make, while others may excel particularly with one or two wines. As a general consumers' guide, at the head of each entry I've singled out the wine (or wines) that I think are particularly outstanding at that particular winery, followed in the text by a brief description of those wines. In previous editions, I've categorized proprietary names of individual wines in this list — Bedell's "Cupola," for example, or Barboursville's "Philéo." But because many wineries frequently change the name, the style, and/or the composition of these wines, I have decided that this is an unreliable way to recommend them in a book whose information can quickly be out of date. Instead, I've made an effort to recommend wine generically: a glance at the text will show that in highlighting, say, Pindar, I am also recommending "Mythology," which is usually a blend of Cabernet Sauvignon and Merlot.

In making decisions about which wines to target for specific recommendation, I had occasional help from other wine professionals, but the ultimate calls are a reflection of my own judgment and tastes. Because the quality of wine in any given winery is constantly influenced by factors, such as changes in personnel, equipment, individual vintages, and so forth, I urge readers to use all of this as a very general guide rather than an unimpeachable assessment of the wines. Your own taste buds will always be the best guide to what you like.

Touring East Coast Wine Country

A Guide to the Finest Wineries

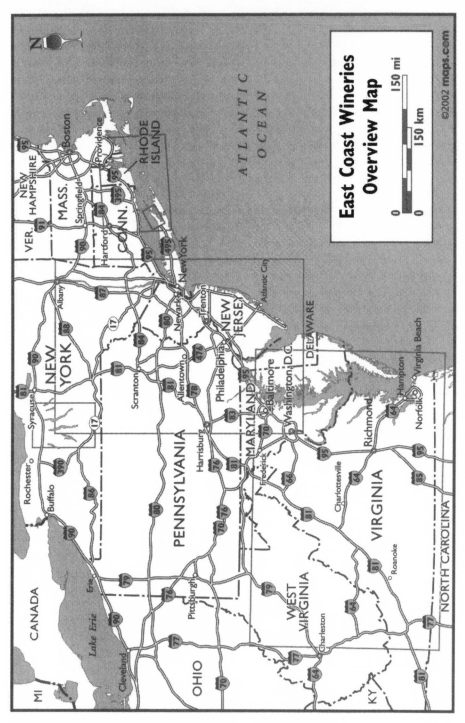

Detailed maps for areas marked by boxes can be found on pages 192–196.

CHAPTER ONE
History, Grapes & Marketing

Marguerite Thomas

Ruins of the house, once belonging to James Barbour, Governor of Virginia, and designed by Thomas Jefferson, near Barboursville, Virginia.

From Peach Wine to Pinot Noir, from Scuppernong to Sauvignon Blanc, every state in the union produces wine of one sort or another. Our winemaking origins date back to the beginning of our history as a nation. The Jamestown colonists started vinifying local grapes as soon as they got here, and we've been trying to make decent table wine ever since.

The colonists had no lack of native fruit to work with. In A.D. 1000, the Norse explorer Leif Eriksson was so impressed by the riot of grape vines that he saw cascading from the trees in North America that he dubbed the place "Vinland." In fact, more grape varieties grow naturally between the Atlantic coast and the Rocky Mountains than in any other place on earth.

The problem, from the early settlers' thirsty point of view, was that the fermented juice of native grapes had a powerful, musky smell and a stronger, more aggressive flavor than the more refined wines that they were used to drinking. Had the European settlers simply acquired a taste for wine made from grapes in their adopted land, they wouldn't have spent the next 350 years trying to coax European vines into growing in the harsh conditions of the New World.

The English monarchy, and eventually the individual states, worked to establish a viticultural industry in the New World. Both invested heavily, with the hope of reaping substantial economic returns. European vine cuttings were first imported to Virginia about 1619. From then on, determined viticulturists all along the Atlantic seaboard imported vines from every major wine-producing region in Europe.

For reasons that were not understood at the time, these vines always died. But since hope is part of the job description of a winemaker, the trials continued. French vignerons were imported to Virginia as consultants, French Huguenot exiles came to the Carolinas, and German winemakers immigrated to Pennsylvania. None of these experts, however, could get *Vitis vinifera* to grow in the New World.

THE RAVAGES OF DISEASE

While they never gave up trying, European vineyard specialists were forced to acknowledge that European vines would not do well in the new country. The vines that didn't die in the freezing winters would inevitably be killed off by American diseases, against which they had no inherent immunity. Native American grapes, by contrast, were resistant to Pierce's disease, black rot, phylloxera, and a variety of mildews and other fungal problems.

Of all the problems besetting the American vinifera wine industry, phylloxera was its ruin. This minuscule, yellow louse attacks vines by sucking the life out of the plant through its roots. California's vinifera-based wine industry, which had been thriving in the 19th century, was decimated by phylloxera. To make matters worse, the disease was inadvertently imported into France on the roots of American vines around 1860. There, phylloxera spread like the plague it was, almost wiping out most of the major wine-producing regions of France. In fact, few winemaking regions in the world escaped. The insect invaded the vineyards of Russia, South Africa, Australia, and New Zealand, as well as those of other European countries.

Finally, in the late 1800s, it was discovered that native American vines were resistant to phylloxera. Eventually, grafting of vinifera vines onto native American rootstock became the established method of combating phylloxera. Today, most of the world's grape vines grow on native American roots.

Even after the threat of phylloxera diminished, raising vinifera vines remained an extraordinary challenge in the Eastern states, although they flourished in California's mild climate. In the search for hardy grapes that would also produce palatable wines, viticulturists in the East turned to French-American hybrids. These new strains, developed in France after the phylloxera devastation, are American vine species crossed with European vinifera vines. They are more disease resistant than traditional vinifera, while their fruit is less pungently flavored than native American grapes. Thanks to these hybrids, the Eastern wine industry finally began to grow. Leading production centers developed around Lake Erie, in Michigan and Ohio, and in New York's Finger Lakes region.

By 1900, the future looked good. As Leon D. Adams wrote in *The Wines of America*, "Winegrowing was a full-grown, proud American industry. The brands of leading California, New York, Ohio, Michigan, and New Jersey wineries were competing with European vintages on many of the best restaurant wine lists."

PROHIBITION

J ust when the wine industry was reaching maturity, however, a disaster
far more deadly than disease or climatic catastrophe struck, as America
headed into Prohibition. In 1919, 55 million gallons of wine were produced
in the United States; by 1925, the figure had dropped to barely 3.5 million
gallons.

It is hard to imagine how rapidly this new calamity advanced, but the
seeds of destruction had been gathering for almost 100 years. Temperance
societies and religious organizations lobbied Congress and terrorized the
American public into accepting Prohibition. At first, local communities and
cities went "dry"; then, in 1851, Maine became the first state to declare
itself alcohol free. In 1920, the 18th Amendment to the Constitution of the
United States, prohibiting the manufacture, sale, transportation, or impor-
tation of alcoholic beverages, was passed. Intoxicating liquor, as defined by
Congress, was any beverage that contained 0.5 percent alcohol and
included all wine and beer. Some uses of wine were still permitted: for religious ceremonies, for medicinal purposes, for food flavoring, and for other
nonbeverage purposes.

Abuse of the law was rampant, however, and enforcement virtually
impossible. In 1933, the 21st Amendment, repealing the 18th, was ratified.
But, as *The Oxford Companion to Wine*, edited by Jancis Robinson, observes,
"Unfortunately, the [21st] Amendment left to the separate states the entire
regulation of the liquor traffic within their borders, with the result that the
U.S. liquor laws, including local and state prohibitions, remain a crazy quilt
of inconsistent and arbitrary rules, another lastingly destructive effect of
national prohibition . . . . Liquor — wine very much included — continues
to be an object of punitive taxation, of moral disapproval, and of obstructive
legislation in the United States today."

During the 13 years of Prohibition, thousands of wineries across the
nation went out of business. No one in the wine industry received any
compensation for losses. In addition to personal and financial tragedies,
the economic loss to local communities and to entire states was disastrous.

California ventured forward on the road to recovery immediately after
Repeal, thanks in part to a more enlightened government than in most
states. But in the East, the wine industry lay in a coma for nearly half a century, until the 1960s and 1970s, when it finally began to emerge from its
long slumber and reinvent itself. While hardly the "Vinland" that dazzled
Leif Eriksson, the winegrowing regions of the Eastern United States today
are beginning to prosper again. Most of us would even consider much of

the wine produced in the East to be above average in quality. And, more and more frequently, a truly great wine emerges.

FROM VINEYARD TO TABLE

Numerous factors affect the production of wines and our enjoyment of them. But no factor is as influential as the quality of the wine grapes themselves. The history of Eastern winemaking has been very much a story of shifting preferences in fruit. As Eastern winemaking evolved from a fledgling industry into maturity, European grape varieties grew in popularity and now dominate the field. In regions whose climate is too harsh for the grapes' survival, however, vintners rely on hybrid and native American vines.

GRAPE TYPES

Vinifera: The world's most common wine grape comes from the vine species called *Vitis vinifera*, a native of Europe and West Asia. There are approximately 10,000 varieties of vinifera throughout the world. These include Chardonnay, Sauvignon Blanc, Riesling, Pinot Noir, Cabernet

Sauvignon, Merlot, and all the other grapes that are used to make traditional European wines.

Labrusca and rotundifolia: Of the many grape varieties that are native to
America, only two are still used for winemaking in any quantity:

- *Vitis labrusca*, found in the Northeastern United States, produces intensely
  aromatic grapes with a pronounced flavor that is often described as
  "foxy." Grape juice and raw Concord grapes have a typical foxy smell,
  which scientists attribute either to a component called methyl anthrani-
  late, or to o-amino acetophenone. Whatever its cause, "foxiness" is seldom a complimentary term when applied to wine.

  The Concord, from which grape juice and many sweet, kosher wines
  are made, is the most widely planted labrusca grape and the most common grape in the United States after the Thompson seedless table grape.
  Catawba, another well-known labrusca, was for many years the leading
  wine grape in America. It is still used today, especially to make sparkling
  wines that have a pronounced grapy flavor. Longfellow described this
  wine as "dulcet, delicious, and dreamy." Today's sophisticated wine buff
  generally turns his or her nose up at these aggressively flavored wines,
  yet well-made sweet Catawba and Concord can be uniquely delicious.

- *Vitis rotundifolia*, a native of the Southern states, rotundifolia produces
  the Scuppernong grape, which yields a sweet, musky wine that is being
  eclipsed by other varietals, but is still popular in some parts of the South.

Hybrids: French-American hybrid grapes are crosses between two grape
varieties, usually vinifera and labrusca. The earliest vinifera vine cuttings
imported from Europe sometimes survived here for a few years. During
that time, a natural hybridization took place by exchange pollination
between the imported vines and the local American species. The earliest
offspring of these crosses, first noticed in the mid-18th century in
Pennsylvania, became known as the Alexander. This grape was the basis
for the first commercially successful winery in North America.

In the early 1800s, many more of these accidental crossings were discovered, and by the middle of the century, controlled hybridization began in
America. By the late 19th and early 20th century, after the devastation of
the French vineyards by phylloxera, French hybridizers developed a host
of hardy, flavorful grapes — Seyval and Vidal Blanc, Chambourcin, Baco,
and Rayon d'Or among others. For many years, these vines were planted
all over France; since 1955, however, French planting regulations have dis-
couraged vine varieties that are associated with inferior wines, including

many of the hybrids. While hybrid plantings have been phased out throughout most of France, they remain popular in regions of the United States where vinifera can't grow.

In the 1930s, a hobbyist winemaker named Philip Wagner began experimenting with French-American hybrids in his vineyard in Maryland. At the time, it seemed unlikely that vinifera grapes could ever survive anywhere in the Eastern states, while the flavor of labrusca grapes would never be accepted. The better hybrids that Wagner helped to develop and popularize seemed an exciting alternative.

When the revival of the Eastern wine industry got underway in the 1960s, hybrid grapes were ubiquitous. Today, however, more and more wine producers are ripping out hybrid vines and replacing them with vinifera; most new vineyards are planted exclusively with vinifera grapes. The switch resulted from a number of factors, among them the evolution of hardier vinifera vines and the use of more advanced technology in combating disease. New understanding about vineyard management, including new forms of trellising and pruning, also helps to keep the vines healthy. Generally milder winters for the past few years have been another factor in increased vinifera plantings. Furthermore, most contemporary American vintners, like their French cousins, believe vinifera grapes make the best wines. Why work with mediocre grapes, they argue, when vinifera grapes have proven to be the best for winemaking?

On the other hand, not all wineries have rushed to raise Chardonnay, Pinot Noir, Sauvignon Blanc, Merlot, and other European grapes. A number of vintners believe that the best wines made from superior hybridized

grapes, such as Seyval and Vidal Blanc, can hold their own in any company. And a few stalwart folks also cling to the notion that wine made from hybrid grapes has a unique American flavor, with as much varietal appeal as any other wine. They also worry that the European vines will not survive here over the long haul. History, they point out, has not been on the side of vinifera in the East.

From an economic standpoint, however, vinifera clearly has the edge. No matter how good the wine from hybridized grapes might be, just marketing these wines is an uphill challenge. Skeptics might well wonder how, in a world awash in wine, the consumer can be persuaded to buy a bottle of Baco over Merlot, or an obscure Aurora rather than a familiar Chardonnay. In addition, while hybrid vines are less challenging to grow, vintners are not blind to the fact that wines from vinifera grapes command higher prices.

Grape vines at Barboursville Vineyards in Virginia.

Some viticulturists in the Eastern states still hedge their bets by planting both vinifera and hybrids. In many ways, this diversity is fortunate for consumers, who can taste and test their way through a wide range of wines: from simple country hybrids — many of which, in spirit and sometimes in palate, resemble some of France's regional *Vins de Pays* — to

Direct Shipping
Why you can't get home delivery — and what you can do about it

Have you ever tried to send a case of wine home from a winery that you were visiting or called an out-of-state winery to have wine shipped? It is a lot of fun to do, if you can. But if you have tried, the chances are you have been told either that it's illegal to ship to your state, or that the common carriers won't deliver wine to individuals because state regulations are too complicated.

More than half of our states either forbid or partially restrict direct shipment of wine to consumers. These laws are not just obsolete relics of the Prohibition era, many have been retained on the books despite reasonable efforts to remove them, and several states have enacted them in recent times. Sad to say, some liquor distributors and retailers, fearful of losing their market share of wine sales, have played upon public fears of underage access and the potential loss of state tax revenue to persuade state legislatures to forbid direct home shipment of wines. Both concerns are provably unfounded, but in the absence of any organized voice on behalf of the consumer, the law sustains an antiquated distribution oligopoly.

As the number of wineries all over the country increases (from 377 in 1963 to more than 2,000 today) and the number of distributors decreases (from 10,900 in 1979 to fewer than 2,750 today), the possibility of buying a favorite wine at your friendly local wine emporium is decreasing drastically. Direct purchase and shipment from winery to consumer is clearly the answer. It works very well, meets an obvious need, and creates no illegal access or tax evasion problems in the states where it is permitted. Indeed, as wineries collect and forward state alcoholic beverage taxes (easily done in this electronic era), the states benefit from expanded commerce in wine. And it doesn't really hurt distributors. In those states where direct shipment is permitted, the distributor/retailer network still accounts for 95 percent of wine sales.

Winemakers and wine lovers are beginning to speak up for fair treatment. This is especially important for winemakers and consumers in the Eastern states. Winemaking is flourishing in more and more locales, and wine lovers are awakening to the pleasures of the wines of the Eastern states, but are unable to purchase any but a small fraction of them. There are so many wineries, most of them with an output too small to attract the attention of distributors, especially out-of-state distributors. There are so many states, and thus so many potential restaurants and bars to direct delivery. Direct sale from winery to consumer is the logical answer. If you care about it — do something!

The Wine Institute and winemakers associations have organized **Free the Grapes** as a body to lobby for unfettered direct shipment of wine throughout the country. Contact: Free the Grapes (707-254-9292; www.freethegrapes.org). Add your voice to those of other wine lovers all over the United States who are reshaping the debate on this issue.

midrange, moderately priced wines and all the way up to beautifully crafted examples of premium wines made from both hybrids and the world's noblest grapes.

I was once accused by a wine writer in one of the Eastern states of having a pro-California bias. What she meant, I think, is that I have an admittedly pro-vinifera bias. There are, to be sure, scores of wines produced from hybrid and native American grapes that I have found to be every bit as appealing as vinifera-based wine. Incidentally, certain grape varieties of this type produce much more successful wine than others, for example, Chambourcin, Seyval, Vidal, and Vignoles. On the other hand, I've tasted far too much wine made from nonvinifera grapes that is overly sweet, lacking complexity, and redolent of that bizarre and unpleasant characteristic known as "foxiness."

MARKETING WINE

It is still a challenge of Sisyphean proportions to market wine made in the East. The first obvious difficulty is promoting an unknown product. The relatively small production of Eastern wineries, ranging from a few hundred cases to a couple of thousand, is another. Add to this a complex web of licensing, distribution, taxation, and retail regulations, and one begins to understand why growing grapes is considered the easy part of winemaking! Distribution problems are compounded when a winery sells and transports its wines from one state to another. As one New England winemaker described the convoluted logistics of interstate wine distribution, "If your hat blows off in Rhode Island and lands in Connecticut, you have to apply for a license to go get it."

For all these reasons, and because Eastern wineries still produce relatively small quantities, most Eastern wine is sold only in the state where it's produced. All Eastern wineries sell their own product at the winery, and for many, the wine is available *only* through the winery. Increasingly, however, regional wines are available in local restaurants, while a handful of the most successful wineries, such as Bedell, Chaddsford, and Sakonnet, may be featured on wine lists throughout their own state. The biggest producers, such as Rhode Island's Sakonnet Vineyards or Virginia's Williamsburg, are served in a few fine restaurants across the country. Several audacious wineries, such as Long Island's Palmer, have even begun to crack the European market. An increasing number of Manhattan's finest restaurants, such as Jean-Georges, Gramercy Tavern, Judson Grill, and Home (to single out but a few), now proudly promote New York wines.

CHAPTER TWO
New England
CONNECTICUT, MASSACHUSETTS, & RHODE ISLAND

Marguerite Thomas

Beautiful landspcaping at Sakonnet Vineyards

The viticultural district of Southeast New England includes the coastal sections of Connecticut, Massachusetts, and Rhode Island. The region sits on a vast bench of sand, sediment, and stone that was formed by the debris left behind by a massive melting glacier that drifted across the land tens of thousands of years ago. These benchland soils are typically low in most trace minerals except silica, and in some areas they may be gravelly.

The Atlantic Ocean and Long Island Sound raise the temperature several degrees above the relatively frigid country only a few miles inland. The climate is further tempered by the jet stream. Situated just above latitude 40° (making it slightly more southerly than France), New England ought to have reliable, moderate weather — but it doesn't. Mark Twain wrote about New England's weather: "In the spring, I have counted 136 different kinds of weather inside of 24 hours." Most vintners in this part of the world know exactly what he meant.

And yet, despite winter freezes, schizophrenic springs, steamy summer heat, and vine-flattening hurricanes, people have been making wine here since 1632, when the first vineyard was planted on Governor's Island in Boston Harbor. Today, for those would-be vintners blessed with enough cash and a determined Yankee spirit, the odds in favor of producing wine sometimes even outweigh the risks. An obsessive desire to succeed certainly helps. As Bob Russell, owner of Massachusetts's Westport Rivers Vineyard & Winery puts it, "Anyone going into the wine business has to do it because they love it — because they have a dream, a passion."

The land closest to the coast, protected as it is by the Atlantic, has proven to be the most suitable place for growing vinifera grapes in New England. The Chardonnay grape that is harder to grow further inland does well here because of a relatively long growing season — about 190 days, compared to the average of 145 days in other parts of New England. Other white wine grapes, especially Seyval and Vidal Blanc, also thrive along the coast.

While white wine predominates, New England is beginning to prove that it can produce some above-average red vinifera wines, too, with Cabernet Franc and, in some instances, Merlot, showing particularly well. Overall, however, the wine industry in this region has had a slow start. Most of the leaders in the field (Chamard, Sakonnet, Westport) have been around since the 1980s; Sharpe Hill appeared in the 1990s. But since then there's not been the explosion of new wineries that New York and Virginia have seen. Part of the reason for this is the tepid support viticulture receives from local governments. At the dawn of a new century, however, the picture may be changing. In Connecticut alone, a handful of new wineries are under construction, and 500 new acres have been planted in vines to the delight of local vintners who are crying out for more grapes. One of the most promising of the new ventures is Priam Vineyards (860-267-8520; 11 Shailor Hill Rd., Colchester, CT 06415). This burgeoning venture is owned by Gary Crump and his wife Gloria Priam (the estate is named after Gloria's Hungarian grandfather, who was forced to abandon his vineyards when he fled Hungary during the Communist takeover). The couple bought an old farm in 1997 and have so far planted about six acres of Chardonnay, Cabernet Franc, Riesling, and a handful of hybrid varieties. Their tasting room is slated to open before the end of 2002.

Virtually all of the original serious vintners in New England have made stunning progress in the quality of their wines. The second generation has, by and large, been struggling to catch up stylistically, but vineyards are expanding, cellar practices are improving, and the wines are getting better all the time. There can be little doubt that this promising viticultural region will surely attract more new wineries.

In addition to its wines, Coastal New England offers a memorable travel destination, filled with charming villages and historic houses, antique stores and art galleries, picturesque farmland undulating down to the sea, colorful harbors and ports, wildlife refuges, woodlands, and beaches. Newport alone draws people from all over the world, who peer back through history for a glimpse of the place Henry James described: "They danced and they drove and they rode," he wrote, "they dined and wined and dressed and flirted and yachted and polo'd and Casino'd . . . past the low headlands I saw their white sails verily flash, and through the dusky old shrubberies came the light and sound of their feasts." All that was missing from this picture as they "dined and wined" was a good local wine. Today's feasts won't have that problem.

CONNECTICUT

CHAMARD VINEYARDS
860-664-0299;
    fax 860-664-0297.
www.chamard.com.
info@chamard.com.
115 Cow Hill Rd., Clinton, CT 06413.
Directions: From I-95, take exit 63 to Rte. 81 north. Just past the Clinton Crossing Outlet Complex, turn left onto Walnut Hill Rd., which merges into Cow Hill Rd. after 0.8 mile. Continue to winery on left.
Owner: William Chaney.
Open: Year-round: Wed.–Sat. 11am–4pm.
Price Range of Wines: $9.99–$14.99.

Chamard's 20 acres of vines are picturesquely framed by classic New England stone walls. An agrarian pond sparkles outside the tasting room. All in all this is a charming country setting, but happily, there is no rural clumsiness in these sophisticated wines.

The winery's owner, William Chaney, is also chairman of the board and CEO of Tiffany & Co. In the mid-1980s, he began searching New England for a place to plant a vineyard when, by a stroke of luck, he found a 40-acre farm for sale in Clinton, Connecticut, the same coastal community where he owned a weekend house. Now the Kansas-born Chaney spends weekends and vacations in the vineyards or in the winery working alongside winemaker and general manager Larry McCulloch. After training as a horticulturist, Larry learned winemaking at Benmarl, a Hudson River winery. Both men share the

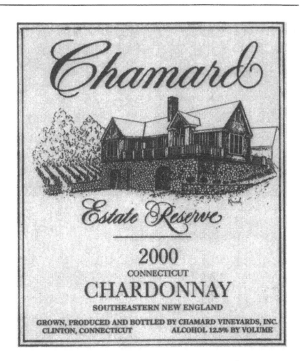

- Chardonnay
- Cabernet Sauvignon
- Merlot
- Cabernet Franc

strong belief that great wines come from great vineyards. "We've proven that if you pick the right site and put your mind and money into it, you can make nice wine. It may not be easy, but it can be done," Larry insists.

Chamard's exceptional recent Chardonnays have a concentration of fruitiness balanced by high levels of acidity and a pronounced mineral aftertaste. Very fine Estate Cabernet Sauvignon and Merlot are also produced here in limited amounts. The outstanding Cabernet Franc, says Larry McCulloch, is great with spicy ribs and Cajun shrimp or chicken. Larry has recently been experimenting with small amounts of Pinot Noir, and he is encouraged by the results so far. Chamard Vineyards' total production is 7,000 cases. The wines are consistently distinguished by a good flavor balance of fruit, oak, acid, and alcohol, plus the mystery and intangibles that make fine wines so alluring.

SHARPE HILL
VINEYARD
860-974-3549;
  fax 860-974-1503.
www.sharpehill.com.
sharpehill@snet.com.
108 Wade Rd., P.O. Box 1,
  Pomfret, CT 06285.

Sharpe Hill burst on the scene in the late 1990s, producing astonishingly good wines from the very beginning. Owner Steven Vollweiler, whose first career was in the metal-recycling business, realized a 20-year-old dream with this winery. Current production is about 8,000

Directions: From I-395, take exit 93. Drive west on Rte. 101 (which becomes Rte. 44) for 7 miles to Rte. 97 (in Abington district of Pomfret). Drive south on Rte. 97 exactly 4 miles to Kimball Hill Rd. Turn left and drive 1.8 miles to winery. From I-84, take exit 69. Drive east on Rte. 74 to end. Make a left onto Rte. 44 east and drive to Abington district of Pomfret. Turn right onto Rte. 97 south and proceed as above.

Owners: Steven & Catherine Vollweiler.
Open: Fri.–Sun. 11am–5pm.
Price Range of Wines: $9.99–$19.99.
Special Features: Café and Fireside Tavern.

- Chardonnay
- Cabernet Franc
- Seyval
- St. Croix
- Vignoles

cases, and the vineyard has expanded from seven acres to 16. It's a long drive from almost anywhere to get to Sharpe Hill (but, trust me, well worth it) along a curving rural road, past woods and farms and a great number of authentic Colonial houses. You might want to stop off in Pomfret for some antiquing, if that's your thing. In Sharpe Hill's tasting room, fashioned after an 18th-century taproom complete with antique furnishings and decorations, sample "Ballet of Angels," a white wine that manages to be both crisp and slightly sweet, with heavenly aromas. Made from Seyval and Vignoles grapes, this award-winning wine makes a nifty aperitif and is also a good accompaniment to spicy foods. The elegant Chardonnays and the earthy, peppery Cabernet Francs are outstanding. "Red Seraph," a pleasing light red wine made from a cold-hardy hybrid grape named St. Croix, plus a dash of Merlot and a whisper of Cabernet Franc is, like the Beaujolais it somewhat resembles, best served slightly chilled. The Select Late Harvest wine, made only in the best years (I tasted both the 1996 and 1997), is sublime, one of the best dessert Vignoles in the East — or anywhere else, for that matter. Too many dessert wines are syrupy and cloying — this one is endlessly lively and bright in the mouth.

Don't even think of going anywhere else for lunch. Sharpe Hill's wine garden is nicely situated at the base of the eponymous slope of vines. Work up an appetite before lunch with a stroll up the hill through the vineyard for a fabulous view over Connecticut, Massachusetts, and Rhode Island. Catherine Vollweiler's light but flavorful fare will tickle any wine taster's fancy. Okay, the service can be slow — but how many other places do you know where the butter is flown in from France, the Stilton from England?

Howard Burson

"I've been working in the wine industry for over a quarter of a century," says Howard Burson. "I've been involved in it everywhere, from China to South Africa to the Finger Lakes." Like many people, Howard stumbled into his profession more by accident than by design. As a graduate student polishing up his doctoral dissertation in philosophy at Cornell University, he found a part-time job swabbing out tanks at Bully Hill Vineyards in the Finger Lakes region of New York. "It was fun, and it was a good place to learn about wine. I got to do everything there." Although he ended up as Bully Hill's cellar manager, Howard hadn't quite severed his ties with academia. After two years of teaching at Wells College, however, he finally decided to dive into the wine business full-time. Travels, especially to France and Spain, played an important role in his career, giving him critical familiarity with the world's best wines. "It has been my good fortune to pick up a few tricks along the way," he adds modestly.

Howard and his wife spent time in India, adopting first one daughter and later a second baby. In 1980, the family moved to Pomfret, Connecticut, where Howard started up, designed, and ran Hamlet Hill Winery. There he sharpened his skills and was awarded many prizes for his wines, but the venture simply wasn't profitable enough; in 1990, Hamlet Hill went out of business. Howard, at the age of 43, went back to school to study grape tissue culture, with the ultimate goal of opening a biotech-based grape vine nursery. As it turned out, he couldn't quite pull off the start-up financing for the project, but at about that time Steven Vollweiler came on the scene looking for a winemaker for Sharpe Hill Vineyards. "I jumped back into winemaking with a vengeance. It really is what I love to do," says Howard.

Howard is characteristically humble when it comes to explaining the success of his wines. Noting that a good winemaking facility is important, Howard mentions almost as an aside that he designed Sharpe Hill's winery himself. Good equipment, he adds, especially the right choice of barrels, counts. Good vineyard management is essential, as is the right choice of grapes. Some grapes, such as Cabernet Sauvignon, are impossible to grow in this particular climate; therefore, Howard says Sharpe Hill concentrates on grapes that adapt to the region. Among the grape varieties that appear to be successful here are Cabernet Franc and the white wine varieties Chardonnay, Pinot Blanc, Pinot Gris, Gewürztraminer, Riesling, and Melon de Bourgogne. "If you can coax these grapes to grow here, their fruit is absolutely incredible," says Howard. At Sharpe Hill, it seems that Howard Burson has been doing an excellent job of coaxing.

STONINGTON VINEYARDS
800-421-WINE;
    fax 860-535-2182.
www.stoningtonvineyards.
    com.
stoningtn@aol.com.
523 Taugwonk Rd., P.O.
    Box 463, Stonington, CT
    06378.
Directions: Heading east on
    I-95, take exit 91. Turn
    left on Taugwonk Rd.

Stonington Vineyards, set in the hills a few miles inland from the borough of Stonington, provides an informal rural setting in which to picnic or simply sample wines. Nick Smith, who arrived in the wine world via international banking, believes strongly in maintaining the individual character of regional wines. While 50 percent of his grapes are grown on the Stonington property (13 acres of vineyards), the rest are purchased from other New England vineyards.

and follow signs 2.5
miles to winery on left.
Owners: Happy & Nick
Smith.
Open: Daily 11am–5pm.
Price Range of Wines:
$8–$14.99.
Special Features: Art
gallery.
Special Events: Oct. and
May sale and barrel
tasting.

• Gewürztraminer

Under the supervision of winemaker Mike McAndrew, the wines at Stonington Vineyards continue to improve year after year. The Chardonnay sometimes has a beguiling aroma of jasmine. "Seaport White" is a user-friendly blend of Chardonnay, Vidal, and Seyval, which Smith describes as "a real New England wine, great with scallops and lobster." Fumé Vidal has a slight oakey edge. Gewürztraminer, with its powerful perfume, has become one of Stonington's leading wines. While this has always been primarily a white wine house, the owners are excited about the success so far of recent plantings of Cabernet Franc.

Stonington's production is currently at about 7,000 cases. Nearby, Stonington Borough is a lovely seaport village, with many fine historic houses and an outstanding collection of antique shops, art and craft galleries, and restaurants. Mystic Seaport Aquarium, one of the best in the East, and Mystic Seaport are a 15-minute drive from Stonington.

MASSACHUSETTS

**WESTPORT RIVERS
    VINEYARD & WINERY**
508-636-3423, 800-993-9695;
    fax 508-636-4133.
www.westportrivers.com.
retail@westportrivers.com.
417 Hixbridge Rd.,
    Westport, MA 02790.
Directions: From I-95, take
    Rte. 88 south to
    Hixbridge Rd. Turn left
    to winery.
Owners: The Russell family.
Open: Daily 11am–5pm.
Price Range of Wines:
    $10–$85.
Special Features: Historic
    art gallery, wine and food
    education center,
    Buzzard Bay Brewery.

Set on an old Massachusetts farm, on a spit of land facing Rhode Island, Westport Rivers is a family-run winery. Bob Russell decided to leave the security of his job as a metallurgical engineer for the uncertainty of operating a winery almost 25 years ago. The decision was based partly on the Russells' desire to find an interest and occupation where "we could grow old together." The Russells also were influenced by long discussions with Carol's father, who had owned Germania Wine Cellars in Hammondsport, New York. "With my father's memories, our love of food and wine, our common concern for environmental issues, and a long-standing desire to preserve working agricultural land, a vineyard and winery were an obvious choice," explains Carol.

Special Events: Annual
  Chardonnay Festival
  (Aug.), Annual Sparkling
  Wine Gala (June),
  Thanksgiving Weekend
  Open House, other
  seasonal events.

• Riesling
• Chardonnay
• Sparkling wine

The Russells could have gone anywhere — California, Oregon, Australia — but they opted for this corner of the world for one simple reason: They loved the New England landscape. By 1982, the Russells had purchased a farm, where their son Rob planted the first vines in 1986. Their other son, Bill, apprenticed with Eric Fry at Long Island's Lenz Winery before joining the family business as winemaker. Rob is now the full-time vineyard manager. Ninety-five percent of Westport Rivers' wine is made from grapes that are raised on the property. Eighty acres of vineyards are planted on the estate's permanently preserved, historic farmland (150 acres at the Buzzards Bay Brewery property). All of the estate wine is made from vinifera grapes. Chardonnays and Rieslings exhibit the classy character of cool-climate wines, but can also be lush and ripe in warmer years.

Sparkling wine is what Westport Vineyard is known for. All of it is vintage dated, all made from the estate's own grapes, and all produced in the *méthode champenoise*. The Blanc de Blancs is pure and fresh. The Brut Cuvée RJR is a classic that is sure to please all true Champagne lovers, and the Blanc de Noirs is creamy and delicious. "Imperial Sec," made from Riesling grapes, is distinguished by floral aromas and by a delicate touch of sweetness. The Russells are particularly proud of their specialty releases, such as the rare "Maximilian Cuvée." About 10,000 cases of wine are produced each year at Westport Vineyard.

Westport Rivers led the way in New England for the production of sparkling wine made from vinifera grapes using traditional French Champagne vinification techniques. These wines tend to be charming, with fruity flavors, bracing acidity, and tiny, persistent bubbles. These sparklers also tend to age well. Anyone who doubts that sparkling wine is a good match for food should sign up for one of the events at Westport Vineyard's Long Acre House (an educational center for wine, beer, and food), where resident chef Kerry Downey Romaniello specializes in food and wine pairings.

Buzzard Bay Brewery, which opened in 1998, is turning out American versions of British Pale Ales as well as lagers. The Russells will be growing their own hops and barleys for the beers.

Westport's setting, deep in picturesque farmland, is lovely. The Russells' commitment to the environment remains strong: From 1993 on, a portion of the profits from every bottle of wine has been donated to an organization dedicated to the preservation of farmland.

Oysters

New England's commercial fishing fleet is still productive and so is a new breed of farmer: The aquaculturist, or farmer of the sea, raises fish and shellfish in inlets and salt ponds near the shore. While most of the local seafood is well suited to Eastern wines, there is nothing quite so delicious as the taste of sweet and briny oysters fresh from the sea accompanied by one of the lively white wines from the Atlantic coastal regions.

Like grapes, the flavor of oysters varies tremendously, depending on where they are raised. No one yet understands all the factors that contribute to this variation in flavor, but it is safe to assume that the degree of salinity, as well as the fluctuations in water temperature, may affect both the oysters and the microscopic algae, called phytoplankton, upon which they feed.

While oysters from different locales along the East coast have individual flavors, they all, except for the French Belon oyster, originate from the same oyster family. Whether they are called bluepoint, Peconic Bay, Wellfleet, Fishers Island, or Cotuit, virtually all oysters raised on the East Coast are grown from the seed of the American oyster.

CUTTYHUNK SHELLFISH FARMS (508-990-1317 in summer, 508-636-2072 in winter; Bayview Dr., P.O. Box 51, Cuttyhunk Island, MA 02713; raw bar open May–Oct.) One of the most notable oyster farms is located just off the coast of Massachusetts, not far from Westport Rivers Vineyard & Winery. Oyster farms, like vineyards, are vulnerable to weather patterns, explains owner Seth Garfield. In addition to oysters, Cuttyhunk also harvests wild quahog clams. The plan is to gradually begin cultivating these clams as they become less available in the wild. Cuttyhunk oysters may be enjoyed in many East Coast restaurants, from Boston to New York. Visitors are welcome at the farm. A ferry travels to the island from New Bedford.

MOONSTONE OYSTERS (401-783-3360; oyster@ids.net; 264 Foddering Farm Rd., Narragansett, RI 02882; open by appt. only) Moonstone supplies its trademarked oysters to some of the best restaurants in the East, including Manhattan's acclaimed Le Bernardin and the Oyster Bar in New York's Grand Central Station. Both native species and Belon oysters are raised in coastal salt ponds at Moonstone; scallops are grown as well.

FISHERS ISLAND (631-788-7899) Fishers Island oysters are raised in nets off the harbor bottom on Fishers Island, NY, a private island nestled between Connecticut and Long Island in Long Island Sound. Ninety percent of the oysters go to restaurants in Manhattan, while the rest are reserved for other East Coast restaurants. Not open to the public.

RHODE ISLAND

GREENVALE VINEYARDS

401-847-3777.
info@ greenvale.com.
www.greenvale.com.
582 Wapping Rd.,
 Portsmouth, RI 02871.
Directions: From Fall River, take Rte. 24 south. Cross the Sakonnet River and take exit 1. Drive under highway and merge with Rte 138 south. Pass State Police barracks and take a left onto Sandy Point Ave. Take first right onto Wapping Rd. Winery driveway is 0.9 mile on left. From Newport, take Rte. 138 north. Just past the "Entering Portsmouth" sign, take a right onto Braman's Ln. At the end, take a right into Wapping Rd., then a left onto winery driveway, Greenvale Ln.
Owners: Cortlandt & Nancy Parker.
Open: Mon.–Sat. 10am–5pm, Sun. 12noon–5pm.
Price Range of Wines: $9–$22.

• Cabernet Franc

Picture a tranquil river winding through fields, marshes, and vineyards. Picture a charming Victorian house and stable-cum-tasting-room designed by famed Boston architect John Sturgis in the 1860s (the buildings are listed on the State and National Registers of Historic Places). Now put yourself in the picture, sipping the zesty, berrylike Cabernet Franc. This scene is set at Greenvale Vineyards, which has been in the same family since the farm first started in the 19th century. Nancy and Cortlandt Parker and their daughter, Nancy Parker Wilson, first planted grapes in 1982, as a means to develop a productive use of their family farm. At first, they sold grapes to Sakonnet Vineyards, but in the 1990s, they began making their own wine. Winemaker Larry Perrine, now at Channing Daughters on Long Island, got them off to a good start. Currently Richard Carmichael, formerly at Williamsburg Winery, is making the wines. Greenvale currently produces about 3,500 cases of wine a year from its 18-acre vineyard.

NEWPORT VINEYARDS

401-848-5161;
 fax 401-848-5162.
www.newportvineyards .com.
info@newportvineyards .com.
909 East Main Rd. (Rte. 138), Middletown, RI 02842.
Directions: From Newport, drive east on Memorial

The Nunes family bought the former Vinland Cellars vineyards and winemaking facility in 1988. The subsequent purchase of a local potato farm expanded the vineyard by 20 acres. With the possible exception of some Cayuga and Vidal, all the new plantings are vinifera grapes, including Merlot, Cabernet Franc, Cabernet Sauvignon, and Pinot Blanc (all the vines and rootstocks come from Ontario). The purchase of

NEWPORT VINEYARDS

ALC. 12% BY VOL

Cabernet Franc

Vintners Select 2000 RHODE ISLAND

Blvd. past Easton's Beach, then north on Aquidneck Ave. (Rte. 138A) to East Main Rd. (Rte. 138). Turn right and drive 0.75 mile to the winery. From Providence, drive east on Rte. 195 to Rte. 24 south. Take exit 1, bear right and follow Rte. 138 south for 10 minutes. Winery is on left.
Owner: John F. Nunes, Jr.
Open: May–Oct.: Mon.–Sat. 10am–5pm, Sun. 12noon–5pm, tours Sat. & Sun. 1pm and 3pm; Nov.–Apr.: by appt.
Price Range of Wines: $7.95–$24.95.

the Perry potato farm, incidentally, was made possible through a public-private partnership that took advantage of a state program to buy development rights and keep agricultural land green. The winery has recently expanded its operations and has begun upgrading its barrel program. Popular Newport wines include an off-dry blend of various white grapes and "Gemini," a smoky red wine made from Merlot and Maréchal Foch grapes. With 30 acres under cultivation, the winery produces 7,000–10,000 cases annually.

SAKONNET VINEYARDS AND WINERY
401-635-8486, 800-998-8486; fax 401-635-2101.
www.sakonnetwines.com.
sakonnetri@aol.com.

Sakonnet Vineyards is ideally situated on one of the handful of Rhode Island peninsulas poking out into Narragansett Bay. Established in 1975, Sakonnet is New England's largest winery, with an annual production of 50,000 cases. Owners Susan and Earl Samson came to the wine

162 West Main Rd. (Rte. 77), P.O. Box 197, Little Compton, RI 02837.
Directions: From I-195, take Rte. 24 south and continue to Tiverton-Little Compton/Rte. 77 exit. Drive south on Rte. 77 through traffic light at Tiverton Four Corners. Sakonnet is 3 miles from this junction on left.
Owners: Susan & Earl Samson.
Open: June–Oct.: daily 10am–6pm; Nov.–May: daily 11am–5pm.
Price Range of Wines: $6–$29.95.
Special Events: Cooking classes, food and wine events throughout the year.
Special Features: The Roost, a B&B.

• Chardonnay
• Gewürztraminer
• Vidal
• Sparkling wine

business from backgrounds far removed from anything resembling agriculture — she from the Broadway theater, he from the world of investments and capital venture — but they have embraced Sakonnet Vineyards as a way of life as much as a commercial undertaking. Vineyard manager Joetta Kirk has been here since 1983. Most of the grapes for the winery's premium wines are from Sakonnet's own 45-acre vineyard, although some additional grapes are purchased, mostly from local vineyards.

Particularly noteworthy among Sakonnet's overall excellent wines is the Gewürztraminer, with a powerful, floral aroma, rich flavor, and fleshy body; it's a good sipping wine and an excellent accompaniment to a variety of foods, from smoked salmon to spicy Chinese menus. Vidal Blanc has flavors reminiscent of ripe peaches and melons, plus enough acidity to make it a fine accompaniment to shrimp, oysters, and other seafood. The barrel-fermented Fumé Blanc (Vidal with a mellow hint of oak) is another classy food-friendly wine, with flavor that lingers like the glow of a perfect sunset. Chardonnay tends to be round and rich. The sparkling wine combines power and finesse — it's as impressive a non-Champagne bubbly as one could ask for.

Sakonnet also produces a few inexpensive, agreeable, lightweight wines for its "Newport" series, including "America's Cup Red," "America's Cup White," and "Eye of the Storm," a fruity Blush named after the hurricane that devastated much of the surrounding area, while sparing the Sakonnet vineyards a few years ago. Sakonnet's "Seaborne" series is a blend of domestic wine, plus wines brought in from other wine regions, sometimes as far away as France or Chile. As many Eastern winemakers struggle to find an adequate supply of grapes, this type of venture may become more common in the future.

Sakonnet is set in a particularly attractive location, and Little Compton is a charming and attractive New England village. Swimming beaches, fishing, and historic attractions are nearby. The Roost, a bed-and-breakfast, is located in the original farmhouse on the property of Sakonnet Vineyards.

Joetta Kirk

Joetta Kirk never set out to become a vineyard manager. On the contrary, her career path began evolving in a perfectly ordinary, conventional way. First she was a hairdresser, then a salesperson in a shop, followed by a stint in an advertising agency. Along the way, she fell in love, got married . . . and divorced.

At the time of the divorce, she was living in a cottage on an estate in rural Massachusetts, where she agreed to do groundswork in exchange for rent. Her fate was sealed as she embarked on her lifelong love affair with agriculture. Characteristically, Joetta first learned everything she could about managing an agricultural property, from property management to equipment maintenance. Then, on a whim, she contacted Jim and Lolly Mitchell, the original owners of Rhode Island's Sakonnet Vineyards, after reading an article about their winery. The Mitchells, who happened to be looking for someone who knew how to operate a tractor, invited her to lunch, and the rest, as they say, is history.

Joetta Kirk became not just Sakonnet's vineyard manager, but also one of the most respected authorities on cool-climate vineyards, especially those in the Atlantic coastal states. For more than two decades, she has spent her life in the vineyards, habitually putting in seven-day weeks. "It was stupid and crazy," she sighs, "but I needed to learn a lot. And I did learn a lot, and I also witnessed many extraordinary changes during that time."

What are some of these changes? "One is that the technology of growing grapes in marginal regions has advanced significantly in the last 10 years," Joetta explains. "The difference between the early 1980s and the 1990s is dramatic. Take the advancement of clonal selection: We've found that the most popular Chardonnay clone in California isn't that good here. Then there is the issue of canopy management that I first heard about at an international symposium in New Zealand in 1988. [Canopy management refers to pruning and trellising techniques that allow sunlight to reach all parts of the vine.] If some parts of the vine are shaded, it's defeating itself. You want the plant to photosynthesize properly, and we now know you have to supply sunlight to the leaves, the shoots, and the fruit. You should not allow the vines to droop to the ground."

Although Joetta talks about building more of a personal life after all these years of devotion to the vine, it is clear that the vineyard still enthralls her. "I can't imagine another crop that would be as fascinating as vines," she confesses. "A vineyard is a controlled environment that wants to run amok. There's an emotional bond there. It's a contest between grower and vine and you wonder who's going to win; who's going to be happy. Of course, I want both to win."

Joetta mentioned another worker at Sakonnet who trims the hedges around the vineyard. "He comes in sometimes to tell me the vines look happy. So we go out and stand there admiring them. And you know, they do look happy."

TOURING NEW ENGLAND

CONNECTICUT

New England displays its charms in every season, but autumn is everybody's favorite time of year, made all the more appealing in Connecticut when the splendor of fall foliage is combined with the excitement of the grape harvest. Begin a day of wine tasting in Connecticut at Chamard, in the coastal town of Clinton. Continue driving up the coast, stopping for lunch, perhaps, at one of the bistros or other restaurants around the village green in Guilford. Cross the Connecticut River and make a detour into Old Lyme, the center of American Impressionism. This classic New England village boasts galleries, art academies, and a museum devoted to the painters who spent their summers here during the heyday of American Impressionism.

A few miles farther up the coast is New London. Once a thriving seaport that fell on hard times toward the end of the 20th century is now experiencing a revival with shops, galleries, and restaurants and is flourishing. Just before the Rhode Island border, stop in at Stonington Vineyards' tasting room. Then, if it's one of the Friday nights when the restaurant at Sharpe Hill Vineyards is open, veer inland for dinner at their Fireside Tavern.

CHAPTER THREE
New York State
LONG ISLAND, THE FINGER LAKES, & THE HUDSON RIVER VALLEY

Marguerite Thomas

Wine casks at Raphael.

A merica's third largest grape and wine-producing state, New York, has undergone an impressive growth spurt in recent years. Of its 160 wineries, 141 were established after 1976. New York's four major viticultural areas are Long Island, the Finger Lakes, the Hudson River Valley, and the Lake Erie Region. The grape and wine industry brings in more than $500 million in gross sales and attracts some 2 million tourists annually — and is growing.

LONG ISLAND

L ong Island is a 120-mile-long bed of gravel and silt left behind by a gla-cier sliding in slow motion over the land some 10,000 years ago. Look-ing at the flat and almost treeless land today, it is hard to believe that when the first Europeans arrived, they found a thickly forested place inhabited mostly by bears and snakes. A small population of Native Americans planted corn and tilled the fields lying beyond the sandy beaches.

Like their predecessors, the European newcomers discovered that because of its well-drained soil and temperate climate, Long Island was a good place to grow a variety of crops. Many of the early settlers raised table grapes on arbors near their houses. In the 1950s, John Wickham planted the first experimental vinifera grapes on his farm in Cutchogue, on Long Island's North Fork. Rather than attempt to make wine, he sold the grapes at his farm stand.

Today, 20 of Long Island's 24 wineries are on the North Fork, a 159-square-mile band of well-drained soil. Surrounded on three sides by water, with the moderating Gulf Stream paralleling the island some 50 miles off-shore, this region has the longest, coolest growing season of any viticul-tural region in the Northeast. Because the water cools down slowly in the winter, reflecting heat back onto the land for a long time, the severe freezes that threaten other regions are mostly unknown here. In the summer, the water warms up gradually, keeping temperatures from soaring disas-trously.

Long Island's North Fork is the sunniest part of New York State, with at least 210 growing days per season (compared to 150 days in the Finger Lakes). This long and sunny season allows vinifera grapes, whose ripeness is often unpredictable from year to year in other areas in the Northeast, to ripen consistently here. Furthermore, the constant sea breezes that blow across the vineyards discourage the formation of molds and mildew on the grapes.

This is not to say that the area is trouble-free. In addition to the usual vagaries of weather and pests that threaten viticulture everywhere, Long Island's vineyards are particularly susceptible to damage from wind and hurricanes, as well as from great flocks of birds who love nothing better than to dine on grapes.

Long Island's first commercial winery was established in 1973 by Alex and Louisa Hargrave (Hargrave Vineyard is now Castello di Borghese). There were four more wineries by 1980, when the first big flush of vine-yard planting on Long Island began in earnest. During the economic slump of the late 1980s, things slowed down, but during the 1990s the boom was back. By 2001, there were some 49 vineyards covering a total of 3,000 acres, with 24 wineries operating on Long Island. The first generation of vintners, who had acquired their properties for a few hundred thousand dollars are now selling them for millions.

Virtually all the grapes grown on Long Island are vinifera. White grapes include Chardonnay, Chenin Blanc, Gewürztraminer, Pinot Blanc, Pinot Gris, Riesling, Sauvignon Blanc, and Viognier. Among the reds are Cabernet Franc, Cabernet Sauvignon, Dolcetto, Lemberger, Malbec, Merlot, Petit Verdot, Sangiovese, and Shiraz (Syrah).

The remarkable improvement in Long Island wines over the past few years can be at least partially explained by the increased age of the vines, as well as by better vineyard management that allows the grapes to ripen more completely on the vine. Better winemaking techniques have certainly contributed to the steady rise in quality wine, and the recent influx of capital has financed the upgrading of winery equipment. A string of recent good vintages in the 1990s and into the 21st century has helped lift Long Island wines to world-class stature. After a difficult 1992 vintage, the superb 1993 is probably what started to put Long Island wines on the map. The years 2000 and 2001 are probably the best vintages in Long Island's history. After an almost perfect growing season in 2001, with the right balance of rainfall and heat over a longer than usual summer, the good weather held throughout the harvest. This allowed the grapes to reach full maturation as they were allowed to hang longer than usual on the vines. "The 2001 reds are going to have tremendous colors and full rich flavors," says Kip Bedell. Mark Lieb adds, "Our whites are the best that we have ever harvested." Raphael's Richard Olson-Harbick says, "All our reds were harvested with levels of ripeness that I have never seen in 20 years of winemaking here." And from Jamesport's Ron Goeler, Jr., we hear, "Vintage 2000 was believed to be one of the best ever, but 2001 looks as though it will be even better."

Long Island wines are generally more intense in color and flavor than those from New York's Finger Lakes, and they are more delicate and restrained than wines from California. Many Long Island vintners consider France's Bordeaux region their model, citing similarities in climate and soils. At the same time, they are quick to insist their product does not mimic Bordeaux's famed wines — "Our wine has a *Long Island* style, not Bordeaux, not California," is a constant refrain.

Critics agree that the best of the Long Island Chardonnays are as good as any in the world, and the 1990s and early 2000s are proving that the potential for reds is equally strong. "I think we'll be known first for our Merlot," says winemaker Kip Bedell. "The grape ripens just after Chardonnay, and it is our most consistent producer. Eventually, I think we'll be known for our Cabernet Sauvignon and Cabernet Franc, too. In good years, we already make world-class red wines."

In a little over a quarter of a century, the Long Island wine industry has grown into a multimillion dollar business. It is a key to the region's economic and agricultural well-being. It produces almost $65 million in gross annual sales, generates $3.5 million in annual sales tax revenues, and employs (directly and indirectly) over 4,000 people. Furthermore, its growth has stimulated support industries and encouraged travel and tourism while helping to preserve open space and the East End's rural character in a region with heavy development pressures. Despite the ever-present threat of development, the region's farmland remains agricultural as potato fields continue to metamorphose into vineyards.

With the added bonus of its proximity to New York City, the most sophisticated and largest per-capita wine consumption center in the East, Long Island has a unique marketing advantage.

One exciting development on Long Island is the appearance of the **Premiere Wine Group,** a unique custom-crush winery that opened in 2000. One of only 12 custom-crush facilities in the world, the purpose of this organization is to contract with vintners who don't have their own winemaking facilities, or whose winery might get overloaded with an unexpected amount of grapes (as happened to many with the abundant 2000 harvest). **PWG** will provide services "from soup to nuts" as Kathy Lieb, one of the company's partners, describes it. "We'll do everything from simply crushing the grapes all the way through the entire winemaking process, from grape to bottle," Lieb explains. Pellegrini's talented Russell Hearn makes the wines at **PWG** and is also an owner, along with partners Bernard Sussman (an investor) and Kathy and Mark Lieb (who are also the proprietors of Lieb Family Cellars).

Long Island's wine country is approximately a two-hour drive from Manhattan, and an hour and a half by ferry from Connecticut. Twenty wineries are located on the North Fork, along a 35-mile-long strip of land that is scarcely five miles wide. The drive to the three wineries on the South Fork will take approximately three hours from Manhattan. They can be reached from the North Fork by driving through Riverhead or by taking the ferries that connect to Shelter Island.

Profile: Mad for Merlot

Most Long Island vintners make Chardonnay. A good many of them swear that Cabernet Franc is ideally suited to the *terroir*. Cabernet Sauvignon, while not quite ubiquitous, is a component in most serious Bordeaux-style red blends. But every Long Islander is mad for Merlot. It's the queen of wines, according to Pellegrini's Russell Hearn, who explains that Merlot is "supple and soft, not as hard and closed as Cabernet." "Merlot has the best affinity for our soils," Raphael's wine-maker Richard Olson-Harbick points out, adding, "It's also the most enjoyable grape to work with." "We have the ability here to make Merlot in a uniquely soft and elegant style," asserts Mark Lieb (Lieb Family Cellars).

Merlot is the popular grape associated with the classic wines of St. Émilion and Pomerol. It is Bordeaux's most planted red grape, but it has also become an important part of the finest red wine blends around the world, from Tuscany to Napa to Australia. Unlike other red wines, such as Cabernet Sauvignon or Pinot Noir, whose distinct characteristics can be readily identified by experienced tasters, Merlot resists easy pegging. It is reputed to be smooth — yet young Merlots frequently scour the tongue with aggressive tannins. It is said to be fragrant and fruity — but all too often Merlot is suffused with unappealing weedy or green pepper aromas. At it's best, however, and Bordeaux's famed Château Pétrus is a good benchmark, Merlot seduces the senses with its glorious rich, ripe, plump, and plummy fruitiness.

Fashion plays an undeniable role in Merlot's sudden visibility. We can all take a guess as to why Merlot has become the darling of the day — it isn't hard to pronounce, it's easy to drink, it has been well marketed. But since the logic of trends remains the genesis behind Merlot's sudden popularity, it remains largely unfathomable. And of course fashion is fickle — today's hottest car could be tomorrow's Edsel. Merlot, however, is no flash in the pan. The grape's long lineage dates back at least to 1784, when it was first documented in the Libournais section of Bordeaux. By the mid-1800s it was already a common ingredient in standard Bordelais-blended reds, with its lush fruitiness providing a good counterpoint and adding suppleness to the more austere Cabernet Sauvignon.

Merlot is susceptible to early spring frosts, but because it ripens earlier and can therefore be harvested at least a week before Cabernet, it is better suited to the eastern states, where sudden early frosts can wipe out a Cabernet crop. It also is more tolerant of the colder, damper soils of regions such as Long Island and Pomerol. But gauging the correct moment to harvest Merlot is perhaps even more critical than with Cabernet, for unripened Merlot can be green and astringent.

Overcropping is another common problem, particularly in the East Coast's cooler climate, for too much fruit left on the vines can prevent the grapes from fully ripening, reduce their overall sugar content, and lower their color and flavor. But when Long Island vintners get it right — and increasingly they are doing just that — few wines can compete with the delectable aroma and complex flavors of marvelous Merlot.

North Fork

BEDELL CELLARS
631-734-7537;
fax 631-734-5788.
www.bedellcellars.com.
wines@bedell cellars.com.
Main Rd. (Rte. 25),
Cutchogue, NY 11935.
Directions: From I-495, take
exit 73 in Riverhead.
Continue east on Old
Country Rd. (Rte. 58) to
Rte. 25 east. Continue
east to winery.
Owner: Michael Lynne.
Open: Daily 11am–5pm.
Price Range of Wines:
$7.49–$30.

• Riesling
• Chardonnay
• Cabernet Franc
• Merlot
• Cabernet Sauvignon
• Viognier
• Dessert wine

In 1999, Bedell was purchased by Michael Lynne, the CEO of New Line Cinema. Since Kip Bedell stayed on as winemaker and general manager, the quality of these absolutely top-rated wines is guaranteed. The tasting room has been transformed from a simple, turn-of-the-century, refurbished potato barn into a hospitable and elegant space, where the color scheme is dominated by New York-chic black and gray, and visitors gather around a sleek stainless steel bar to taste the wines. The winemaking facility will likewise benefit from the millions of dollars that Michael Lynne is sinking into this project. Major expansion includes a big, new barrel cellar geared to hold 750 barrels and a state-of-the-art bottling line. About 30 acres of fields are planted with grapes, and production is up to about 9,500 cases.

Bedell wine labels have undergone slight changes under the new ownership, but they are still easily recognized by the stylized pair of swans on a black-and-white background. Kip Bedell explains that the original symbol reflected his desire "to represent some of Long Island's marine bird life on the label."

The most popular Bedell white wine, called "Cygnet," is an alluring blend dominated by Riesling and Gewürztraminer grapes. "It's as close to a blush wine as we'll ever get here," says Kip with a smile. But this luscious and somewhat sweet wine is far more complex and classy than any blush could hope to be. "Main Road Red," a blend of 80 percent Cabernet Sauvignon/20 percent Merlot, is an easy-drinking wine that's just the thing to have with pizza, burgers, and other informal foods. The label on this wine depicts Kip's old, red 1951 Ford pickup.

Reserve Chardonnay is soft and elegant with discreet, rather than overbearing, vanilla flavors picked up from oak barrels and malolactic fermentation (Kip says this is a particularly good wine to serve with chili). A new departure for Bedell is Viognier, which Kip describes as a fickle grape, prone to "shatter" (a vineyard problem that results in the grapes not setting properly). Because of these difficulties, Viognier will be made only in good years (and only in small lots of two or three thousand cases), but it is well worth seeking out. Bedell's Viognier is a flashy beauty showing off all the peach and honeysuckle aromas characteristic of the grape and is better balanced and more elegant than most American versions of this classic white wine from the Northern Rhône region. "Eis," a Riesling dessert wine, is a heady dessert wine packed with flavors resembling dried apricots and peaches.

Bedell Merlot is one of the three or four best Merlots in Long Island, and for that matter in the entire East. The Merlots are beautifully balanced wines that linger for a long time on the palate. Look for aromas that can be smoky and meaty. Sniff at the wine again and catch whiffs of black pepper and coffee. In lighter years, a distinct fragrance of red berries (raspberries perhaps) is detected.

Like the Merlot, "Cupola," a Bordeaux-style blend based on Cabernet Sauvignon and Cabernet Franc (the proportions vary from vintage to vintage), has complex flavors, and it has the intense, almost herbal, aromas typical of Cabernet Sauvignon. "I still think Cabernet is the king of grapes," reflects Kip. "The only trouble is, it can't be done successfully on Long Island every year." But oh, those good years are worth waiting for.

Kip Bedell

It was a slow journey from running a fuel oil business to opening a winery, but John (Kip) Bedell inched along his chosen path patiently. After buying a potato farm in Cutchogue in 1980, Kip and his wife, Susan, spent the next 10 years commuting from their home in Garden City to Long Island's North Fork. Gradually, they began planting grapes and tending the vineyard. When he arrived on the North Fork, Bedell became one of only five pioneering wineries, along with Hargrave, Lenz, Pindar, and Peconic Bay. Barely aware of what the others were doing, they each invented their own rules for growing grapes and turning out wine, learning by trial and error what would work in this particular environment. This first wave of founding fathers served as a beacon for the next generation of Long Island winemakers.

Having been a home winemaker before purchasing the Cutchogue property, Kip Bedell made his first commercial wines in 1989. He had, as it turned out, almost inadvertently selected the perfect site for a vineyard. He also was blessed with an unusually fine palate and a considerable talent for creating superior wine. "Nobody — nobody — is more gifted," wrote the *New York Times* writer Howard G. Goldberg in *Fine Wine Folio*.

In 1990, after 10 years of juggling winemaking and marketing with the family fuel oil business, he sold the oil company. He and Susan moved to Cutchogue, and he became a full-time winemaker. "I'm still in a business that depends on the weather. And I'm still just pumping liquid from one container to another," he jokes, "but at least now I can drink the product."

Kip Bedell is a winemaker's winemaker, a widely respected technician and experienced vintner to whom others turn for inspiration and advice. No one would argue that he makes some of the best wines in the region. "There's no doubt that some of our earlier wines weren't great," he acknowledges. "Our vines were young, and we made some mistakes. We're still fine-tuning some of our viticultural practices, but there's been a great improvement over the past few years."

Making fine wines is the first hurdle, marketing them is the next big challenge. "We're sitting next to the biggest market in the world, which we've only just begun to tap," Kip explains, cocking his head in the direction of New York City. Bedell wines are now sold in several Manhattan stores and served in many of the city's finest restaurants. "The Long Island style is evolving. We'll be able to define it better when our region gets a little more time under its belt. We're poised right on the edge of a very exciting time."

The exciting times have taken a new direction since 1999 when Bedell Cellars was purchased by Michael Lynne, New Line Cinema's CEO. Under the terms of this transaction, Kip Bedell stays on as winemaker and general manager. He is also involved in several other Long Island projects, including overseeing the red wines made at Michael Lynne's other new property, Corey Creek. With more economic freedom now to push the quality envelope even further, Kip is throwing himself wholeheartedly into the physical expansion of Bedell Cellars. His fans await Kip's future vintages with keen anticipation.

CASTELLO DI BORGHESE/ HARGRAVE VINEYARD
631-734-5111, 800-734-5158; fax 631-734-5485.
www.castellodiborghese.com.
North Rd. (Rte. 48), P.O. Box 957, Cutchogue, NY 11935.
Directions: From I-495, take exit 73 in Riverhead. Continue east on Old Country Rd. (Rte. 58) to Rte. 25. Continue east to Cutchogue. Rte. 48 is just north of Rte. 25 and parallel to it.

Hargrave was the first commercial vineyard and winery on Long Island, founded by Louisa and Alex Hargrave. After searching up and down both the east and the west coasts for an appropriate spot to make the French-style wines they loved, the couple heard about John Wickham, a farmer who was raising a small experimental plot of vinifera grapes in Cutchogue, on the North Fork of Long Island. If he could do it on a modest scale, they reasoned, why shouldn't they succeed on a larger one?

The Hargraves planted their first vines in 1973. "We were here eight years before anyone else came. At that time, we weren't thinking of this

Marguerite Thomas

The welcoming sign at Castello di Borghese.

Owners: Anne Marie & Marco Borghese.
Open: Daily 11am–5pm; summer months: daily 11am–6pm.
Price Range of Wines: $7–$45.
Special Events: Concerts, opera, Summer Festival.

- Chardonnay
- Pinot Noir

becoming a viticultural region someday," Louisa once said. "One reason we came here is that it was a farm community, so we knew we could get tractor parts," she added with a touch of irony. The Hargraves went on to prove that vinifera grapes could indeed thrive on Long Island and that critically acclaimed wines could be produced from them.

In October 1999, almost three decades after planting their first vines, the Hargraves sold the property to Italian-born Marco Borghese and his American wife Anne Marie, who previously owned a successful import/export business. Marco Borghese's family tree extends back to 9th-century Italy and includes princes and even a Pope, as well as several winemakers. Marco grew up on the self-sustaining family estate in Tuscany, which made its own wine. It is this winemaking heritage that sparked his interest in carrying on the work that the Hargraves began on Long Island.

The Borgheses have expanded the vineyard plantings to 25 acres, with another 10 on the way. In addition to the original Chardonnay and Pinot Noir, the new owners are proudly identifying their heritage by planting Italian grape varieties, such as Sangiovese, Nebbiolo, and Dolcetto.

While the overall character of the original tasting room (which like so many other Long Island wineries began life as a potato barn) has not changed all that much, the space has expanded to give visitors a little more elbow room as they savor the Chardonnay's well-balanced fruitiness and the Pinot Noir's smoky aroma and hint of chocolate and mint on the palate. The Borgheses have also added a gallery where painting exhibitions are displayed and operas are performed. Not only does the Borghese presence seem to indicate that this pioneering winery is coming into step with modern tastes and Long Island's winemaking potential, but it also adds a touch of cultural class to the region.

COREY CREEK VINEYARDS
631-765-4168;
fax 631-765-1468.
www.coreycreek.com.
info@coreycreek.com.
Main Rd. (Rte. 25), P.O. Box 921, Southold, NY 11971.
Directions: From I-495, take exit 73 in Riverhead. Continue east on Old Country Rd. (Rte. 58) to Rte. 25 east. Continue east to Southold.
Owner: Michael Lynne.
Open: Daily 11am–5pm.
Price Range of Wines: $10.50–$18.

• Chardonnay
• Merlot

Michael Lynne purchased Corey Creek in August 1999, and he bought Bedell Cellars the following year. While Corey Creek wines had never been particularly noteworthy, the airy tasting room overlooking the vineyards was charming, and the vineyards are among the oldest on Long Island. More vineyards have recently been purchased (bringing the total to about 90 acres); the vineyards are now managed by the team from Lenz Winery. Corey Creek does not have its own winery, but the wines are crafted by some of the best in the business, including Kip Bedell and Pellegrini winemaker Russell Hearn. A couple of years of meticulous attention to the vineyards and cellar already shows results. Corey Creek's fine Chardonnays tend to be characterized by bright fruitiness balanced by a crisp acidity. Look for notes of dark chocolate and cedar in the altogether satisfying Merlots.

GALLUCCIO ESTATE VINEYARDS/ GRISTINA WINERY
631-734-7089;
fax 631-734-7114.

Like so many other vineyards on Long Island, this estate was a potato farm before the Gristina family purchased it in 1983. Today, it is a modern vineyard and state-of-the-art winery

www.gristinawines.com.
Main Rd. (Rte. 25), P.O. Box
   1269, Cutchogue, NY
   11935.
Directions: From I-495, take
   exit 73 in Riverhead.
   Continue east on Old
   Country Rd. (Rte. 58) to
   Rte. 25. Continue east to
   winery.
Owner: Vincent Galluccio.
Open: Daily 11am–5pm.
Price Range of Wines:
   $9–$26.

• Chardonnay
• Cabernet Franc
• Cabernet Sauvignon
• Merlot

owned by Vincent Galluccio, who acquired the property in August 2000. A telecommunications mogul with a long history working overseas with companies, such as IBM, British Telecom, and Metromedia Fiber Network, Galluccio had for some time contemplated buying a winery in Europe. When personal issues brought him back to the U.S., he acquired the exemplary Gristina property for a reported 5.2 million dollars.

Among the strengths of this estate are the "Andy's Field" wines (named for vineyards planted in 1984), which demonstrate the depth and complexity that fruit from mature vineyards can bring. Andy's Field Chardonnay is made in a new-world style, which is to say with plenty of fruit and oak showing on the palate, but it is still refined and by no means a bang-in-your-face wine. Andy's Field Merlot is also nicely balanced, with good depth of flavor.

At the other end of the Galluccio spectrum are the "Point House" wines, a new lower-priced second label. These wines are simpler in style than the high-end Andy's Field, but with their clean, straightforward character they can certainly hold their own in any company.

Both the vineyard acreage and the wine production have expanded to 180 acres and 10,000 cases, and still growing. Galluccio's team is entirely French, from winemaker Charles Girad to vineyard manager Bernard Ramis. There has also been input from renowned consultant Michel Rolland, famous for the rich, ripe, supple wines he has helped craft all over the world. Another change that will surely affect future Galluccio wines is a gradual transition to organic viticulture as of 2002. "We are stewards of the land," says Vince Galluccio explaining this decision. "It is a precious resource."

**JAMESPORT
   VINEYARDS**
631-722-5256;
   fax 631-722-5256.
www.jamesport-
   vineyards.com.
842 Main Rd., P.O. Box 842,
   Jamesport, NY 11947.
Directions: From I-495, take
   exit 73 in Riverhead.

No winery on Long Island has made such a tremendous leap in quality as Jamesport. While Jamesport has always been a popular tourist destination, the wines never aspired to greatness in the past. Beginning in the late 1990s, however, Jamesport suddenly became truly competitive. A good part of the force behind this evolution is Ron Goerler, Jr., the dedicated vineyard

Continue east on Old Country Rd. (Rte. 58) to Rte. 25. Continue east to winery.
Owners: Ron Goerler, Sr. & Ron Goerler, Jr.
Open: Daily 10am–6pm.
Price Range of Wines: $9.95–$45.

• Chardonnay
• Cabernet Franc
• Merlot
• Pinot Noir
• Late Harvest Riesling

manager who is now a partner in the winery along with his father. In addition to caring passionately about the quality of his wines, Ron, Jr. is endowed with another essential quality concern for the future. "Can we pass this along to our children?" he wonders aloud, sweeping his hand around to indicate the vineyards, the winery, the tasting room. "Any good wine region in the world depends on this."

In addition to contemplating the future, Ron is also able to cast a discerning eye over the past to analyze the impact of both climate and winemaking skills on the region. "Unlike California, no two years are alike here. After all, we're sticking 110 miles out into the Atlantic Ocean — we're never going to be California," he says. "And until recently, with inexperienced winemakers and vineyard managers, we just haven"t been up to snuff." The result has been wildly uneven vintages that, even in the best of circumstances were apt to be found lacking. "The decade of the 1980s was particularly wet. Then along came the warmer decade of the 1990s, which helped breed consistency," Ron recalls.

The combination of recent good weather and improved viticultural techniques is apparent in the wines. Some Jamesport Chardonnays offer a delicate interplay between fruit and oak, while others present a bolder, broader expression of this varietal. Cabernet Franc delivers a mouthful of plum flavors riding on a wave of soft tannins. The best Merlots are packed with ripe berrylike elements, and in some vintages (1998, for example), a little edge of funkiness will appeal to experienced palates. The regular Pinot Noir is pleasant and uncomplicated, giving off whiffs of cranberry and strawberry, while the unfiltered "Sarah's Hill" (from a single vineyard named after Ron's daughter) has surprisingly classic Pinot aromas and flavors. The 2000 Sarah's Hill is proof that, in the right hands and with the right weather, excellent Pinot can be made on Long Island. "Mélange de Trois," a Cabernet and Merlot-based blend (some vintages include Syrah), is ripe, complex, and luscious; it's made only in the best years. When Late Harvest Riesling is produced from the grapes of an exceptional warm vintage, one's senses are rewarded with an explosion of honey-coated fruit and a long, mellow finish. Alas, since there is only a single acre of these particular grapes, only small amounts of the outstanding wine are made.

**LAUREL LAKE
   VINEYARDS**
631-298-1420;
   fax 631-298-1405.
www.llwines.com.
info@llwines.com.
3165 Main Rd. (Rte. 25),
   Laurel, NY 11948.
Directions: From I-495, take
   exit 73 in Riverhead.
   Continue east on Old
   Country Rd. (Rte. 58) to
   Rte. 25 east. Continue
   east to winery.
Owners: Caesar Baeza,
   Francisco Gillmore,
   Alejandro Parot & Juan
   Esteban Sepulveda.
Open: Daily 11am–6pm.
Price Range of Wines:
   $7.99–$17.99.

• Merlot

L aurel Lake was the first Long Island winery to profit from foreign investment when, in July 1999, a group of Chilean partners purchased the estate. Laurel Lake was originally established in 1997, and the first vines were planted in 1980. Both the wine production and the vineyards are expanding under the new ownership, and while it is still too early to predict the ultimate outcome of all this, Laurel Lake is definitely a winery to keep an eye on. Chardonnay, Cabernet Sauvignon, Syrah, and a fairly sweet Rosé are being produced, as well as "Credence," a Cabernet-based red blend (first vintage released in 2002). "Windsong" is a summertime blend of white wines.

*Winemaker Eric Fry prepares
to sample his wine.*

Marguerite Thomas

LENZ WINERY
631-734-6010,
    800-974-9899 (NY only);
    fax 631-734-6069.
www.lenzwine.com.
Main Rd. (Rte. 25), P.O. Box
    28, Peconic, NY 11958.
Directions: From I-495, take
    exit 73 in Riverhead.
    Continue east on Old
    Country Rd. (Rte. 58) to
    Rte. 25. Continue east to
    winery.
Owners: Peter & Deborah
    Carroll.
Open: Daily 10am–6pm;
    winter months: daily
    10am–5pm.
Price Range of Wines:
    $7.99–$55.

• Chardonnay
• Gewürztraminer
• Pinot Gris
• Pinot Noir
• Cabernet Sauvignon
• Merlot

Originally founded by a pair of local restaurateurs, for the past decade Lenz has been owned by British-born Peter Carroll and his wife Debbie, who had the good sense to hire winemaker Eric Fry as soon as they came on board. Eric got his start in California at the Robert Mondavi and Jordan wineries under the tutelage of the legendary André Tchelistcheff. Following stints in Australia and then in New York's Finger Lakes region and at Westport Rivers in Massachusetts, he came to Lenz in 1989.

Working side by side with vineyard manager Sam McCullough, Eric has overseen the revitalization of the vineyards and has set a winemaking standard that has placed Lenz up along the very top rung of Long Island wineries. One of the biggest surprises when he first came to work in the East, Eric recalls, was the amount of acidity in Eastern wines. "What's the drug of choice for Eastern winemakers?" he asks. "Acid. First it shocked me. Then I began to get used to it. Now, I want more and more of it all the time, like any true junkie. One advantage of acidity is that it adds to wine's compatibility with food."

Indeed, that flash of acidity is what separates Lenz wines from their flabbier, less vivacious peers. The ultra brut sparkling wine, for example, is particularly crisp, made in the lean, bright style Eric favors. Lenz Gewürztraminer is lushly aromatic and bursting with flavor, yet bracingly clean on the palate; "I like Gewürztraminer to just slap people in the face with flavor," grins Eric.

Eric is not the type of winemaker to coddle his grapes. His approach is to let them ripen in the vineyard to a maximum degree, then he proceeds to "mash the hell out of them to extract every bit of color and flavor," he says. The results are red wines that do indeed have good color and flavor intensity. Case in point is the rich Cabernet Sauvignon, characterized by cherry flavors and a pleasant, long finish. Tasting back through several vintages of Merlot, one discovers a consistent depth and breadth in the rich, round, and complex wine.

With close to 70 acres of vines, Lenz produces about 10,000 cases a year. The informal tasting room is a Long Island classic, housed in a converted potato barn.

LIEB FAMILY CELLARS
631-298-1942;
    fax 631-734-1113.
www.liebcellars.com.
35 Cox Neck Rd.,
    Mattituck, NY 11952.
Directions: From I-495, take
    exit 73 in Riverhead. Drive
    east on Old Country Rd.
    (Rte. 58) to Rte. 25 east.
    Turn left on Rte. 105. Turn
    right on Rte. 48 to winery
    at corner of Rte. 48 and
    Cox Rd.
Owners: Mark & Kathy
    Lieb.
Open: Daily 11am–6pm.
Price Range of Wines:
    $15–$30.

• Sparkling wine
• Pinot Blanc
• Chardonnay
• Merlot

This promising new winery opened on Memorial Day weekend 2000. Owners Kathy and Mark Lieb, both with Wall Street backgrounds, represent a new generation of vintners — sophisticated, savvy, well schooled in business practices, and deep-pocketed. Mark, an investment banker, is also the owner of a money management firm based in Stamford, Connecticut. After working at a friend's California winery one summer in the 1980s, he decided that some day he would have a winery of his own. When he first met Kathy, who was then a vice president at Salomon Brothers, he warned her about this dream, but she married him anyway.

After they had looked at property in the Hudson River region and in the Finger Lakes, fate eventually led the couple to Long Island. If she ever had any doubts about wanting to be involved in winery ownership, they have clearly

Marguerite Thomas

Kathy and Mark Lieb, owners of Lieb Family Cellars.

vanished. Today, with abundant energy and good cheer, she handles the winery's sales and marketing.

Lieb wines are made by the Premium Wine Group, the custom-crush operation in which Mark and Kathy are also partners, along with investor Bernie Sussman and Russell Hearn (Pellegrini's winemaker). The Lieb tasting room, incidentally, is attractively sleek and modern.

The vineyard purchased by the Liebs in 1992 is one of Long Island's oldest, planted in 1983. Thirty more acres have been added to the original 13. The Liebs have eliminated the use of all herbicides in the vineyard and are enhancing the soil by mechanically tilling around the vines. These practices, they report, have strengthened the vines and improved the quality of the grapes. The grapes are all hand-picked and sorted.

This scrupulous care is paying off. Wines (about 4,000 cases so far) include a succulent Pinot Blanc from vines that are about 20 years old. This wine, with hints of pear and other delicate fruits, is an excellent match for seafood (in fact, says Kathy, local chefs are crazy about the wine). Lieb Chardonnay delivers a full throttle of aroma, fruit (pears and pineapple), and oak, all of it beautifully balanced. Merlot is soft and well structured. A Meritage blend will be released sometime in the future.

MACARI VINEYARDS
631-298-0100;
fax 631-298-8373.
www.macariwines.com.
macari@peconic.net.
150 Bergen Ave., P.O. Box 2, Mattituck, NY 11952.
Directions: From I-495, take exit 73 in Riverhead. Continue east on Old Country Rd. (Rte. 58) to Rte. 25 east. Turn left (north) on Rte. 105 and continue to Rte. 48. Turn right on Rte. 48 and continue east. From Rte. 48, turn onto Bergen Ave. and continue straight to winery.
Owners: The Macari family.
Open: Daily 11am–5pm.
Price Range of Wines: $7.99–$35.99.
Special Events: August Tapas & Wine Weekend.

• Chardonnay
• Sauvignon Blanc

Joe Macari, Sr. and his son, Joe, Jr. come to the North Fork wine world from a lifetime in the real estate business. The Macaris seem to be giving new meaning to the old cliché that the best way to make a small fortune is to take a large one and start a winery. With money seemingly no object, they've built an immensely attractive tasting room designed by architect Carol Vinci (who has produced some of Manhattan's hot/chic restaurants, such as Patria and Citrus). They've purchased one of the largest vineyard sites in the region, a vast former potato farm. With a total of 500 plantable acres, 180 are already under vine. The vineyard land was scrupulously prepared. "We've used 150,000 tons of fish so far, plus other organic materials for compost," says Joe, Jr., adding that the ultimate goal is to be completely organic. They've installed $40,000 worth of bird netting and invested in state-of-the art planters, harvesters, and computers. With this much money and care

Marguerite Thomas

Macari Vineyards tasting room, designed by Carol Vinci.

- Sparkling wine
- Rosé
- Cabernet Franc
- Cabernet Sauvignon

poured into the operation, the only thing missing was a dependable winemaker, and the Macaris seem to have finally solved this problem in the person of Jose Montilla. Born in Barcelona, Jose seems to have injected some of his own intense personality into some of the recent Macari releases. The unoaked Chardonnay is lean yet redolent of tropical fruit flavors, while the Reserve Chardonnay spreads a big, buttery layer of flavor over that same fruit. Sauvignon Blanc tends to be stylistically crisp and grassy. Nonvintage sparkling wine is equally crisp, with a beguiling aroma. Red wines are invariably well balanced, with ripe fruit flavors showing through; the exemplary Cabernet Franc has a distinctive edgy quality that distinguishes it from some of the more vapid manifestations of this varietal. "Bergen Road," a Bordeaux-style red wine blend made only in exceptional years, is a powerful potion with shots of ripe plum and berry streaking though it. Macari's total production hovers around 11,000 cases and will surely expand. There's no doubt that this winery has established itself as one of the leaders in the field.

MARTHA CLARA VINEYARDS
631-298-0075;
fax 631-298-5502.
www.marthaclaravine yards.com.
P.O. Box 124, Mattituck, NY 11952.
Directions: Take I-495 to exit 71. Turn left on Edwards Ave. Continue on Edwards to end, then turn right onto Sound Ave. Head east approx. 10 miles to winery.
Owners: The Entenmann family.
Open: Mon.–Sat. 11am–6pm, Sun. 12noon–6pm.
Price Range of Wines: $8.99–$25.

One of the North Fork's newest wineries is Martha Clara, owned by Robert Entenmann and his daughter, Jacqueline Entenmann Connolly. And yes, these are the same Entenmanns as the famed bakery (while the bakery no longer belongs to the family, Robert continues to put in time there as a consultant). Martha Clara was Robert Entenmann's mother, who is famous in her own right for having invented the "window" on bakery cake boxes.

Out of about 200 potential vineyard acres, the first five were planted in 1995. Over the next few years, a variety of vines, including Chardonnay and Merlot along with more unusual grapes such as Viognier and Sémillon, will be planted over 23 acres. Martha Clara's first vintage, released in 2000, was made by Wölffer Estate's Roman Roth. Another winemaker, Gilles Martin, will also help craft Martha Clara's wines, which until the winery is built are being made at Premium Wine Cellars. A big new tasting room will replace the current modest structure (a former polo horse barn). Long Island's biggest cave is being dug out to house the planned winemaking facility. A couple of sparkling white wines had already been released at the time of this writing, as had the "White Blend" for Martha Clara's second label, Glaciers End. Cabernet Franc, Cabernet Sauvignon, Meritage, and a couple of dessert wines are also in the works. Big things seem to be in store here.

OSPREY'S DOMINION
631-765-6188;
fax 631-765-1903.
www.opsreysdominion .com.
winemakr@ ospreys dominion.com.
44075 Main Rd. (Rte. 25), P.O. Box 275, Peconic, NY 11958.
Directions: From I-495, take exit 73 in Riverhead. Continue east on Old Country Rd. (Rte. 58) to Rte. 25 east. Continue east to winery.

Named after the majestic fish hawks that soar over Long Island skies, Osprey's Dominion is owned by Bud Koelher and Bill Tyree, who have been growing grapes since 1983. Today, they control 90 acres of their own vines, and they lease and operate an additional 20 acres. Initially the partners sold their fruit to various New York wineries, but in 1991, they began producing their own wines. Annual production is now at about 15,000 cases.

Chardonnay tends to be a big, friendly wine, equal stylistically in some ways to the robust

Owners: Bud Koehler & Bill
  Tyree.
Open: Mon.–Sat.
  11am–6pm, Sun.
  12noon–6pm.
Price Range of Wines:
  $10–$26.

• Chardonnay
• Gamay
• Meritage (Cabernet
  Sauvignon, Cabernet
  Franc, Melot)

Cabernet Sauvignon. Fans of Gamay will appreciate this lively version of it, which may in fact be Long Island's only Gamay. The Merlot is soothing and uncomplicated, while "Flight," the Meritage blend (Cabernet Sauvignon, Cabernet Franc, and Merlot) offers a more complex mouthful of wine.

PALMER VINEYARDS
631-722-9463, 631-722-4080;
  fax 631-722-5364.
www.palmervineyards.
  com.
palmervineyards@mail
  .com.
Sound Ave. (Rte. 48), P.O.
  Box 2125, Aquebogue,
  NY 11931.
Directions: From I-495, take
  exit 73 in Riverhead.
  Continue east on Old
  Country Rd. (Rte. 58) to
  4th traffic light,
  Osbourne Ave. Turn left
  on Osbourne and
  continue to end. Turn
  right onto Sound Ave.

Robert Palmer, a former advertising exec and marketing genius, has parlayed Palmer Vineyards into what is arguably Long Island's most recognized winery. Proof of his marketing acumen is that Palmer wines are poured in some 23 states and several foreign countries. While it is not one of the oldest wineries (its 10th anniversary was celebrated in 1996), Palmer wines were among the very first on Long Island to show true quality.

Stylistically, the wines made by Tom Drozd tend to be big and bold. Chardonnay offers up a swirl of butterscotch and apple flavors, further enhanced by a layer of vanilla in the barrel-fermented version. Pinot Blanc and Gewürztraminer

and drive 6 miles to winery on left.
Owner: Robert Palmer.
Open: Apr.–Oct.: daily 11am–6pm; Nov.–Mar.: daily 11am–5pm.
Price Range of Wines: $9.99–$29.99.
Special Events: Annual Yard Sale (wine bargains), Mem. Day Celebration, Fourth of July Hot Dog Event, Harvest Festival, cooking series, and live music.

• Pinot Blanc
• Chardonnay
• Gewürztraminer
• Sauvignon Blanc
• Merlot

both show the classic lush characteristics of their Alsatian counterparts. Cabernet Franc has bright, red cherry flavors, while the "Barrel Select Red" (a blend of Cabernet Sauvignon, Merlot, and Cabernet Franc made only in excellent years) is more apt to be reminiscent of dark cherries and blackberries. Harvest Select Gewürztraminer is an opulent late-harvest sweetie that Tom Drozd aptly describes as "dessert in a glass." Palmer's total production is about 20–25,000 cases, not big by global standards but fairly sizable for the region. About 100 acres are planted in vines.

Visitors love Palmer's English pub-style tasting room, furnished with Victorian booths that really were once part of an English pub.

Open to the constant sea breezes that help keep vines dry and disease-free, Palmer's site seems an ideal place for a vineyard. Winter temperatures are relatively mild out here on the North Fork, and summers are cooler than on the mainland. Like any paradise, however, there is a downside, and in this case that downside is covered with feathers and sports voracious, stiletto-sharp beaks. Like many vineyards on the east end of Long Island, Palmer is in the path of a North-South flyway for migratory birds. To protect the grapes from the ravages of the winged gluttony, every acre must be covered by bird netting — a labor-intensive and expensive proposition. Yet another potential threat to the crop between late Aug. until Oct. is from the occasional hurricane that can whip across the land tearing fruit off the vines in its path. Well, nobody ever said growing grapes was a piece of cake.

PAUMANOK VINEYARDS
631-722-8800;
    fax 631-722-5110.
www.paumanok.com.
mail@paumanok.com.
Main Rd. (Rte. 25), P.O. Box 741, Aquebogue, NY 11931.
Directions: From I-495, take exit 73 in Riverhead. Continue east on Old Country Rd. (Rte. 58) to

Lebanese-born Charles Massoud, Paumanok's owner woke up one morning a couple of decades ago and realized that he would never become the president of IBM, where he was then an executive. With that sobering realization in mind, he set about looking for something else that would provide an interesting and creative outlet for his interests and skills. Since Charles and his wife were passionate about wine, and since they had built-in consultants in the form of

Rte. 25. Continue east to winery.
Owners: Charles & Ursula Massoud.
Open: Mon.-Sat. 11am–6pm, Sun. 12noon–6pm.
Price Range of Wines: $14.99–$39.
Special Events: Sunset at the Vineyard (music, gourmet dishes from local restaurants, wine tastings), classical music, jazz concerts, Harvest Festival, Christmas music and wine tasting.

• Chenin Blanc
• Merlot
• Cabernet Sauvignon
• Riesling
• Late Harvest Sauvignon Blanc

Ursula Massoud's family (who have been in the wine business in Germany for generations), winegrowing seemed the answer. The Massouds elected to settle on Long Island's North Fork, where they began planting vines in 1983. They decided to call their new venture "Paumanok," Long Island's native name. In 1992, Charles left IBM, and from then on it was full steam ahead for the winery.

Charles has long claimed that once the vines were mature enough, his wines would be exceptional. Time, along with good winemaking skills, has proven him right. Initially, Paumonok's strength was in white wines, which continue to impress. Chardonnay, Riesling, and Chenin Blanc are all impeccable. The dessert wines — Late Harvest Riesling and Sauvignon Blanc — could convert all skeptics who think they don't like sweet wines. A tasting tip from Charles: "Don't swallow sweet wines too quickly. Let them sit in your mouth for a moment while you look for the dried fruit flavors."

In the last few of years, Paumanok reds have caught up in quality to the whites, and they may now be counted among the very top labels on Long Island. Most of the reds are unfiltered and aged in both French and American oak. The "Grand Vintage" (Merlot and Cabernet Sauvignon) is big, bodacious, and beautifully balanced. The winery has 50 acres under cultivation, producing 8,000 cases a year.

PECONIC BAY WINERY
631-734-7361; fax 631-734-5867.
www.peconicbay.com.
31320 Main Rd. (Rte. 25), P.O. Box 818, Cutchogue, NY 11935.
Directions: From I-495, take exit 73 in Riverhead. Continue east on Old Country Rd. (Rte. 58) to Rte. 25 east. Continue east to winery.
Owners: Paul & Ursula Lowerre.

New owners Paul and Ursula Lowerre purchased Peconic Bay in the winter of 1998. They have expanded the vineyard to 140 acres (with a total of 200 potential acres). Charlie Hargrave, brother of Long Island's pioneering vintner Alex Hargrave, manages the 21-year-old vineyard, where he has been more or less completely overhauling the old vines. This much-needed attention has already had an impact on the wines. Local "Flavor White" (a Chardonnay, Riesling blend) is an informal, approachable wine. Peconic Bay Chardonnay packs a pretty good wallop of

Open: Daily 11am–5pm.
Price Range of Wines:
$8.99–$19.99.

• Chardonnay
• Riesling
• Cabernet Franc
• Cabernet Sauvignon
• Rosé

**PELLEGRINI
VINEYARDS**
631-734-4111;
  fax 631-734-4159.
www.pellegrinivineyards
  .com.
pellegrinivineyards@msn
  .com.
23005 Main Rd. (Rte. 25),
  Cutchogue, NY 11935.
Directions: From I-495, take
  exit 73 in Riverhead.
  Continue east on Old
  Country Rd. (Rte. 58) to
  Rte. 25. Continue east to
  winery.
Owners: Joyce & Bob
  Pellegrini.
Open: Daily 11am–5pm.
Price Range of Wines:
  $8.99–$26.

• Chardonnay
• Merlot
• Cabernet Sauvignon
• Cabernet Franc
• Dessert wine

oak in the fragrance, but generous fruit on the palate balances it nicely. The outstanding Riesling, with its mixed bouquet of ripe pineapple, honey, figs, and grapefruit, leads one to wonder why American wine drinkers don't gravitate more towards fine Riesling. Rosé is another category that is mysteriously underappreciated by American consumers. Peconic Bay's version may resemble blush wine in some ways, but its polished finish lifts it out of mediocrity, and it's a dandy food wine to boot. Nothing wrong with Peconic Bay's soft, fruity Merlot either.

Pellegrini is across the street from the site of Fort Cutchogue, where some of Long Island's first European settlers lived in the 17th century. Were any of those early Cutchogue residents able to time-travel forward into today's world they would surely be astonished to discover that one of Long Island's finest, most serious wines is located a stone's throw from where the fort stood.

Bob Pellegrini grew up in a wine-drinking Italian family in New York. "I thought everybody drank wine," he says ruefully. As a young adult, Bob dabbled in home winemaking. Soon, as he puts it, "the hobby ran amuck" — to the point where he eventually became the owner of a Long Island winery. Working with his talented winemaker Australian-born Russell Hearn, Bob had distinct notions from the get-go about the kind of wine he wanted to produce. Take Merlot: "We were never looking to make a soft and easy Merlot," he says. "Too many of them today are simply fruity and not at all complex." Pellegrini Vineyards has a long track record for creating red wines, including Merlot, Cabernet, and a Bordeaux-style blend that lie stylistically between the finesse, structure, and complexity of top French wines and the big, fruity lushness characteristic of California.

Pellegrini white wines are as exceptional as the reds. The lush Vintner's

Pride Chardonnay, for example, delivers a big burst of fresh pear and sweet spice flavors tempered by enough acidity to make it an unusually good food wine. "Finale" is a beautiful, silky dessert wine made from late-harvested Gewürztraminer and Sauvignon Blanc grapes that are frozen before pressing.

Pellegrini is owned by Joyce and Bob Pellegrini — she's a retired teacher, he's the owner of a successful New York graphic design business. Everything about this winery reflects the good taste of a superior designer, from the handsome, stylized wine labels to the modern, cathedral-like tasting room, where a few café tables and chairs provide a nice spot to relax and sip. The building itself, which opened in 1992, was the North Fork's first truly stylish winery. Designed by local architects Samuels and Steelman, it is built around a grassy courtyard flanked by white columns. Outdoor balconies allow visitors to look down into the tank room, where between 10,000 and 12,000 cases of wine are processed each year. Recent vineyard purchases have added 50 acres to the original 32 acres under cultivation.

PINDAR VINEYARDS
631-734-6200;
   fax 631-734-6205.
www.pindar.net.
grapegod1@aol.com.
Main Rd. (Rte. 25), P.O. Box
   332, Peconic, NY 11958.
Directions: From I-495, take
   exit 73 in Riverhead.
   Continue east on Old
   Country Rd. (Rte. 58) to
   Rte. 25. Continue east to
   winery.
Owner: Dr. Herodotus
   Damianos.
Open: Daily 11am–6pm.
Price Range of Wines:
   $7.99–$34.99.
Special Events: Outdoor
   summer concerts.

• Chardonnay
• Sparkling wine
• Merlot
• Riesling
• Dessert wine

Pindar was founded in 1979 by Dr. Herodotus Damianos, a Stony Brook internist. As one might expect from a place named after a Greek poet, Pindar is a winery of heroic proportions. It has a larger production, with about 90,000 cases, and more land, some 500 acres planted in vines, than any other winery on Long Island. Even the number of people that its picnic pavilion can accommodate (300) is larger than other wineries. Pindar outdoes its neighbors in other ways as well. The variety of grapes planted is greater: fourteen in all, including the standard Chardonnay, Cabernet, and Merlot, as well as somewhat more unusual varieties, such as Malbec, Viognier, and Pinot Meunier. Winemaker Mark Friszolowski, a Long Island native, has been at Pindar since 1994.

Pindar's top tier wines have achieved a level of excellence that was unimaginable even a handful of years ago. Some 20 different wines are produced in all, including "Mythology," which was Long Island's first blended red wine. Recent vintages of this classic Bordeaux blend of Cabernet Sauvignon, Cabernet Franc, Merlot, Petit Verdot, and Malbec, while perhaps not quite Bordelais in style, have been remarkably smooth and appealing. "Pythagoras," a simpler version of the blend, is a tasty everyday wine. The impressive Reserve Merlot has matured into a graceful, fruity, and complex example of just how good this grape can be when properly grown and handled on Long Island.

I've long been partial to Pindar's Cuvée Rare, an outstanding sparkling wine that is bone-dry yet full of pleasing, yeasty flavors. This elegant sparkler is made from 100 percent Pinot Meunier grapes, one of the traditional varietals used in France as a Champagne-blending grape.

PUGLIESE VINEYARDS
631-734-4057;
    fax 631-734-5668.
www.pugliesevineyards
    .com.
Main Rd. (Rte. 25), P.O.
    Box 467, Cutchogue, NY
    11935.
Directions: From I-495,
    take exit 73 in Riverhead.
    Continue east on Old
    Country Rd. (Rte. 58) to
    Rte. 25 east. Continue
    east to winery.
Owners: The Pugliese
    family.
Open: Daily 10am–5pm;
    summer months: daily
    10am-6pm.
Price Range of Wines:
    $7.99–$21.99.

• Sparkling wine

It would be hard not to like this straightforward winery and the Pugliese family who run it. Ralph Sr. declares proudly, "I've been making wine since I was a kid." His son, Peter, has lately been taking over the winemaking duties from his dad. Ralph's wife, Patricia, hand-paints special bottles with nail enamel. (I don't usually like gussied-up bottles, but these are surprisingly pretty.) Ralph Jr.'s fine landscape photography adorns the tasting room walls.

The best thing at Pugliese is the sparkling wine, especially the Blanc de Noirs (100 percent Pinot Noir), and the Blanc de Blancs Brut with its pervasive aroma of green apples. Pugliese is undoubtedly the only producer on Long Island (or perhaps in the entire country) to make Sparkling Red Merlot. It's an acquired taste to be sure, but fans of Australian Sparkling Shiraz (and I'm one of them) will like this fun sparkler from Pugliese. I imagine the wine would be a festive and savory accompaniment to Thanksgiving or Christmas turkey.

Pugiese has 50 acres under cultivation and produces about 7,000 cases annually.

RAPHAEL
631-765-1100;
    fax 631-765-1991.
www.raphaelwine.com.
info@raphaelwine.com.
39390 Main Rd., Peconic,
    NY 11958.
Directions: From I-495, take
    exit 73 in Riverhead.

This newest of the North Fork wineries has had just about everything going for it even before the doors first opened in July 2001: generous cash flow, good vineyard land, an accomplished winemaker, and a world-class French consultant (Paul Pontallier of Château Margaux). The monumental winemaking and tasting room

Continue east on Old
Country Rd. (Rte. 58) to
Rte. 25. Continue east to
winery.
Owners: John & Joan
Petrocelli.
Open: Daily 12noon-6pm.
Price Range of Wines:
$14–$20.

• Sauvignon Blanc
• Merlot

facility looks more like the kind of grand place
you'd see in Napa Valley than out on the North
Fork where potato-barn chic has been the norm.

Winemaker Richard Olson-Harbick brings a
wealth of experience to the task of launching this
ambitious winery. After catching the wine bug as a
student at Cornell, he first went to work for Hermann Wiemer in the Finger Lakes. Then, following stints at various wineries around the world,
including South Africa's exquisite Plaisir de Merle,

Raphael — The Newest Kids in Town

The Long Island wine industry is still in its infancy, but by the time Jack and Joan
Petrocelli opened their winery in June 2001, winemaking in this region already had
enough of a track record to enable them to avoid many of the mistakes made by the
first and second waves of North Fork vintners. Since the Petrocellis had no need to
reinvent what had already been learned, they were free to embroider upon the fab-
ric already in place. They planted the kind of grapes that had proven over 20 years
to be successful and hired a winemaker, Richard Olson-Harbick, who had witnessed the entire evolution of winemaking on Long Island.

From the very beginning, Joan and Jack Petrocelli were adamant about wanting
to make the best wine the region could yield. Because all good wine depends on
quality grapes, their first concern was how to turn what had once been a vegetable
farm into the best possible vineyard. "The first thing we had to decide was what
kind of world-class wine this region could produce," recalls Richard Olson-Harbick. All the data they gathered indicated that in terms of soil composition, climate,
and length of the growing season, their site resembles Bordeaux more than any
other established wine region. Soils on the property consist mostly of loam based
on a layer of clay, much like the land in Bordeaux's winegrowing region; the Sauvignon Blanc grows on a patch of vineyard dominated by sand and gravel — very
much the conditions favored by Bordeaux Sauvignon Blanc. According to an
ancient Bordeaux proverb, "Only vines overlooking the water are capable of producing wines of great quality." Happily, Raphael's vineyards are a mere 2,000 feet
from the relatively temperate waters of Peconic Bay. With all this in mind, the Petrocellis brought Paul Pontellier, managing director at Bordeaux's famed Château
Margaux, on board as consultant. His advice was followed every step of the way,
from the optimum amount of space needed between the rows of vines to the most
suitable clones for Raphael's particular site. He suggested the best way to plant the
vines and gave his opinion on how the finished bottles should be packaged.

To ensure the highest possible quality in this demanding region, rigorous vineyard techniques are practiced at Raphael. For example, because too much fruit
hanging on the vines dilutes the overall quality of a wine, when premium wine is
the goal, grape bunches are usually pulled off at various stages before the harvest.
To put this in some kind of perspective, compare grapes grown for bulk wine in

*Raphael winemaker,
Richard Olson-Harbick.*

Marguerite Thomas

California's Central Valley, which may come in at 12 or even more tons per acre to grapes destined for fine wine in Napa, which might be reduced to four tons/acre. Raphael's ultimate goal is to thin the grapes to about two tons/acre. All Raphael grapes are picked by hand, an unusual practice for Long Island where machine harvesting is the norm. Furthermore, the fruit that comes into the winery is all sorted by hand to eliminate less than perfect bunches.

Along with the luxury of profiting from the experiences of their predecessors and from the combined skills of their winemaker and French consultant, Jack and Joan have the further advantage of being able to afford to make their dream come true in high style. The Petrocellis, whose primary business is a construction company specializing in building churches and cathedrals, were inspired for the design of their winery by monasteries near Naples, where the Petrocelli family originated (Raphael, by the way, was the name of Jack's father). With its soaring stone arches and meticulous attention to design detail, Raphael looks more like a traditional cellar in Bordeaux than the state-of-the-art, new-world winery it actually is.

The Petrocellis and their team took the admirable decision to concentrate principally on Merlot, Bordeaux's most planted red grape, and to a lesser extent on Bordeaux's prime white grape, Sauvignon Blanc. Their goal is to make the finest wine that this region is capable of producing, a wine that will reflect both the traditional character of fine Bordeaux, as well as the unique qualities imparted by Long Island's own *terroir*. It will be many years before the vines mature, and the wines age, but meanwhile, the wines already coming out of Raphael are a treat.

Richard made his way back to Long Island, where he had first started working at the age of 19.

Raphael's ultimate goal is to remain small, producing a maximum of 12,000 cases — about twice as much wine as they make today. "What we're about is how good the wine is, not about how much we make," says Richard. Raphael has 42 contiguous acres already under vine, with another 20 acres that may be planted in the near future. While Raphael's own vines are maturing, grapes are purchased from North Fork growers known for quality grapes.

Raphael's first white wine, the 2000 Sauvignon Blanc, was made from the property's own three-year-old vines. While more mature vines will clearly add greater structure and depth of flavor, this soft, slightly spicy wine is already pretty classy. The 1997 Merlot, made from purchased grapes, shows off ripe fruit, well-balanced tannins, and good complexity and length. The 1999 — the first red wine made from Raphael's own grapes — has a hint of dried fennel intermingled with fruit flavors and a good distribution of soft tannins.

TERNHAVEN CELLARS
631-477-8737.
www.ternhaven.com.
harold@ternhaven.com.
331 Front St., P.O. Box 758,
  Greenport, NY 11944.
Directions: From I-495, take
  exit 73 in Riverhead.
  Continue east on Old
  Country Rd. (Rte. 58) to
  Rte. 25. From beginning
  of Rte. 25, drive 20 miles
  to Greenport. Winery is
  on right after enter
  village.
Owner: Harold Watts.
Open: Apr.–Dec.: Fri.–Sun.
  11am–6pm; Jan.-Mar.: by
  appt.
Price Range of Wines:
  $11.25–$21.75.

Ternhaven, which opened in the summer of 1998, is owned by Harold Watts, professor emeritus (economics) at Columbia University. Harold, who began making wine in his Manhattan apartment, says that his goals are modest — he aims to keep production small (he currently makes about 650 cases). The wines, made from his own five prime acres of 14-year-old vines, are all red and include Cabernet Sauvignon, a sweet and juicy Merlot, and the flagship Claret, a full-flavored red blend. The tasting room is handily located in downtown Greenport.

South Fork

CHANNING DAUGHTERS
631-537-7224;
  fax 631-537-7243.
www.chaningdaughters
  .com.

Walter Channing has done lots of things right at Channing Daughters (named for his four girls). First of all, he was prepared to invest money — lots and lots of money — into

1927 Scuttlehole Rd., P.O.
  Box 2202,
  Bridgehampton, NY
  11932.
Directions: From I-495, take
  exit 70. Follow County
  Rd. south to Montauk
  Hwy. (Rte. 27) through
  Southampton
  commercial district to
  Water Mill. After about
  0.5 mile, watch for sign
  for Sag Harbor at
  Scuttlehole Rd. Winery is
  about 3 miles from Rte.
  27.
Owners: Walter & Molly
  Channing.
Open: Daily 11am–5pm.
Price Range of Wines: $13
  for Scuttlehole
  Chardonnay–$19 for
  Brick Kiln Merlot.

• Chardonnay
• Merlot

starting his winery. As a venture capitalist involved in health care and medical technology, his financial resources could withstand the tremendous expense of starting a vineyard and winery. Another thing he's doing right is making wines from an established vineyard. Every credible winemaker in the world will tell you that good wine begins in the vineyard, so if you want to produce successful wine, make sure you have great grapes, they say, preferably from older vines. Walter, who began planting vines in 1982, now owns some of the oldest vineyards on the South Fork.

Walter has teamed up with an experienced winemaker, Larry Perrine, a seasoned Long Island vintner. "In sculpting our project into the future we're trying to focus on bright, fresh lighter wines," says Larry. "We're not trying to imitate Pomerol. We want wines in tune with summer dining." All Channing Perrine wines are made from small lots of fruit from older vines. The mild-mannered Chardonnay is designed to go with seafood and other delicate dishes, while the fresh Red Merlot is a light, summery libation that is great with burgers and other foods hot off the grill.

Channing Daughters tasting room is set in the middle of the vineyards. Walter Channing's wood sculptures are displayed around the winery and vineyards, adding a touch of beauty and fun to the wine-tasting experience.

DUCK WALK
VINEYARDS
631-726-7555;
  fax 631-726-4395.
www.duckwalk.com.
231 Montauk Hwy., P.O.
  Box 962, Water Mill, NY
  11976.
Directions: Take Rte. 27
  (Montauk Hwy.) through
  Southampton to winery
  on left.
Owner: Dr. Herodotus
  Damianos.

If it's true that the third time is a charm, Duck Walk Vineyards is in for a good run, and indeed, its wines get progressively better vintage after vintage. Formerly Le Rêve, then Southampton Winery, Duck Walk was launched in 1994 by Pindar's proprietor, Dr. Herodotus Damianos. Duck Walk owns about 38 acres of vines in Southampton plus 50 acres in Mattituck and produces about 30,000 cases of wine a year. "Dr. Dan's" son, Jason, has recently taken over as winemaker here after pursuing an enology degree at

Open: Daily 11am–6pm.
Price Range of Wines:
 $7.95–$34.95.
Special Events: Summer
 weekends, live music on
 patio.

• Merlot
• Dessert wine

the University of California in Fresno, followed by further schooling at the University of Bordeaux. Jason's first Duck Walk vintage was in 2001. Another Damianos son, Alex, is the winery's general manager and vice president. It is heartening to see the second generation of the founding families moving into position in this region, a measure of just how solid the Long Island wine industry has become.

Since the beginning, one of Duck Walk's big successes has been the Merlot Reserve, an unfiltered, complex wine packed with the ripe flavors of dark plums and cherries. "Aphrodite" is a very popular dessert wine that can be stunning in good years. Made from late-harvested Gewürztraminer grapes, this sweet concoction shows off elements of honeysuckle, peach, and apricot. Like its sister winery Pindar, Duck Walk uses colorful, eye-catching labels (one of my favorites is Aphrodite, a depiction of a lovely goddess of heroic proportions).

WÖLFFER ESTATE
631-537-5106;
 fax 631-537-5107.

Conditions for growing grapes on the South Fork can be more challenging than on the North Fork, for it's a flatter and siltier place,

www.wolffer.com.
wolferwines@hamptons
.com.
139 Sagg Rd., P.O. Box 9002,
Sagaponack, NY 11962.
Directions: From I-495, take
exit 70 in Manorville.
Drive south to Rte. 27.
Take Rte. 27 east to
Bridgehampton. At first
traffic light after leaving
Bridgehampton, turn left
onto Sagg Rd. Winery is
0.25 mile on right.
Owner: Christian Wölffer.
Open: Daily 11am–6pm.
Price Range of Wines:
$10.50–$35.

• Chardonnay
• Sparkling wine
• Merlot

with somewhat cooler temperatures. Grapes that require lighter soils, such as Cabernet Sauvignon, definitely do better on the North Fork, says winemaker Roman Roth. "But in the hot and dry years," he continues, "the South Fork has the advantage with its heavier, loamier soils that hold moisture. The grapes retain more acidity, so we can let them hang longer on the vine with less danger of disease."

Raising grapes wasn't what owner Christian Wölffer had in mind when he first moved out to the South Fork in 1977. When he purchased a 14-acre potato farm, his goal was to create a horse farm. Today, his property — 173 acres in all — includes 13 acres of jumping rings and the largest indoor riding ring on the East Coast. This enterprise has helped make equestrian pursuits one of the Hamptons' hottest hobbies. Christian also built a nursery, but when Hurricane Gloria blew down all the trees in 1988, he decided to plant a vineyard instead. The first wines were released in 1992, and today, the production from 55 acres of vines is about 15,000 cases a year.

Christian Wölffer, a native of Hamburg, Germany, made his fortune in real estate and venture capital investments in South America and Canada. He still travels constantly, racking up a million Frequent Flyer miles a year, while remaining deeply involved in his Long Island projects. When a writer once asked him how he managed to keep up the pace, Christian answered — only half jokingly I suspect — "I drink a lot of wine and ride a lot."

Wölffer wine is among Long Island's very best. The vines have aged enough to yield wines of greater complexity, and Roman's skills, like those of the other first generation of top Long Island vintners, have grown along with their understanding of their particular *terroir*. Vineyard manager Richard Pisacano has also brought improvements to the venture. Wölffer's market has broadened considerably over the past years, and the wines are now served at many top Manhattan restaurants.

Roman's goal has always been to make wine for food. "The whole structure of wine is meant to accompany food," he insists. The palate-cleansing acidity that tempers the fruit-rich flavors of the Chardonnays and Merlots does, indeed, make them ideal food wines. The Reserve Chardonnay typically presents a resonant chorus of flavors evoking both fruit and the kind of mineral quality often found in fine Burgundy whites. The Reserve Chardonnay has concentrated flavors and a velvety texture, but finishes with crisp apple nuances. The Merlots have lip-smacking cherry flavors backed up by complexity derived from long maceration on the skins (up to 28 days, compared to the 15 days averaged by many of Roman's Long Island colleagues). A second label, Réserve St. Martin, features wines that have simpler flavor profiles, but are well-made, imminently pleasurable, fruit-dominant quaffs.

I applaud this winery's approach to making fewer types of wine, but making them well. More wineries in the East would benefit from scaling back their overly long list of different wines, concentrating instead on a few wines beautifully made.

OTHER LONG ISLAND WINERIES

BANFI OLD BROOKVILLE VINEYARDS (office: 800-645-6511, 800-626-9200; info@banfi.com.; 1111 Cedar Swamp Rd., Old Brookville, NY 11545) Banfi is the only commercial vineyard in Nassau County (and also has the claim of being the closest vineyard to Broadway). Planted in 1982, the 45-acre vineyard is dedicated exclusively to Chardonnay. While there is no winery or tasting room here, approximately 1,200 cases of "Old Brookville Chardonnay" are custom-produced and bottled on the North Fork by Russell Hearn. The wine, available nationwide, retails for about $15.

SCHNEIDER VINEYARDS (631-727-3334; www.schneidervineyards.com; info@schneidervineyards.com; 2248 Roanoke Ave., Riverhead, NY 11901) Christiane Baker Schneider and Bruce Schneider have been producing top-notch wines from other peoples' vineyards for several years. Now they have their own vines (about 22 acres, planted in the spring of 2000). They'll also be opening their winery at long last. With the guidance of consulting winemaker Sean Capiaux, the Schneiders will continue to focus on their Cabernet Franc, their much-acclaimed signature wine.

THE FINGER LAKES

Most of the wineries in upstate New York are clustered around three of the Finger Lakes: Cayuga is the longest of the lakes (40 miles);

Keuka, the most scenic, is known as "the jewel of the Finger Lakes" because of its unusually clear and clean waters; and the deepest lake is Seneca (630 feet deep in some places), where wineries line both shores in such profusion that one may easily visit several of them in a single day.

The whole region is one of spectacular scenic beauty, where vine-covered hills roll down to the edge of the water. Hundreds of examples of the Greek Revival architecture that once dominated the Finger Lakes region still stand. Many of them are open to visitors, including Rose Hill Mansion, one of the most beautiful Greek Revival houses in America (Route 96A, Geneva, NY).

Originally, the Finger Lakes region was home to the Seneca and Cayuga Indians of the Six Nations, whose lands were devastated by the Clinton-Sullivan military expedition of 1779. The area opened up for settlement after the American Revolution. When the Erie Canal linked Cayuga and Seneca Lakes in 1830, the population grew, and industry flourished.

More recent history has played a role here as well. The region prides itself on being the birthplace of women's rights as the first Women's Rights Convention was held in Seneca Falls in 1848. This is also the cradle of American aviation since Glenn Curtiss pioneered the first flying airplanes here in 1908. And the Finger Lakes is where the modern wine industry in the Eastern United States was born.

The Finger Lakes region is blessed with a climate moderated by the lakes and by soils that are a good host for grapes. It has another advantage as well. "One of our great secret weapons is Indian summer," says Willy Frank, son of the legendary vintner Konstantin Frank, referring to the exceptional warm period that arrives in late fall to prolong the growing season. Because of these favorable conditions, the Finger Lakes region was able to produce strong-flavored, sweet wines made from native American labrusca grapes, such as Niagara and Catawba, for generations. Native labrusca was what everyone focused on since it was universally believed that Chardonnay, Riesling, and other European vinifera grapes could not survive New York's freezing winter climate.

The first person to challenge the labrusca tradition was Charles Fournier, who at the end of Prohibition left his post as chief winemaker for the French Champagne firm Veuve Clicquot to come to the Finger Lakes to work at the Urbana Wine Company, which later became the Gold Seal Wine Company. Fournier experimented with the hybrid grapes that had been developed in France to withstand phylloxera and other vine diseases. As a result of his work, other vintners began focusing on hybrids. Important though this advancement was, however, Fournier's most lasting contribution was the trust that he put in Dr. Konstantin Frank, the German-born Russian emigré whom he hired in 1953 to help plant vinifera grapes at Gold Seal.

Konstantin Frank had managed vineyards in the Ukraine, where it was not unusual for winter temperatures to drop to 20°-30° below zero. If vinifera grapes could survive those temperatures, Frank reasoned, they ought to be able to thrive here as well. First at Gold Seal, and later at his own winery on Keuka Lake, Dr. Frank proved that vinifera vines could indeed be grown in upstate New York. Frank's influence on the entire Eastern wine industry is inestimable. He inspired, encouraged, and educated leading trailblazers Philip Wagner (Maryland's Boordy Vineyards), Louisa and Alex Hargrave (Hargrave Vineyard on Long Island), and John Dyson (Millbrook Winery in the Hudson Valley), among scores of others.

The second important pioneering European immigrant was another German, Hermann J. Wiemer, who arrived in the Finger Lakes in 1968. Wiemer first made wine from hybrid grapes at Bully Hill Vineyards, but he switched to vinifera when he acquired his own vineyard and winery in 1979. He also established one of the nation's largest grape nurseries. In addition to producing some of the region's most successful wines, Wiemer provides rootstock to vineyards all over the country.

Many of the Finger Lakes leading vintners are descended from farmers who began by raising labrusca grapes for the Taylor Wine Company, and who then replanted with hybrids to keep pace with demand. For years, the powerful Taylor Wine Company was the major player in the Eastern wine business, and most Finger Lakes viticulturists sold their grapes to this giant. When Taylor was taken over by Coca-Cola, many growers resisted becoming a link in the impersonal and exploitative chain of corporate farming. By contrast, the family-run Taylor Company was widely perceived as being benevolent and fair.

By the early 1980s, tastes in New York State, as elsewhere, had shifted from sweet wines toward drier, European-style wines, with an analogous decline in the labrusca and hybrid grape industry. Many of the growers who did not make the switch to vinifera had trouble staying afloat economically. "One of the unspoken reasons why hybrid wines are still around is that the grapes are a cinch to grow," one vintner told me a few years ago. "Vinifera is definitely harder work, and a lot of growers just don't want to make the extra effort." Now, at the dawn of the 21st century, all serious commericial winegrowers are making the effort, and vinifera rules.

Riesling

Of the many vinifera grape varieties thriving in the Finger Lakes region today, Riesling still stands out as the brightest star in the firmament. Other grapes, such as Chardonnay, Gewürztraminer, and Cabernet Franc, are showing great promise in this relatively cool region, but it would be hard to find Riesling anywhere in the country that surpasses the best from the Finger Lakes.

For a variety of reasons, Riesling is a misunderstood and underappreciated wine in the United States. Part of this has to do with the belief that all Riesling is sweet, a perception dating back to the days of bland, mass-marketed Liebfraumilch. A lot of Riesling *is* sweet, ranging in style from spineless schlock to some of the greatest dessert wines in the world, notably Germany's *Trockenbeerenauslese.* But the trend worldwide — Riesling is grown in virtually every wine-producing country on earth — is toward a drier wine that is adaptable to a variety of foods.

The Riesling grape is believed to have originated in Germany, where the Romans probably cultivated it. Many connoisseurs consider Riesling the noblest of all wines. While Germany, Austria, and Alsace have traditionally produced the ultimate Rieslings, a handful of vintners in the Finger Lakes have been making Rieslings that can arguably stand side by side with the great Rieslings of Europe.

One of the charms of an excellent Riesling is its beguiling aroma that, in youth, is fresh and floral, becoming more subtle and intriguing with maturity. With a touch of age, it may develop a gasolinelike bouquet known as "petrol." To the novice, this may sound unappealing, but one whiff of it is enough to quicken the pulse of Riesling devotees.

Riesling's character depends, more than most grapes, on *terroir,* or the site on which it is grown. Mediocre Riesling can vary from watery, insipid versions to those that are cloyingly sweet. Fine Riesling, on the other hand, will range from the light and racy elegance found in wine from Germany's Moselle region to the firm, vivacious elixir from the Rheingau. Flavors range from fresh lime peel to ripe plum and honey. All good Rieslings, whether dry or sweet, finish with a refreshing flash of acidity.

One of Riesling's many attributes is its ability to age well. Unfortunately, most top-grade Riesling today is consumed in its infancy, before it has the chance to develop the full charm and multifaceted personality of an adult wine.

Riesling is one of the best wines to drink with food. "A dry Riesling is the most versatile wine you have in the house," asserts Vinifera Wine Cellars' Willy Frank. Crisp, dry Riesling is an excellent match for simple seafood or chicken, for certain sausage and other pork preparations, and for such classic dishes as *choucroute* (sauerkraut). Slightly less dry Rieslings are excellent accompaniments to spicy Cajun, Mexican, and Thai cuisine. When it carries a hint of sweetness, Riesling is a far more satisfying aperitif than most bone-dry wines — "Better than a dry martini," says Willy Frank. Late-harvested or other dessert-style Rieslings are uniquely satisfying at the end of a meal.

There is nothing mysterious about why Riesling grapes are well suited to the Finger Lakes. Despite their small, tightly clustered berries that are vulnerable to injury and disease, Riesling vines also have thick bark and a habit of budding late that enables the plant to resist freezes. Riesling grapes depend on cool nights to develop their characteristic bracing acidity and on warm days for their honeyed sweetness. These grapes do particularly well when the growing season is long enough for flavors to develop slowly. If the weather is too warm, as in many parts of California, grapes ripen before the full balance of fruitiness, acidity, and finesse is complete. California winemakers often add acidity to make a palatable wine. On the other hand, when Riesling is grown in a climate that is too cool, the grapes don't ripen completely and they lack flavor, as well as sufficient alcohol, to produce a harmonious wine.

Finger Lakes vintner Scott Osborne says, "We can get the acids we need here to balance the sugars. That's what makes Riesling great. The fact that we can get up to 12 percent alcohol adds to the overall balance."

Another factor favoring Finger Lakes Riesling are substances called monoterpenes. These various compounds, which are responsible for the perfume of certain aromatic grapes, such as Riesling and Gewürztraminer, are particularly prevalent in this region's grapes.

"The Finger Lakes is Riesling country," Willy Frank has long claimed. "We produce some of the most delicate and elegant Rieslings in the world." Fox Run's winemaker, Peter Bell, concurs, "We can make Rieslings that can exceed anyone else's."

Most winemakers in the Finger Lakes agree with these sentiments. So, finally, can discerning consumers.

Today, a new generation of talented winemakers and knowledgeable wine drinkers has raised the quality bar for Finger Lakes wines. Many growers have decided to take control of their own destiny by founding their own wineries. As a result, the Finger Lakes district is unique among Eastern wine regions in that, rather than being dominated by wealthy "outsiders," many of the upcoming stars here are vintners who know the land intimately from working it for generations. They have experienced all the ups and downs of the region's winemaking history, and they are determined to make the kind of serious wines that will garner world recognition.

Contemporary Finger Lakes wines reflect the touch of both the pioneers and the new activists. No ambitious winemaker in the region today has been untouched by the example of Willy Frank and Hermann Wiemer, who steadfastly led the charge toward excellence and who continue to turn out extraordinary wines. Among the Finger Lakes younger crop of visionary wineries are Anthony Road, Fox Run, Red Newt, Shalestone, and Sheldrake Point.

The strength of the Finger Lakes region rests in the type of wines that are characteristic of cool weather regions, notably Riesling, Chardonnay, and Champagne-style sparkling wine. But one fascinating change sweeping through the vineyards is the increased planting of red wine vinifera grapes, challenging the notion that only white wine can flourish here. Cabernet Franc and Pinot Noir, which in the late 1990s were just beginning to put in a shaky appearance, seem now to be proving their worth with a couple of good solid contemporary examples. The potential for Cabernet Sauvignon and Merlot is, as yet, less convincing. While a couple of surprisingly excellent wines from these varietals have been produced by the most skillful winemakers, in general, these grapes require a longer growing season, more heat, and less extreme winter temperatures than the Finger Lakes consistently affords. On the other hand, even five years ago decent Cabernet Franc seemed an unlikely possibility, so perhaps one should never say "never" in the Finger Lakes.

Since the late 1990s, as vinifera vines matured and winemakers and vineyard managers learned more about the region's idiosyncrasies, there has been a quantum leap in quality in the Finger Lakes. Riesling continues to impress, as does Chardonnay; an advanced trellising technique that allows more sun to reach the fruit is one of the reasons that the best producers are now turning out crisp but flavorful Chardonnays that are well balanced and utterly pleasing. Visitors to the region will find an abundance of satisfying white wines and a few that are dazzling. Outstanding red wines are fewer and farther between —many still have a green, cedary flavor that is a result of many factors, including the youth of the vines and grapes that are harvested before they're fully ripe. Although the Finger Lakes region, which is one of the world's most beautiful viticultural areas, is still in its infancy, it already has attractions galore for discerning wine lovers with open minds and a thirst for new discoveries.

Seneca Lake

ANTHONY ROAD WINE COMPANY
315-536-2182,
   800-559-2182 (NY only);
   fax 315-536-5851.
www.anthonyroadwine
   .com.
anthonyroad@flare.com.
1225 Anthony Rd., Penn
   Yan, NY 14527.
Directions: From I-90, take
   exit 42 to Rte. 14 south,
   turn east on Anthony Rd.
   to winery.
Owners: John & Ann
   Martini, Phillip & Nancy
   Martini.

Anthony Road continues to surprise and delight. The spacious new hospitality center provides a stunning backdrop for tasting the wines. The production, which continues to grow, is up from 9,000 cases a couple of years ago to 11,000, and still growing. Winemaker Johannes Reinhardt is working some magic here, and the wines — always promising — just get better and better. Cabernet Franc and Riesling are outstanding. The top-of-the-line wines are named "Veritas." I guarantee you that the Veritas Late Harvest Vignoles, with its complex and succulent fruit flavors and welcome dash of acidity on the

Johannes Reinhardt,
winemaker at Anthony Road
Wine Company.

Marguerite Thomas

Open: Mon.–Sat.
  10am–5pm, Sun.
  12noon–5pm.
Price Range of Wines:
  $6.99–$34.
Special Features: Large
  tasting room and well-
  stocked gift shop.
Special Events: September
  Federweisser Festival
  with wine, bratwurst,
  and polka band, and
  spring Veritas Festival.

• Cabernet Franc
• Late Harvest Vignoles
• Riesling

finish, can compete with any of America's leading dessert wines.

One sure sign pointing to the coming of age of an emerging wine region is when outside investors begin to arrive. The fact that Robert Young — a noted grape grower in California whose Chardonnay fruit has helped put Chateau St. Jean on every wine lover's map — is a shareholder in Anthony Road and has recently bought 105 acres along Seneca's shoreline, seems further proof of the Finger Lakes promise.

Johannes Reinhardt

Anthony Road's winemaker Johannes Reinhardt grew up in Franconia, Germany, in a family that has been producing wines there since 1438. In the family winery, he gained a solid background in the practical and technical aspects of winemaking. He then went to work in an organic winery, specifically to experience firsthand more about the role nature plays. "I learned a great deal there about how important it is to work with nature through proper canopy management and other vineyard practices. I would say this was the most important experience of my entire professional life," he asserts now.

In 1999, just as Johannes was contemplating leaving Germany to seek experience in another country, he picked up a German newspaper and happened to read a classified ad from Dr. Frank's Vinifera Wine Cellars. He had never heard of the Finger Lakes, let alone Dr. Frank, but 10 weeks later he found himself in Hammondsport, New York, starting a yearlong winemaking internship. The main thing he got out of this experience, says Johannes, was a firm belief in the possibility of making top-quality wine in this region.

Back in Germany after his sojourn in the Finger Lakes, Johannes managed a small German winery, but that job soon proved unsatisfying. Once again, fate in the form of the Finger Lakes intervened in a timely fashion when Anthony Road's owner John Martini called and asked Johannes if he'd like to come back to the U.S. "I'd never heard of Anthony Road," he confesses, "so it was a very hard decision." But one interview and eight sleepless nights later, Johannes accepted John's offer. In August 2000, he started his new job in the Finger Lakes.

One of the reasons he came here Johannes explains is because Anthony Road has such a good winemaking facility. He was also impressed by the quality of the vineyards, and today, he works closely with vineyard manager Peter Martini (John and Ann's son). "My opinion is that the less treatment you give the vines the better," Johannes says. "I believe in respecting what nature gives you in quality. I would never try to make a great vintage out of an average year. I think what winemaking is all about is integrity."

This is an especially significant point of view in a cool growing region, where many vintners try to wring flavor from their delicate fruit by overriding it with masses of oak, malolactic fermentation, and other winemaking procedures. Johannes' approach is more subtle: "I try to get as much elegance as possible from the fruit itself rather than from trying to do it in the cellar."

Johannes is not impressed by the indigenous and hybrid grapes that once dominated this region — with one exception. "I was amazed by Vignoles," he exclaims. "It has a nice acidity in the background, and it ripens to a wonderful sweetness." Vignoles, however, isn't entirely easy to work with as the stems tend to add a jarring bitter note when they're crushed. But Johannes figured out a way to press the grapes gently enough to avoid bruising the stems: "I trod them with my feet for eight hours. The next day I did it a few more hours. By the time I was finished, there was no trace of bitterness, and the sugar levels were up six degrees more."

Now approaching his mid-thirties, Johannes gazes out toward Seneca Lake as he contemplates his future. "My dream is to some day have my own business. I don't know yet where that will be," he muses, "but I have to say the Finger Lakes is a good place to make wine. A *very* good place."

CHATEAU LAFAYETTE RENEAU
607-546-2062, 800-469-9463.
www.clrwine.com.
clrwine@aol.com.
Rte. 414, Hector, NY 14841.
Directions: From Rte. 17, take exit 32 to Rte. 14 north. In Watkins Glen, take Rte. 414 north. Winery is 7.4 miles northeast of Watkins Glen.
Owners: Dick & Betty Reno.
Open: May–Oct.: Mon.–Sat. 10am–6pm, Sun. 11am–6pm; Nov.–May: Mon.–Sat. 10am–5pm, Sun. 12noon–5pm; Jan.–Feb.: by appt.
Price Range of Wines: $7.50–$39.95.
Special Features: The Inn at Chateau LaFayette Reneau.

• Chardonnay
• Riesling
• Seyval
• Cabernet Sauvignon
• Pinot Noir

One of the hazards of visiting the Finger Lakes region is that people are sometimes so charmed by the place that they end up buying a vineyard here. That's what happened to Dick and Betty Reno almost two decades ago. They purchased their lakeside parcel in 1985 and commuted to the site on weekends while they replanted the old vineyard and rebuilt the winery.

The Renos hired winemaker David Whiting, whose stylish, well-crafted wines helped place Chateau LaFayette Reneau near the top of the region's quality producers. While David has since gone on to open his own winery (Red Newt), Reneau continues to win awards and has become particularly well known for its red wines. While the wines seemed to dip somewhat after Dave's departure, the current winemaker Tim Miller has got them back on track. The Riesling is particularly noteworthy with its good structure and rich peach and melon flavors. The Cabernet Sauvignon tends toward opulent red fruit flavors with a kick of licorice on the palate.

The winery maintains 44 acres of vines, from which 30,000 cases of wine are made annually. With its good wines and alluring wide deck flung out above the beautifully tended vineyards facing the lake, Chateau LaFayette Reneau is one of the region's most popular destinations for Finger Lakes visitors.

FOX RUN VINEYARDS
315-536-4616, 800-636-9786.
www.foxrunvineyards.com.
info@foxrunvineyards.com.
670 Rte. 14, Penn Yan, NY 14527.
Directions: From I-90, take exit 42 to Rte. 14 south. Winery is on Rte. 14 bet. Geneva and Dresden.
Owner: Scott Osborne.
Open: Mon.–Sat. 10am–6pm, Sun. 11am–6pm.

Fox Run owner Scott Osborne and winemaker Peter Bell have played an important role in setting the standards for contemporary Finger Lakes wines. Scott is soft-spoken and modest. He is also hardworking, smart, and ambitious, and he's recognized as a leader who is working to propel the Finger Lakes into the national spotlight as a premium wine-producing region. He has absolute confidence in his cause.

Shortly after Scott and his late partner Andy

Marguerite Thomas

The view from the deck at Fox Run Vineyards is breathtaking.

Price Range of Wines:
$4.99–$27.
Special Features: The Café
at Fox Run.
Special Events:
Winemakers' dinners
throughout the year. An
annual August Garlic
Festival (food, wine,
music, crafts).

• Chardonnay
• Riesling
• Gewürztraminer
• Pinot Noir
• Merlot
• Cabernet Franc
• Cabernet Sauvignon

Hale purchased Fox Run in 1993, Scott hired
Peter Bell, a talented Canadian winemaker with
a degree in enology from Australia. In the past
few years, Peter's skills have catapulted the
wines into a new and exciting dimension.

Peter is a firm believer in the influence of climate and soil on Finger Lakes wine. "For example, wine made from Riesling grapes grown on
Keuka Lake tastes different than wine made
from grapes grown on Seneca Lake. Both are
excellent; they're just different," he says. "Both
are aromatic and steely, but those from Seneca
have more apricot and tropical fruit flavor elements. The wines from Keuka have more apple
blossom, lime peel, and slate. I have really gotten
into Riesling since I came here." He is scarcely
less enthusiastic about the potential of Fox Run's
Pinot Noir, even though he describes this grape
as his "biggest challenge." Despite the chal-

lenges, Pinot Noir has become one of Fox Run's signature wines. One of the other exciting Fox Run reds is Meritage, a Cabernet Sauvignon, Cabernet Franc, and Merlot blend. With hints of mint and an intriguing earthiness, it is medium-bodied and characterized by elegance rather than power. It is simply one of the best Meritage-style wines in the East.

"Arctic Fox," an inexpensive, light, off-dry Chardonnay-based wine with the fragrance of a juicy melon, is a perennial crowd pleaser. Fox Run's Gewürztraminer is dry but lushly textured, with seductive aromas of rose petals and sweet spice.

Fox Run maintains 55 acres of vines and produces 17,000 cases of wine annually. The winery has recently expanded into a new 2,100-square-foot space. From the broad deck, the vista of vines sweeping down a gentle slope toward the lake is gorgeous in any season.

GLENORA WINE CELLARS

607-243-5511, 800-243-5513; fax 607-243-5514.
www.glenora.com.
wine@glenora.com.
5435 Rte. 14, Dundee, NY 14837.
Directions: From I-90, take exit 42 to Rte. 14 south. Winery is east of Dundee.
Owners: Ed Dalrymple, Gene Pierce & Scott Welliver.
Open: Jul.–Aug.: daily 10am–8pm; Sept.–Oct.: daily 10am–6pm; Nov.–Apr.: Mon.–Sat. 10am–5pm, Sun. 12noon–5pm; May–June: daily 10am–6pm.
Price Range of Wines: $7.99–$19.99.
Special Features: Restaurant and Inn.
Special Events: Summer Jazz Concert Series, Leaves and Lobsters (autumn festival), and much more.

• Sparkling wine
• Chardonnay
• Pinot Blanc
• Riesling
• Cabernet Franc

Founded in 1976, right after the passage of the New York Farm Winery Act, Glenora Wine Cellars was the first winery on Seneca Lake. Surrounded by vineyards sweeping down to the lake's deep waters, Glenora boasts one of the most magnificent views in the region.

Glenora's owners were quick to recognize that the local climate and soils were ideal for Chardonnay and Pinot Noir, the classic Champagne grapes. The winery has carved out a distinctive niche for itself by focusing on sparkling wine made from these grapes and produced in the same manner as classic French Champagne.

Over the past few years, Glenora's owners have been expanding their empire. They launched a new winery, Logan Ridge, directly across the lake from Glenora, and they also acquired the venerable Knapp Vineyards on Cayuga Lake. With its combined land holdings, the partnership now owns 423 acres of vines. Glenora itself produces about 40,000 cases of wine a year.

Under the direction of winemaker Steve DeFrancesco, most of Glenora's fine sparkling wines tend to be light and delicate in style rather than rich and complex. One of my favorites is the dry, but never boring Brut, made from a blend of Pinot Noir and Chardonnay, plus a touch of Pinot Blanc. Glenora also makes a semidry sparkler whose hint of sweetness makes it a good match with wedding cake. Among the non-sparkling wines, the round and friendly Riesling is always pleasurable. The popular "Jazz" — an uncomplicated Chardonnay/Riesling blend — comes in a blue bottle with a cheerful, brightly colored label.

HAZLITT 1852 VINEYARDS
607-546-9463, 888-750-0494;
fax 607-546-5712.
www.hazlitt1852.com.
hazlitt@lightlink.com.
5712 Rte. 414, P.O. Box 53, Hector, NY 14841.
Directions: From Rte. 17, take exit 32 to Rte. 14 north. In Watkins Glen, take Rte. 414 north. Winery is north of Hector.
Owners: The Hazlitt family.
Open: Mon.-Sat. 10am–5pm, Sun. 12noon–5pm.
Price Range of Wines: $6.65–$18.
Special Features: Schooner for charter on Lake Seneca.

• Chardonnay
• Riesling
• Merlot
• Cabernet Sauvignon
• Cabernet Franc

The Hazlitt family has been growing grapes in this region since 1852, which makes theirs one of the oldest vineyards still held by its original family. Elaine and Jerry Hazlitt opened a winery in 1985 when the grape market declined. "But making wine was nothing new to us," says Elaine. "We'd always made our own wine at home." Today, they produce about 33,000 cases.

Hazlitt represents a classic example of the evolution of Finger Lakes wines. Initially specializing in sweeter wines made mostly from hybrid and native grapes, the winery has shifted in recent years toward drier vinifera wines reflecting an overall change in tastes. "We like the older-style sweeter wines," says Elaine Hazlitt. "Our sons and daughters, however, prefer the dry, red table wines."

The 55-acre Hazlitt Vineyards also mirror this shift in taste. Whereas they were previously planted in grapes like Cayuga and Catawba, today, Merlot, Cabernet, and Gewürztraminer dominate. The Hazlitts are highly regarded grape growers who sell fruit to several of the best wineries in the region.

The Hazlitt tasting room is housed in a rustic barn that resembles a hunting lodge, with animal and fish trophies decorating the walls. Stepping through the doorway into this room is like being transported to a big, friendly party. Energetic young folks belly up to the bar to trade jokes and stories. The aroma of freshly popped corn perfumes the air. The wines, which have evolved impressively over the past few years, include an oakey but nicely balanced Chardonnay. "Schooner White" and "Schooner Red," both soft, sweetish blends, are reminders that Doug Hazlitt is also the Captain of *Malabar 10,* a Seneca Lake schooner that is available for charter. The best-selling red wine is the eternally popular "Red Cat," a blend of

Catawba and Baco Noir, that according to the Hazlitts, is associated with hot tubs and moonlight.

LAKEWOOD VINEYARDS
607-535-9252;
  fax 607-535-6656.
www.lakewoodvineyards
  .com
lwoodwine@aol.com
4024 Rte. 14, Watkins Glen,
  NY 14891.
Directions: From I-90, take
  exit 42 to Rte. 14 south.
  Winery is bet. Dundee
  and Watkins Glen.
Owners: The Stamp family.
Open: May-Dec.: Mon.-Sat.
  10am-5pm, Sun. 12noon-
  6pm; Jan.-Apr.: Fri.-Sat.
  10am-5:30pm, Sun.
  12noon-5pm; weekdays
  by appt.
Price Range of Wines:
  $5.99-$29.
Special Features: Children's
  indoor play area, swings
  outdoors.
Special Events: Steak and
  wine dinners, other food
  and wine pairings.

• Chardonnay
• Riesling
• Cabernet Sauvignon
• Cabernet Franc
• Pinot Noir
• Ice wine

Lakewood is a family-operated winery, and it is family-friendly as well. Visitors bring their kids, who dive happily into the toys piled on the floor while their parents taste wine.

Four generations of the Stamp family have farmed these sloping lakeside vineyards where the first vines were planted in 1952. The Stamps began as growers selling their grapes to local wineries and juice companies, but today, they are making their reputation as winemakers. Monty and Beverly Stamp now run the place. Their son David manages the vineyards, and Christopher, the oldest son, is the winemaker. Chris graduated from Cornell with a degree in food sciences and then trained at Glenora Wine Cellars.

Lakewood has 70 acres under cultivation, and production is 16,000 cases annually. Chris Stamp makes a particularly lush and lovely Riesling. He also turns out some of the region's best ice wines and other dessert wines. Lakewood produces notable native labrusca wines, such as Delaware, Niagara, and White Catawba. The popular "Long Stem Red" is a dry blend of the hybrids Baco Noir and Leon Millot.

LAMOREAUX LANDING WINE CELLARS
607-582-6011;
  fax 607-582-6010.
www.fingerlakes.net/
  lamoreaux.
llwc@capital.net.
9224 Rte. 414, Lodi, NY
  14860.
Directions: From Rte. 17,
  take exit 32 to Rte. 14
  north. In Watkins Glen,

Lamoreaux Landing produces a variety of wines that have consistently won awards since the first vintages appeared in the early 1990s. Mark Wagner founded his winery in 1990, and in 1992, the striking Lamoreaux Landing tasting room and winemaking facility was built. Designed by architect Bruce Corson, who has offices in Ithaca and California, the building bears a resemblance to a Greek temple — an appropriate reference to Bacchus. "I always liked

take Rte. 414 north. Winery is south of Lodi. Owner: Mark Wagner. Open: Mon.–Sat. 10am–5pm, Sun. 12noon–5pm. Price Range of Wines: $8.79–$20.

• Sparkling wine
• Chardonnay
• Gewürztraminer
• Riesling
• Cabernet Franc
• Pinot Noir
• Merlot

the Greek Revival architecture that is so prevalent in this area," says Mark. In the earliest planning stages, he and the architect had talked about renovating an old barn on the property, Mark explains. "Then one day Bruce threw this drawing up on the wall and said we could use the barn for the winery and put a Greek Temple on top of it for tasting."

Today, gazing out through the tall windows of the tasting room, one can look 20 miles north over the lake toward Geneva. There are always quality art shows on exhibit here, which is one of the many things that makes this one of the Finger Lakes most attractive spots in which to taste wine.

Annually, 8,500 cases of wine are produced here by French-born winemaker Samuel Alexandre. Among my favorites are the rich, round Riesling, the fragrant, dry Gewürztraminer, the earthy Cabernet Franc, and the nicely balanced, smooth Chardonnay Reserve.

"People didn't think of Chardonnay growing here, but we're finding that with proper canopy management, you can get some really good flavors," says Mark, whose family has been growing grapes in the Finger Lakes region since the 19th century. While both vinifera and French-American varietals thrive in his 130-acre vineyard, Mark sells the hybrids to other wineries and reserves the vinifera grapes for his own wines. (Mark, incidentally, is only distantly related to Bill Wagner, owner of neighboring Wagner Vineyards.)

LOGAN RIDGE ESTATE WINERY
607-546-6600, 866-546-6486.
3800 Ball Diamond Rd., Hector, NY 14841.
Directions: From Watkins Glen, take Rte. 414 north. Follow winery signs north of Hector.
Owners: Ed Dalrymple, Gene Pierce & Scott Welliver.
Open: Mon.–Sat. 10am–6pm, Sun. 11am–6pm.
Price Range of Wines: $7.99–$14.99.

Logan Ridge was founded in June 2001, by the partnership that owns Glenora Wine Cellars. The tasting room and restaurant is housed in a large, modern edifice that was once the residence of Ed Dalrymple, one of the partners. Hard to envision this vast wood and glass structure as a cozy family home, but its airy rooms and immense glass windows facing the lake do make a splendid setting for a winery. The actual winemaking facility is still under construction (the wines are meanwhile being made at Knapp, a sister winery on Cayuga Lake), but the tasting

Special Features: A large gift shop stocked with unusually handsome ceramics, jewelry, and glassware made by local artisans, and a restaurant, featuring the wines.

- Pinot Blanc
- Riesling
- Estate Blush
- Pinot Noir
- Baco Noir
- Cayuga

room is amply stocked with the dozen or so Logan Ridge wines. Steve DeFrancesco, the winemaker for Glenora and Knapp, oversees Logan Ridge's production as well; about 6,500 cases are currently produced.

Doug Miles, owner of Miles Wine Cellars, with his promising Cabernet Franc.

Marguerite Thomas

MILES WINE CELLARS
607-243-7742;
   fax 607-243-3827.
milesvin@aol.com.

First opened on July 4, 2001, the newest winemaking establishment on Seneca's western shore may well be the oldest winery building on the lake, and it certainly is one of the loveliest.

168 Randall Crossing Rd., Himrod, NY 14842.
Directions: From I-90, take exit 42 to Rte. 14 south. Turn left onto Randall Crossing Rd. to the winery.
Owner: Doug Miles.
Open: Thurs.-Sun. 10am–4pm.
Price Range of Wines: $7.95–$21.75.

- Cabernet Franc
- Cayuga
- Chardonnay
- Riesling

The gracious Federal-style farmhouse, built in 1802 right at the edge of the lake, was extensively restored by Doug Miles and his family, who were careful to preserve the house's monumental Greek Revival front porch and other fine architectural details. Once a bustling dockside where the Seneca ferry stopped, today, this is a tranquil spot where visitors like to sit outdoors on a stone bench or lounge in the shade of a weeping willow tree quietly contemplating a few sailboats gliding by. The earliest vintages of Miles wines, crafted by noted Fox Run winemaker Peter Bell, show great promise. The best wine so far is the plump, round Cabernet Franc.

PREJEAN WINERY
315-536-7524, 800-548-2216; fax 315-536-7635.
www.prejeanwinery.com.
wine@prejeanwinery.com.
2634 State Rte. 14, Penn Yan, NY 14527.
Directions: From I-90, take exit 42 to Rte. 14 south. Winery is south of Dresden.
Owners: Elizabeth & Tom Prejean.
Open: May-Nov.: Mon.–Sat. 10am–5pm, Sun. 11am–5pm; other times by appt.
Price Range of Wines: $5.99–$18.99.
Special Events: Frequent winemakers' dinners.

- Chardonnay
- Gewürztraminer
- Riesling
- Maréchal Foch
- Merlot
- Vignoles

Elizabeth Prejean and her late husband, Jim, started making estate-grown wines when they came to the Finger Lakes in 1986. Today, the winery produces Merlot, Chardonnay, Riesling, Maréchal Foch, Gewürztraminer, Cayuga, and Vignoles, turning out 6,000 cases of wine from its 34-acre vineyard.

Prejean is known for its soft, floral Gewürztraminer. Because it can be a tricky vine to grow, many other Finger Lakes vintners have turned away from Gewürz, but Libby Prejean wouldn't dream of giving it up. "Prejean is a Cajun name," she explains, "and Gewürztraminer is the best wine to drink with Cajun food." Prejean's Gewürztraminer gives off a haunting aroma of rose petals; the unusually powerful scent may arise because the grapes, once crushed, rest on their skins overnight before the juice is drained off (most of the aromas reside in a grape's skin).

In truth, most vinifera grapes in the Finger Lakes region require a certain amount of coddling. "Merlot is another one of our problem children," sighs Libby, "but we feel the rewards are worth it." In good years, Prejean Merlot is among the top four or five in the Finger Lakes.

Sign at Red Newt Cellars welcomes visitors to the winery and bistro.

Marguerite Thomas

RED NEWT CELLARS
607-546-4100;
   fax 607-546-4101.
dwhiting@baka.com.
3675 Tichenor Rd., Hector,
   NY 14841.
Directions: From Rte. 17,
   take exit 32 to Rte. 14
   north. In Watkins Glen,
   take Rte. 414 north. Turn
   right on Tichenor Rd. to
   winery.
Owners: David & Debra
   Whiting.
Open: Mon.–Sat. 10am–
   5pm, Sun. 12noon–5pm.
Price Range of Wines:
   $8–$41.
Special Features: The Red
   Newt Bistro.

• Chardonnay
• Gewürztraminer
• Riesling
• Cabernet Franc
• Cabernet Sauvignon
• Merlot
• Pinot Noir

The Wickham Winery, on Seneca Lake's eastern shore, opened in 1981 and went bankrupt five years later. When the property unexpectedly became available in 1998, David Whiting seized the opportunity to fulfill his dream of having a winery of his own. Renamed Red Newt (in honor of the indigenous salamander that Dave describes as "one of nature's most beautiful but often overlooked creatures"), the winery opened to the public in the summer of 1999. Red Newt has more than lived up to its promise, leaving no doubt that David Whiting is one of the most gifted winemakers in the East. His talents first became apparent in the 1990s when he was a consulting winemaker for Standing Stone, Chateau Lafayette Reneau, and other top wineries in the region.

Dave's mild manner and shy smile may belie his unwavering skill and passionate dedication to winemaking, but the evidence is there in the wines, which are all exceptional. The whites are aromatic and graceful. The reds are arguably more artfully balanced between power and finesse than any others in this region, with none of the peculiar weediness that continues to haunt many of the region's red wines. "Viridescens," a truly elegant Bordeaux-style blend of Cabernet Sauvignon, Cabernet Franc, and Merlot, is stunning. For the moment, Dave owns no vineyards, preferring instead to concentrate his attention and resources on the winemaking itself. He acquires grapes from the best growers around the lake, with whom he has carefully cultivated close relationships over the years. One of his favorite sources is Saw Mill Creek Vineyards, owned by Jim Hazlitt whose family has been growing grapes and making wine in the Finger Lakes for several generations.

Dave marvels over some of the recent Finger Lakes wines. "In the past four years, the changes in quality here have been extraordinary. As a region, we're definitely getting a better handle on our identity," he says with conviction.

Rob Thomas, co-owner and skilled winemaker at Shalestone Vineyards.

Marguerite Thomas

SHALESTONE VINEYARDS LLC
607-582-6600.
shalestonevineyards@
yahoo.com.

Open since Labor Day 1998, Shalestone was hailed as one of the most exciting wineries in the region from the very beginning. All of the grapes come from Rob and Kate Thomas's own

9681 Rte. 414, Lodi, NY 14860.
Directions: From Rte. 17, take exit 32 to Rte 14 north. In Watkins Glen, take Rte. 414 north to winery.
Owners: Rob & Kate Thomas.
Open: Apr.–Nov.: Fri.–Sun. 12noon–5pm.
Price Range of Wines: $9–$17.

• Cabernet Franc
• Cabernet Sauvignon
• Merlot

five-acre vineyard. Rob, a skilled winemaker who first made his name at Lamoreaux Landing, has strong and often iconoclastic opinions about winemaking in general and the Finger Lakes in particular. While Lamoreaux Landing's early reputation was based on Rob's white wines, one of the distinctive things about his own winery is that he makes only red wines. Why red wine in what has long been perceived as a white wine region? The answer is simple: Rob has a passion for red wine and a belief that it is important to focus on a single thing. It would be hard to dispute his decision once one has tasted the wines. Try, for example, the Cabernet Franc with its complex flavors balanced by soft tannins. The best vintages of Cabernet Sauvignon (1999 for example) has a concentrated fruitiness and a long finish, while lesser vintages (such as 1998) are more restrained, showing elegance rather than power. "Red Legend," a blend of various vintages and grape varieties, is an easy-sipping, smooth wine with a background of mellow sweetness. "I don't have to speak for my wines," says Rob with a smile. "They're pretty talkative themselves."

STANDING STONE VINEYARDS
607-582-6051, 800-803-7135; fax 607-582-6312.
www.standingstonewines .com.
info@standingstonewines .com.
9934 Rte. 414, Hector, NY 14841.
Directions: From Rte. 17, take exit 32 to Rte. 14 north. In Watkins Glen, take Rte. 414 north. Winery is north of Valois.
Owners: Martha & Tom Macinski.
Open: Fri. 11am–5pm, Sat. 12noon–6pm, Sun. 12noon–5pm.
Price Range of Wines: $6.99–$16.50.

Standing Stone shot out of the starting gate with the clear indications of a winner a few years ago and has never slowed down. One reason for the winery's success, according to owners Martha (Marti) and Tom Macinski, is that their soil is particularly well suited to grapes. Marti claims the wine is already half made when the grapes are harvested.

Standing Stone has been garnering awards as far away as California, especially for the exceptional Gewürztraminer, with its classic Gewürz floral and lychee notes, plus elements of cardamom and other sweet spice. The winery also makes one of the best dry Vidals in the East, which is light and crisp but still has a fairly substantial body. Among the excellent red wines are "Pinnacle," a successful Bordeaux-type blend of Cabernet Sauvignon, Cabernet Franc, and Mer-

Special Features: Wine and
 Cheese Bar.
Special Events: Barrel
 Tastings (by reservation),
 "Own Your Own Barrel"
 program.

• Chardonnay
• Gewürztraminer
• Riesling
• Cabernet Franc
• Merlot
• Late Harvest Riesling

WAGNER VINEYARDS
607-582-6450;
 fax 607-582-6446.
wagwine@ptd.net.
9322 Rte. 414, Lodi, NY
 14860.
Directions: From Rte. 17,
 take exit 32 to Rte. 14
 north. In Watkins Glen,
 take Rte. 414 north.
 Winery is bet. Valois and
 Lodi.
Owner: Bill Wagner.
Open: Daily 10am–5pm;
 last tour and tasting ends
 at 4:15pm; closed
 Thanksgiving,
 Christmas, New Year's
 Day.
Price Range of Wines:
 $5.99–$14.99.
Special Features: Café and
 Brewery.
Special Events: Live music
 Fri. nights in summer,
 Harvest Dinner,
 Valentine's Day Dinner.

• Approx. 30 different
 types of white, red,
 blush, and sparkling
 wine, both sweet and dry.

lot, and Glen Eldrige Merlot, a rich pleaser with overtones of chocolate and cedar. The winery has 35 acres of vines, producing around 6,500 cases of wine a year.

The tasting room is in a handsomely restored chicken coop, enhanced by a large wooden terrace with picnic tables overlooking the vineyards and lake (the chickens never had it this good).

Wagner Vineyards is BIG. It produces 40,000 cases of wine a year. It maintains 240 acres of vines. It is enormously popular — the tasting room and exceptionally large gift shop are perennially crowded with visitors sampling the vast selection of Wagner wines and, more recently, a wide selection of beers produced at the on-site brewery.

This is also one of the oldest wineries in the region. Bill Wagner first got into agriculture in the Finger Lakes in 1947, when he started a vegetable and dairy farm. He also raised grapes that he sold to various wineries, and he continues to sell a substantial amount of his fruit. In the 1960s, he eliminated his other crops to concentrate on grapes. In 1978, he released his first vintage.

Wagner wines are made from native American, French-American hybrid, and European (vinifera) grapes. The assortment includes three different Chardonnays, four or more Rieslings, a bunch of Blushes, and Pinot Noir in various guises. Several wines are produced from grapes unique to the Finger Lakes region. Wagner's "Melody," for example, is made from the Melody grape, a cross between Seyval and Geneva White, which is a cross between Pinot Blanc and Ontario. The Melody grape was developed in the late 1960s by the New York State Experiment Station in Geneva. Winemaker Ann

Rafetto once described the white, intensely fruity "Melody" as "fruit salad in a glass, a perfect summertime wine."

**HERMANN J. WIEMER
    VINEYARD, INC.**
607-243-7971, 800-371-7971;
    fax 607-243-7983.
www.wiemer.com.
wiemer@linkny.com.
Rte.14, P.O. Box 38,
    Dundee, NY 14837.
Directions: From I-90, take
    exit 42 to Rte. 14 south.
    Winery is halfway bet.
    Geneva and Watkins
    Glen.
Owner: Hermann Wiemer.
Open: Apr.–Nov.: Mon.–
    Sat. 10am–5pm, Sun.
    11am–5pm; Dec.–Mar.:
    Mon.–Fri. 10am–5pm.
Price Range of Wines:
    $7.50–$20.
Special Features: Nursery.

• Chardonnay
• Gewürztraminer
• Riesling
• Individual Bunch Select
    Late Harvest Riesling
• Sparkling wine

Not only are Hermann Wiemer's wines among the best in the Finger Lakes, but his Riesling and Gewürztraminer can arguably top just about any other label in the U.S. Most vintages of the dry Rieslings have a steely backbone supporting layer upon layer of apricot and peachy flavors. The semidry Riesling is invariably mellifluous with a racy, crisp finish. The rare German-style Auslese and Trockenbeerenauslese (TBA) wines are beautifully balanced, with heady aromas and deep flavors. A very special Individual Bunch Select Late Harvest Riesling is also made in the TBA tradition from hand-selected grapes that have been affected by the noble botrytis mold.

Today, Hermann Wiemer produces about 15,000 cases of wine and has some 65 acres under vines. The handsome tasting room and winery, designed by Simon Ungers of UZK Architects of Ithaca, is dovetailed into an old dairy barn.

Hermann Wiemer

Among the vintners working in the Finger Lakes today, Hermann Wiemer stands out for his role in shaping the evolution of Finger Lakes wines. While others were still scoffing, he followed in Konstantin Frank's footsteps, steadfastly championing the cause of vinifera grapes. He proved by example that Riesling and Gewürztraminer could be made in this region to stand on an equal footing with the world's best from Alsace and Germany. His contribution to the quality of Finger Lakes wines is inestimable, and indeed, virtually every one of the leading younger crop of winemakers cites Hermann Wiemer as a model for their own success.

Hermann Wiemer's family raised vines and made wine in Germany for hundreds of years. In 1968, he arrived in the United States, where his career here began in earnest when he went to work at Bully Hill Vineyards. Like most Finger Lakes vintners in the mid-1970s, Bully Hill's owner Walter S. Taylor was adamantly committed to French-American and other hybrids, which he believed were the only grapes that could survive the region's cold winters. But Hermann, who came from the cool Moselle region of northern Germany, was convinced that vinifera could grow in the

Finger Lakes, where the hills slope gently to the water as they do in the Moselle, and where the slatey glacial soils likewise reminded him of home. His vision was unquestionably profoundly influenced by Konstantin Frank's success with European vinifera grapes.

In 1979, after his position at Bully Hill was abruptly terminated following one of many disputes with Walter Taylor, Hermann bought an abandoned 145-acre soybean farm on the shores of Seneca Lake, where he began planting Riesling, Pinot Noir, and other vinifera grapes. As the vineyard grew, its initial success was due to the high quality of the young vines it supplied to other vineyards. In this endeavor, Hermann was following the example of his father, who had run Germany's largest nursery and had supervised the replanting of that country's vineyards after World War II.

Hermann Wiemer, owner and inestimable winemaker at the Hermann J. Wiemer Vineyard, Inc.

Marguerite Thomas

Like serious winemakers the world over, Hermann Wiemer is committed to the principle that good wine begins in the vineyard. His nursery is planted along Seneca Lake's scenic shoreline and produces some 300,000 entirely vinifera vines a year. The nursery has supplied plants for vineyards in Latin America and the United States, including such notable California wineries as Buena Vista, Caymus, and Kendall-Jackson. Far from resting on his laurels, Hermann continues to refine his planting, growing, and harvesting practices. He is the first grower in the Finger Lakes to use laser planting in the vineyard, a technique that has resulted in an almost 100 percent survival rate. His vines grow on double trunks to minimize dangers from freezing. For further protection, dirt is laboriously mounded up around each vine in the winter.

Recalling the difficult 2000 vintage, which began with deadly frost early in the year followed by a summer of endless rain, Hermann observes ruefully, "We have some problems with the weather here that just don't exist in California." But later, as we sip flutes of his round and engaging Blanc de Blancs, he beams. "It's still an awful lot of fun to make wines like this," he says.

Keuka Lake

BULLY HILL VINEYARDS
607-868-3610, 607-868-3210;
fax 607-868-3205.
www.bullyhill.com.
bullyhill@ptd.net.
8843 Greyton H. Taylor
Mem. Dr., Hammonds-
port, NY 14840.
Directions: From Rte. 17,
take exit 38 to Rte. 54. In
Hammondsport, take Rte.
54A along west side of
lake to County Rte. 76.
Follow Rte. 76 for 1.5
miles to Greyton H. Taylor
Mem. Dr. and winery.
Owner: Lillian Taylor.
Open: Mon.–Sat. 9am–5pm,
Sun. 12noon–5pm.
Price Range of Wines: $6–$18.
Special Features: Restaurant,
gift shop, museum.

• Whites
• Reds
• Blushes
• Sparkling wine

The saga of Walter S. Taylor and his quirky winery is the stuff of American legend. Taylor's chronicle began in the late 19th century when his grandfather, also named Walter Taylor, arrived in Hammondsport. The elder Taylor purchased a vineyard and established a winery. Taylor's wine was shipped 22 miles up Keuka Lake by steamboat to Penn Yan, then transported across to Seneca Lake and over to the Erie Canal. From there, it made its way to the large markets in New York City.

The Taylor winery expanded rapidly in the 1920s, and it began purchasing grapes from local growers. The original site atop Bully Hill was sold, and the operation was moved to larger quarters. The firm rode out Prohibition by switching to grape juice, which was also shipped down the river in barrels. The elder Taylor audaciously wrote on them: "Please do not add sugar or keep in a warm place or contents will ferment."

By the 1950s, Taylor Wine had become a leader in the New York wine industry, but success was somewhat tarnished for grandson Walter S. Taylor by disputes with the rest of the Taylor clan over the quality of the wine. Walter argued that they should switch from native American labrusca grapes to the more universally appealing hybrid grapes. Furthermore, he believed they should stop adulterating the wine with additives, such as sugar and water. "It's easy to tell when the Taylor Company is making wine," he used to joke, "because the level of Keuka Lake drops several feet." His relatives were not amused.

The Taylor Wine Company, by now made up of numerous relatives who had had enough of Walter's zeal for reform, invited him to leave the firm in 1970. So, Walter and his father, Greyton, bought back the original Taylor site on Bully Hill and began their own winery. Little did Walter know his troubles were just beginning.

When the Coca-Cola Corporation purchased the Taylor Wine Company, they immediately filed, and eventually won, a lawsuit forbidding Walter to use the Taylor name on his wine. So Walter threw a party. He provided his guests with marking pens and plenty of wine to drink, and they spent the night inking out the word "Taylor" on thousands of bottles of wine. Unable to use the family name, Walter proceeded to design labels using portraits of his ancestors instead of their name. When Coca-Cola got a court order forbidding him to do that, he put masks on their faces, but — you guessed it — he was hauled back to court for another losing battle.

In the dramatic denouement, Walter was ordered to turn over everything he owned that related to the Taylor family. He led a motorcade hauling paintings, documents, and a host of other objects down the road to the Taylor Wine Company, where he dumped everything in a large pile on the front steps of the winery. Then he persuaded his goat, named Guilt Free, to pose on top of the heap. "They got my name and heritage, but they didn't get my goat," was Walter's now legendary quip.

Of course, all of these legal wrangles cost Walter a bundle, but did any of it hurt Bully Hill sales? Absolutely not. Walter may have lost the battles, but he won the war. The Taylor Wine Company, which changed hands several more times, has now disappeared. Bully Hill, however, continues to produce enormous assortments of very popular wines.

Walter Taylor died in 2001 at the age of 69. The winery is now run by his extremely capable widow Lillian. Born in Eastern Europe, Lillian's many talents range from business acumen ("She's the smartest businesswoman in the world," says neighboring vintner Willy Frank admiringly) to athletic prowess (Lillian was a ski champion in the former Yugoslavia).

Some of Bully Hill's grapes are grown in the estate's 130-acre vineyard, the rest are purchased from other New York growers. The long list of Bully Hill wines (150,000 cases are produced) includes a few vinifera selections, but most are made from native and French-American hybrid grapes. Gregg Learned has been making the wines here since 1971. The labels on the front of the bottles are famously colorful, and the names of many of the wines reflect the same whimsy ("Sweet Walter White," "Le Goat Blush," "Bulldog Baco Noir"). Bully Hill has thousands of enthusiastic fans who flock here to taste and buy the wines, to eat in the restaurant, go on the entertaining tours, and to browse the abundantly stocked gift shop and visit the museum.

DR. FRANK'S VINIFERA WINE CELLARS/ CHATEAU FRANK
607-868-4884, 800-320-0735; fax 607-868-4884.
www.drfrankwines.com.
frankwines@aol.com.
9749 Middle Rd.,
Hammondsport, NY 14840.
Directions: From Rte. 17,

Vinifera Wine Cellars is where the modern Eastern American wine industry was born, and Dr. Frank exemplifies the story of the American dream come true. A German-born immigrant from the Ukraine, Dr. Konstantin Frank arrived in New York with his family in 1951. Although he was a professor of plant sciences in the USSR, the only job Konstantin Frank could find in

Marguerite Thomas

Winemakers Willy Frank and his son Fred of Dr. Frank's Vinifera Wine Cellars/Chateau Frank.

take exit 38 to Rte. 54 north. Drive north for 6 miles to Hammondsport. Take Rte. 54A north for 6 more miles, then take first left past Hammondsport Motel onto County Rte. 76 (Middle Rd.).
Owners: The Frank family.
Open: Mon.–Sat. 9am–5pm, Sun. 12noon–5pm.
Price Range of Wines: $7–$29.95.
Special Events: Salmon Run Festival.

• Sparkling wine
• Chardonnay
• Gewürztraminer
• Riesling
• Cabernet Franc
• Pinot Noir
• Merlot
• Rkatziteli

America was hoeing blueberries at the New York State Agricultural Experiment Station in Geneva. This is where Charles Fournier, of Gold Seal Vineyards, discovered him.

Recognizing Frank's talents, Fournier hired him to plant and manage the first vinifera grapes at Gold Seal. By 1962, Konstantin Frank had purchased his own land, where he proved to a skeptical world that European vinifera grapes could indeed be successfully cultivated in the Finger Lakes region.

Next he went on to produce critically acclaimed wine from his grapes, including Chardonnay and Riesling, as well as almost 60 other varieties. Soon other prospective Eastern vintners sought Dr. Frank's advice and encouragement. Untold numbers of wineries today owe their success, directly or indirectly, to Konstantin Frank's visionary work.

Vinifera Wine Cellars is now run by Dr. Frank's son Willy Frank and Willy's son Fred. They produce approximately 46,000 cases of Dr. Frank's Vinifera Wine Cellars wine and 4,000 cases of Chateau Frank sparkling wine. Chateau Frank is a separate facility devoted exclusively to sparkling wines; it is not open to the public. Grapes come from the estate's 100-acre Keuka Lake vineyard, plus 40 or so acres on Seneca Lake.

The sparkling wines tend to be refreshing and well balanced, with overtones of green apple and pears. The classic Rieslings are complex and long-lived. Rkatziteli, made from a Russian grape that yields a unique and appealing flavor reminiscent of pineapple, has a devoted following ("We can't make enough of it, it sells out immediately," marvels Willy). The Salmon Run label has long been a favorite of mine with its soft and appealing Riesling and Chardonnay blends. Red wines are beginning to catch up in quality with the whites. Pinot Noir, made from 40-year-old vines, shows surprising richness. The Reserve Merlot has good, rich color, dusty/earthy flavor, and huge tannins, while Cabernet Franc is fruity and harmonious.

HERON HILL WINERY

607-868-4241, 800-441-4241; fax 607-868-3435.
www.heronhill.com.
info@heronhill.com.
9249 County Rte. 76, Hammondsport, NY 14840.
Directions: From Rte. 17, take exit 38 to Rte. 54 north. Drive north 6 miles to Hammondsport. Take Rte. 54A north for 6 more miles, then take first left past Hammondsport Motel onto County Rte. 76 (Middle Rd.). Follow winery signs.
Owners: John & Josephine Ingle.
Open: Mon.–Sat. 10am–5pm, Sun. 12noon–5pm.
Price Range of Wines: $7.99–$24.
Special Features: Box lunches, gift shop.
Special Events: Various programs year-round; call for schedule.

• Chardonnay
• Johannisberg Riesling

Heron Hill is showing the benefits of the much-needed second wind it recently experienced. Most noticeable among the improvements is the lavish winery and tasting room expansion that adds 2,500 square feet of new space and 1,000 feet of remodeled space, plus extensive terraces and open-air pavilions. Charles Warren, a New York architect originally from the Finger Lakes, designed the new building. Impressive though the new structure is, however, the real news here is the improved quality of the wine. The Chardonnays (especially the one made in stainless steel tanks without barrel fermentation) are fruity and very drinkable. The Johannisberg Riesling is aromatic and, with a residual sugar level of two percent, relatively sweet; Heron Hill uses the term "Johannisberg" to indicate sweetness. The handsomely packaged Game Bird series (reds and whites) have distinct appeal, and each bottle comes with an original recipe, created by the winery owners, for preparing game birds. Heron Hill currently has 40 acres of vines, producing 17,000 cases annually.

**KEUKA OVERLOOK
WINE CELLARS**
607-292-6877.
www.keukaoverlook.com.
tab6877@aol.com.
5777 Old Bath Road,
   Dundee, NY 14837.
Directions: From Rte. 17,
   take exit 38 to Rte. 54
   north. Drive north 6 miles
   to Hammondsport. Take
   Rte. 54 north to Rte. 230 to
   winery on left.
Owners: Bob & Terry Barrett.
Open: Mon.–Sun. 11am–5pm.
Price Range of Wines:
   $7.99–$18.99.
Special Features: Bed &
   Breakfast Inn.
Special Events: Year-round
   festivities include
   Chardonnay for Mothers
   Day, Wine & Cheese Pairings, Be Mine with Wine
   (Valentine's Day), Gewürz
   & Brats (Gewürztraminer
   served with bratwursts,
   sauerkraut, and other del-
   icacies).

• Chardonnay
• Gewürztraminer
• Riesling
• Pinot Noir
• Cabernet Franc
• Cabernet Sauvignon
• Dessert wine

Bob Barrett crushed his first grapes in 1994 and opened his winery in a rebuilt barn in May 1995. His solid wines have already attracted a following that buys up just about every last drop of wine he makes, including the floral Gewürztraminer, the plummy Merlot, and the Pinot Noir with its hints of cherry LifeSaver. Semisweet wines, such as "Victorian Red" (a blend of Baco, Rougeon, and Chambourcin that's a great pasta wine according to Bob), also have devoted partisans. Bob is an engaging and entertaining host who loves to regale visitors with his repertoire of jokes. Ask him to tell you the one about the cowboy who went into the bar.

**MCGREGOR VINEYARDS
& WINERY**
800-272-0192;
   fax 607-292-6929.
www.mcgregorwinery.com.
mcg@linkny.com.
5503 Dutch St., Dundee, NY
   14837.
Directions: From Rte. 17,
   take exit 38 to Rte. 54
   north. Drive north 6 miles
   to Hammondsport. Con-
   tinue on Rte. 54 to Hyatt
   Hill Rd. Turn up Hyatt

McGregor Winery has the unusual distinction of raising hardy Russian vinifera varietals, as well as European vinifera grapes. "They seem to tolerate the winters here," observes owner Robert McGregor," and they produce unusually deep-colored and -flavored wines.

Robert, who retired early from Kodak in 1986, had planted vines on this slope of land in 1971. Today, from its 35-acre vineyard, McGregor produces about 7,000 cases of very good wine. "Highlands Red," a blend of various red grapes,

Hill Rd. to Dutch St. Turn
left. Winery is 1 mile
farther.
Owner: Robert McGregor.
Open: Apr.–Dec.: daily
10am–6pm; Jan.–Mar.: daily
11am–5pm.
Price Range of Wines:
$6.99–$30.
Special Features: Adopt a
Barrel Program.
Special Events: Frequent food
and wine pairings.

• Sparkling wine
• Chardonnay
• Gewürztraminer
• Riesling
• Pinot Noir
• Late Harvest Vignoles
• Muscat Ottonel

Cayuga Lake

GOOSE WATCH WINERY
315-549-2599;
fax 315-549-2596.
www.goosewatch.com.
goosewatch@flare.net.
5480 Rte. 89, Romulus, NY
14541.
Directions: From I-90, take
exit 41 to Rte. 414 south.
Follow Rte. 414 south to
Ogden Rd.-County Rd.
124, then take Rte. 89
south 2 1/2 miles south.
Owners: Dick & Cindy
Peterson.
Open: Daily 10am–6pm.
Price Range of Wines:
$7–$16.50.

• Sparkling wine
• Pinot Gris
• Viognier
• Merlot
• Cabernet Franc
• Cabernet Sauvignon

is a particular favorite of McGregor fans. Don't miss the Muscat Ottonel, a luscious sweet wine with citrusy overtones made in limited amounts. Late Harvest Vignoles is another fine dessert wine. Also available are limited amounts of "Black Russian Red" from a blend of Russian grapes named Black Sereksia and Saperavia.

One of the newest wineries in the Finger Lakes, Goose Watch was started in 1997 by the same folks who own the very successful Swedish Hill Winery. The Petersons have also embarked on another new venture, Champagne Wine Cellars, which is devoted primarily to promoting the sparkling wines of these two wineries.

Goose Watch is housed in a 100-year-old barn, with beautiful views of the lake. It is surrounded by one of New York's only commercial chestnut groves; another unique feature at Goose Watch is an aquaculture trout operation. Goose Watch wines are made with the same high standards and care as at Swedish Hill and are stylistically similar.

The distinctive doors of Hosmer's tasting room.

Marguerite Thomas

HOSMER
607-869-3393,
　888-HOSWINE;
　fax 607-869-9409.
hoswine@fltg.net.
6999 Rte. 89, Ovid, NY
　14521.
Directions: From Ithaca,
　take Rte. 89 north for 22
　miles to winery.
Owners: Cameron & Maren
　Hosmer.
Open: Apr.–Dec.: Mon.–Sat.
　10am–5pm, Sun.
　12noon–5pm; closed
　Jan.–Mar. and Easter,
　Thanksgiving, and
　Christmas.
Price Range of Wines:
　$6–$20.
Special Features: Gift shop,
　gourmet foods.

• Cayuga
• Riesling
• Cabernet Franc

This lakeside farm was purchased by the Chicago-based Hosmer family in the 1930s as a vacation retreat. Cameron Hosmer, who studied fruit sciences (pomology) at Cornell, began his current career as a home winemaker. He made wine for friends and family from grapes his father planted in 1972. In 1985, Cameron and his wife, Maren, opened their winery. They now produce 6,000 cases a year from their 40-acre vineyard, and they also supply grapes to other local wineries.

Hosmer wines include Riesling with a pretty, floral aroma and a Cayuga that would be a good match for spicy Asian or Mexican dishes. Hosmer's young Cabernet Franc has bold tannins that will probably mellow with time.

The tasting room, which is entered through a carved door that displays Hosmer's signature grape-leaf pattern, includes a large gift shop where prospective picnickers can stock up on cheese, chips, and snack food.

KING FERRY
　WINERY/TRELEAVEN
　WINES
315-364-5100, 800-439-5271;
　fax 315-364-8078.
www.treleavenwines.com.

Located about midpoint on the east side of Cayuga Lake, Treleaven may be out of the way, but the wines are absolutely worth the long, scenic drive. The Saltonstalls, who have been producing wine here for just over a decade,

treleaven@aol.com.
658 Lake Rd., King Ferry,
   NY 13081.
Directions: From the north,
   follow Rte. 90 on east side
   of Cayuga Lake to Lake
   Rd. From the south, take
   Rte. 90 to 34B. Turn left
   onto Lake Rd.
Owners: Peter & Tacie
   Saltonstall.
Open: Mon.–Sat. 10am–
   5pm, Sun. 12noon–5pm.
Price Range of Wines:
   $8.49–$29.99.
Special Events: Harvest Fest,
   "I Love Chocolate Day,"
   winemakers' dinners, and
   other events.

• Chardonnay
• Gewürztraminer
• Riesling
• Merlot
• Pinot Noir

**KNAPP VINEYARDS
WINERY AND
RESTAURANT**
607-869-9271, 800-869-9271;
   fax 607-869-3212.
www.knappwine.com.
winery@knappwine.com.
2770 County Rte.128,
   Romulus, NY 14541.
Directions: From I-90, take
   exit 41 to Rte. 414. Follow
   Rte. 414 south to Rte.
   20/5. Drive east on 20/5
   to Rte. 414 south, then
   south to County Rte. 128.
   Turn east onto Rte. 128
   (Ernsberger Rd.) to
   winery.
Owners: Gene Pierce, Ed
   Dalrymple & Scott
   Welliver.
Open: Mar.–Dec.: Mon.–Sat.
   10am–5pm, Sun.
   11:30am–5:30pm; Jan.–
   Feb.: open weekends only.
Price Range of Wines:
   $7.95–$18.

clearly know what they're doing as virtually everything they make is outstanding; total production is about 8,000 cases from 22 acres of vines. The barrel-fermented Chardonnay is a textbook example of how the delicacy of cool-climate grapes can be enriched with just a touch — not a wallop — of oak, which allows the clean, bracing fresh fruit character to shine through. The Pinot Noir is light but flavorful, the Gewürztraminer is aromatic and full-bodied, and the Dry Riesling is delicate yet not wimpy. "Saumon" is a somewhat sweet, tasty Rosé-style wine that's simple without being stupid — Treleaven's answer to Blush.

The story of Doug and Suzie Knapp, the winery's founders, is emblematic of the Finger Lakes winemaking history. "Like most growers around here, we were supplying grapes to the Taylor Wine Company," recalls Suzie. "And, like most growers in the region, we were growing native American grapes. These grapes had been the backbone of the American wine industry for 150 years. Besides, most people felt that since we didn't have a Mediterranean climate, we couldn't grow anything else."

By the mid-1970s, everything had changed. The Taylor family was no longer involved in the business. Under the ownership of Coca-Cola, and then Seagram, the company was no longer responsive to local growers. As Suzie explains, the large corporation started allocating grapes and dropping prices."Grapes aren't like corn," she grumbles. "You can't just change your crop from year to year according to the whims of the market. By 1976, a lot of people could see the writing on the wall."

Special Features:
  Restaurant, distillery.
Special Events: Harvest
  Festival, winemakers'
  dinners.

• Chardonnay
• Blush
• Riesling
• Sparkling wine
• Cabernet Franc
• Pinot Noir
• Late Harvest Vignoles

Once the New York Farm Winery Act was passed, a lot of growers started their own wineries. Those growers who were willing to change with the times — the ones who ripped out their vineyards of American grapes, replanted with more popular vinifera varieties, and opened their own winery — have mostly survived. "Of the others, few stayed in business," Suzie says.

Suzie is quick to point out that while the wine industry has reinvented itself in the Finger Lakes region, until now the wineries have not been owned by wealthy investors. Unlike other areas of the country, she says, "We haven't had Wall Street types and advertising executives buying up the vineyards. Here, land remains cheap, and we're still mostly just farmers."

And now a new chapter begins at Knapp. Suzie and Doug have retired, and the same partnership that owns Glenora and Logan Ridge has taken over the winery. It will be interesting to see what changes lie in store at Knapp. For the moment at least, there has been no major shift in style. Knapp's dependable wines still include a Chardonnay that balances fruit and the flavor from oak barrels nicely. "Dutchman's Breeches," a combination of Vidal and Vignoles, has a handsome label and remains understandably popular. Knapp is virtually the only Finger Lakes winery (so far) to produce Sangiovese. The grapes come from local grower Jim Hazlitt, and while the wine may not taste like it originated in Tuscany (Sangiovese's home), it is fruity and pleasing. Knapp distills brandy and grappa in a beautiful still with a hand-hammered copper, onion-dome roof made in Portugal.

LUCAS VINEYARDS
607-532-4825,
  800-682-WINE (NY only);
  fax 607-532-8580.
lucaswyn@epix.net.
3862 County Rd. 150,
  Interlaken, NY 14847.
Directions: From Ithaca,
  take Rte. 89 north to
  County Rd. 150. Travel
  west to winery.
Owners: Bill & Ruth Lucas.

Lucas Vineyards is the oldest winery on Cayuga Lake, founded by the Lucas family in 1974. They moved to the 68-acre site from New York City and planted grapes that they sold to the Taylor Wine Company. In 1980, the Lucases opened their own winery.

Lucas Vineyards currently has 29 acres planted in vines, from which it produces 20,000 cases of wine annually. Lucas' most popular red wine is "Tugboat Red," a semidry blended wine. "Blues,"

Open: Apr.–Dec.: Mon.–Sat.
10:30am–5:30pm, Sun.
12noon–5:30pm,
Jan.–Mar.: Mon.–Sat.
10:30am–5pm, Sun.
12noon–5pm.
Price Range of Wines:
$6–$14.

• Chardonnay
• Riesling
• Seyval
• Vignoles
• Cabernet Franc
• Pinot Noir

another semidry wine handsomely packaged in a blue bottle, is the favorite white.

Marguerite Thomas

Outstanding view from the entrance of Sheldrake Point Vineyard.

**SHELDRAKE POINT
VINEYARD & CAFE**
607-532-9401;
fax 607-532-8967.
www.sheldrakepoint.com.
finewine@sheldrakepoint
.com.

Sheldrake Point is the most prominent point of land on Cayuga Lake's west coast. For centuries, this bucolic spot was the largest encampment of the great Algonquin Indian nation. From 1850 to the mid-1980s, it was an orchard and dairy farm. Today, it is home to one

7448 County Rd. 153, Ovid, NY 14521.

Directions: Follow Rte. 89 north from Ithaca or south from Seneca Falls. Look for signs directing you down County Rd. 139 to Sheldrake. Turn right at 4-way stop onto County Rd. 153 to winery a few hundred yards on right.

Owners: Bob Madill & Chuck Tauck.

Open: Daily 11am–6pm.

Price Range of Wines: $9–$25.

Special Features: Restaurant.

Special Events: Winemakers' dinners, Annual Harvest Fest (Sept.).

• Chardonnay
• Pinot Gris
• Riesling
• Cabernet Franc
• Gamay
• Pinot Noir
• Merlot

of the newest and most promising wineries in the Finger Lakes. The 160-acre vineyard site and handsome new winery and tasting room are positioned right along the tranquil lakeshore.

Owners Bob Madill (a Canadian whose background includes a long stint in the Niagara Peninsula wine industry) and Chuck Tauck (who was first attracted to the Finger Lakes as a graduate student at Cornell's Hotel School) are applying savvy business practices to build a solid foundation for future successes. The wines are still very young, and production is still small (around 5,000 cases), but the future does indeed look promising: The Chardonnay is round and fruity without being over the top; the Dry Riesling is vibrant and aromatic; the Reserve Pinot Noir has depth and personality and lingers long on the mouth. Sheldrake may well be a harbinger of the direction this region is headed.

SWEDISH HILL VINEYARD & WINERY

315-549-8326, 888-549-WINE; fax 315-549-8477.

www.swedishhill.com.
swedhill@flare.net.

4565 Rte. 414, Romulus, NY 14541.

Directions: From I-90, take exit 41 to Rte. 414, follow Rte. 414 south. Winery is 8 miles south of Seneca Falls.

Owners: Dick & Cindy Peterson.

Open: Daily 9am–6pm.

Price Range of Wines: $6.99 Cayuga–$16.99 Vintage Port.

Special Features: Gift shop.

Dick and Cindy Peterson planted their first vines on this site in 1969, while she was still working for a bank and he had a job with the Seneca Falls school system. Their first vintage, produced in 1985, was so successful that the Petersons quit their day jobs to devote themselves full-time to the winery. The wines have been winning awards and garnering critical praise ever since.

Today, the Petersons produce 34,000 cases of wine annually in their high-tech winery; they have 35 acres of vines that provide them with about 40 percent of the fruit that they need (the rest is purchased locally). Swedish Hill has a large tasting room with three separate tasting bars, a well-stocked gift shop, and a selection of home-winemaking equipment for sale.

Special Events: Santa Lucia Day Celebration (Dec. 8).

• Sparkling wine
• Chardonnay
• Riesling
• Delaware
• Vignoles

One key to the Petersons' success is that they have staked out a niche market that they fill better than anyone else: Swedish Hill produces excellent wines from labrusca and hybrid grapes. "Svenska White," made from Catawba, Golden Muscat, and Cayuga White, is grapy, soft, sweet, and flavorful, with little of the aggressive labrusca flavors that often characterize wines made from hybrids. "Svenska Red" (Concord, Ives, Rougeon, Catawba, and Vincent grapes) has equal appeal. The Late Harvest Vignoles is rich and mellow, with tantalizing honeycomb and dried apricot flavors.

THE HUDSON RIVER VALLEY

The Hudson River Valley is the oldest commercial grape-producing region in the United States. As early as the mid-1600s, the Hudson River was recognized as a major trading artery for the New World. English, German, and Dutch farmers in upstate New York used the river to ship their products to the booming market in New York City.

When the French Huguenots arrived in the valley in the 1670s, they established vineyards along the river. Once they learned that European vinifera grapes couldn't tolerate East Coast diseases and climates, they raised table rather than wine grapes.

In 1877, Andrew Caywood moved from Modena, New York, to Marlboro, in the Hudson Valley, where he developed many successful hybrids, most notably the Dutchess grape. Caywood's contributions marked the beginning of this region's foray into commercial winemaking. Prohibition put a temporary halt to the industry, which was revived by Mark Miller when he replanted Caywood's original vineyards in the 1960s (now called Benmarl Vineyards).

The Hudson River Valley is a famously scenic region that attracts antique hunters, art aficionados, history buffs, and nature lovers who come for the hiking trails and water sports. The homes of several of the famous 19th-century Hudson River painters who lived and worked here are open to the public. Historic sites, such as the 17th-century stone Huguenot houses in New Paltz and the museum at George Washington's Headquarters in Newburgh, are also well worth a visit. And, of course, wine lovers can spend a day or a week visiting wineries and sampling local wines in delightful settings. There are 28 wineries in the region, most of them small, friendly, family-run operations. This is a region to keep an eye on, as the potential for excellent winemaking is there. For the moment, two wineries — each very different from the other — stand out.

CLINTON VINEYARDS
845-266-5372;
   fax 845-266-3395.
Schultzville Rd., Clinton
   Corners, NY 12514.
Directions: From Taconic
   Pkwy., take Salt Point
   Turnpike exit. Turn right
   and go straight through
   Clinton Corners. Take a
   sharp left onto Schultzville
   Rd. at the 10 mph sign and
   proceed to winery.
Owners: Ben & Phyllis Feder.
Open: Fri.–Sun. 10am–5pm,
   or by appt.
Price Range of Wines:
   $12.50–$35.
Special Features: Walking
   trails on 100-acre estate.

Clinton is a tiny jewel in the vast New York wine industry. The focus is almost entirely on a single grape variety: Seyval Blanc. Crisp and fruity, this wine is sometimes reminiscent of a light Sancerre from France's Loire Valley. A small amount of charming, dry sparkling Seyval is also produced at Clinton. Like several other Eastern vintners, Ben Feder, formerly a New York City graphic designer, went into the cattle business before turning to grapes. When he did succumb to the lure of Bacchus, Ben decided to plant only Seyval grapes. Recently, however, he added one acre of Riesling to his 15 acres of Seyval, but since the Riesling appears to be too temperamental for his site, it's doubtful he'll expand the plantings.

Special Events: Press Release
Party, summer picnics,
Harvest Party.

• Seyval Blanc
• Sparkling wine
• Fortified dessert wine

Clinton Vineyards produces up to 3,000 cases of wine annually. In addition to the Seyval, Clinton Vineyards also makes a small amount of "Peach Gala," a delightful, dry, and very drinkable sparkling wine. This novel peach-flavored sparkling wine is the Hudson River's answer to Italian Bellini. And don't overlook the trio of seductive fortified dessert wines: "Romance," "Desire," and "Embrace."

MILLBROOK VINEYARDS & WINERY
845-677-8383, 800-662-WINE; fax 845-677-6186.
26 Wing Rd., R.R. 1, Box 167D, Millbrook, NY 12545.
Directions: From Taconic Pkwy., take Millbrook exit to Rte. 44. Take Rte. 44 east to Rte. 82 north and drive 3 miles to Shunpike Rd. (Rte. 57). Turn right and drive 3 miles to Wing Rd. Turn left to winery.
Owner: John Dyson.

One of the best and most innovative wineries in the East, Millbrook was the first vineyard in the Hudson River region to concentrate exclusively on vinifera grapes. The concept for Millbrook Vineyards began in 1976, when John Dyson, then New York State Commissioner of Agriculture, met Dr. Konstantin Frank, the Russian-born winemaker who operated Vinifera Wine Cellars in the Finger Lakes. Frank's success with European vinifera vines greatly impressed John Dyson, who reasoned that the same grapes might also do well in the Hudson Valley, where he owned a farm. He planted an experimental acre and found that his Chardonnay, Cabernet

Open: Daily 12noon–5pm;
  Mem. Day–Labor Day:
  daily 12noon–7pm.
Price Range of Wines:
  $10.99–$22.99.
Special Events: Summer
  concerts, weekend
  vineyard grill, annual
  Harvest Party on
  Columbus Day weekend.

• Cabernet Franc
• Rosé
• Tocai Friuliano

Sauvignon, and Pinot Noir did perform remarkably well. Today, he has 52 acres under cultivation, producing 15,000–16,000 cases annually.

Armed with the success of this experiment, plus the knowledge that vinifera grapes offer considerably higher gross returns than other crops, John bought an old dairy farm in 1979, where he planted 50 acres of vines. (John firmly believes that vineyards can help save family farming in the East.) He converted the dairy barn into a state-of-the-art winery. Next, he invented and patented a new trellising system, and then he hired John Graziano, a talented graduate of Cornell University, as his winemaker.

God may have rested after creating the world, but John Dyson just keeps going. In 1989, he purchased two top-quality vineyards in California's Central Coast region, where he grows grapes for important California wineries, such as Glen Ellen, Robert Mondavi, and Joseph Phelps. As none of these vineyards has winemaking facilities, John began shipping grapes from his California properties to Millbrook to be made into wine, which he markets under the Mistral label. In the mid-1990s, Dyson added Villa Pillo, a vast wine and olive-oil estate in Tuscany, to his holdings. Scarcely pausing for breath, he then stunned the wine world by purchasing Williams and Selyem, the prestigious California winery.

Among the Millbrook wines that carry Hudson Valley and New York State appellations, Cabernet Franc is particularly outstanding, with a rich aroma of berries followed by a blast of long-lasting complex flavors. "Hunt Country Rosé," a blend of Pinot Noir and Chardonnay, smells sweetly of strawberries; while it may look like a blush wine, this Rosé leaves no perception of sweetness in the taste. The Tocai, a grape native to the Friuli region of Northern Italy, is redolent of tropical fruit aromas and flavors and has a luscious full body. Millbrook Proprietor's Reserve Chardonnay is also full-bodied and understandably popular with wine drinkers who appreciate big, opulent wines. Set deep in the countryside, Millbrook's handsome winery and beautiful setting are well worth a visit. But even without all this, the wines alone are enough of a lure for anyone who loves fine wine. Picnic tables overlook the scenic ponds that John created to provide a modifying influence on the climate.

TOURING NEW YORK STATE

LONG ISLAND

Whether you drive out to Long Island from Manhattan or take the more scenic ferry route over from Connecticut, it is possible for truly dedicated wine tasters to visit virtually every North Fork producer during a two- or three-day visit. This does, however, take perseverance and the ability to adhere to a pretty rigorous schedule, so I recommend this all-inclusive approach only to the most serious wine buffs — and only to those who will either have a designated driver along, or who will emulate the universal practice followed by wine professionals, who spit rather than swallow the wines they sample. Many wine country tourists now hire a limo and driver to ferry them from winery to winery; contact any one of the wineries for information about these services.

A more reasonable way to visit the North Fork is to select four or five wineries to visit each day and to spend a leisurely time touring and tasting at each. Regardless of which end of the wine route you start out from, the wineries are virtually all clustered along two parallel highways (Rtes. 25 and 48), each about 35 miles long. There are many restaurants and scores of motels and B&Bs in the region. Local restrictions prohibit wineries from offering accommodations to visitors, but there are several wine-friendly inns here, including the Greenporter Hotel and Spa, which also has a good wine bar, in Greenport (631-477-0066) at the northernmost tip of the North Fork and the romantic Ram's Head Inn on Shelter Island (631-749-9959). Try to fit in a drive across lovely Shelter Island over to the South Fork's three wineries.

THE FINGER LAKES

It would take a good week to do justice to the Finger Lakes region, but a weekend is all that it takes to get a good overview of any one of the lakes. Seneca has more wineries than either Keuka or Cayuga lakes, but because they are spread out in a line all around the lake, it's easy to visit them one after another. If you're planning to visit more than a couple of wineries and you don't have a designated driver, remember the cardinal doctrine of professional wine tasters: swirl, sniff, sip, and SPIT. Either the waterfront Inn at Glenora on the west side of the lake or the bed-and-breakfast at Chateau LaFayette Reneau on the other side would make an ideal base for touring Seneca's wineries. Among the many fine eateries around Seneca Lake are the restaurants at the Glenora, Logan Ridge, and Red Newt wineries. Also, the Ginny Lee Café at Wagner Vineyards always draws big crowds.

LAKE ERIE REGION

The Lake Erie wine-growing region is comprised of three contiguous states: New York, Pennsylvania, and Ohio. With 25,000 acres of vines stretching along the shore of the lake, it is the largest grape-growing district in the Eastern United States (90 percent is Concord, mostly from New York's Chautauqua County, and is used mainly for commericial juice and jelly). New York has eight wineries, Pennsylvania has five, and Ohio has 26. Ohio's Harpersfield sets the standard for quality in the region. Because this wine is so vast (and lies so far east of the Atlantic Coast), it deserves more attention than it can be given in this book.

CHAPTER FOUR
Mid-Atlantic States
NEW JERSEY, PENNSYLVANIA, & MARYLAND

Dr. Michael Fisher, owner of Amwell Valley Vineyard, Ringoes, New Jersey.

Marguerite Thomas

NEW JERSEY

Anyone driving along the urbanized and industrialized New Jersey Turnpike might think that the state's moniker "The Garden State" was some kind of cruel joke, but thanks to good soils and a maritime climate, this was once a land of flourishing farms and gardens. Today, much of the remaining commercial agriculture has evolved into vineyards. Ironically, vines were widely planted in the mid-1700s, when wine-producing grapes were cultivated in New Jersey for the British Empire. Those early efforts were so successful that in 1767, two New Jersey vintners were praised by London's Royal Society of Arts for producing the first bottles of quality wine from the Colonies. After early triumphs, however, things went downhill as American vine diseases brought the state's wine industry to a virtual standstill.

In the mid-19th century, a man named Thomas Bramwell Welch moved to southern New Jersey. Always game for an opportune career change, Welch had begun his professional life as a Methodist preacher in upstate New York and then became a physician in Minnesota before he settled in Vineland, New Jersey, and took up dentistry. An avid gardener, Welch also began raising Concord grapes, which had been recently developed in Concord, Massachusetts, by Ephraim Bull, a goldsmith who, like Welch, liked to fiddle around in the garden.

The cultivated native American grape that Bull developed was a vigorous grower and was fabulously hardy. Concord grapes, however, make dreadful wine. Sticky sweet and aggressive in flavor — the fighting pit bull of wine — it continues to appeal to a tiny segment of the wine-drinking public, but for most oenophiles, wine made from Concord grapes is a distinct turnoff. In any event, Dr. Welch was an ardent Prohibitionist who had no interest in turning his grapes into wine. He was, however, intrigued enough by Frenchman Louis Pasteur's discoveries regarding pasteurization, as it's now called, to speculate that the technique might be used to stabilize fresh grape juice (before pasteurization, there was no way to keep fruit juice from ultimately fermenting and/or spoiling). Welch began experimenting by boiling sealed bottles of grape juice just long enough to prevent fermentation by destroying the natural yeasts, as well as any active bacteria in the juice. The process proved successful, and in 1870, Welch began selling his first bottles of unfermented grape juice. By 1900, the Welch Grape Juice Company had relocated to western New York and was turning out 50,000 gallons of juice annually, with sales more than doubling every year.

As the grape juice industry grew, the wineries were rapidly sinking under the combined forces of vineyard diseases and Prohibition. After Repeal, the New Jersey wine industry was slow to reemerge because, until 1981, state law restricted the number of wineries to one per each one million inhabitants. The Farm Wine Act removed this restriction and also made it possible for wineries to sell their wines at five off-site sales outlets.

Today, with 18 commercial producers in the state and more than 500 acres of vines planted statewide, wine is once again becoming a viable New Jersey product. The state's oldest winery is Renault, dating back to 1864; Renault survived Prohibition by producing sacramental and medicinal "tonics." Most, though by no means all, New Jersey wine is made from vinifera grapes these days. While the wine industry is nowhere near as advanced as Long Island's, it is certainly gaining strength as vintners and grape growers are joining forces to learn from each other and to market themselves as a entire region rather than as individuals operating in the wilderness.

Public support for New Jersey's wine industry is also growing, albeit slowly. With the rapid disappearance of New Jersey farmland, people are beginning to understand that vineyards help preserve the agricultural ambience of the state for today and for generations to come. This kind of local support will undoubtedly help further the development of New Jersey's wines.

Although wineries and vineyards are spread across most of the state, in eight different counties, there are two distinct growing regions, one in the north in Warren and Hunterdon Counties, the other south and west of Atlantic City. A long growing season, plus well-drained, mineral-laden limestone, clay and shale soils washed down from the mountains endow the best New Jersey wines with a beautifully balanced ratio between sweetness, acidity, and alcohol. They are further characterized by delicate fruit flavors, and when the grapes come from the region's very best vineyards, they can have rich and intense flavor components. As with most Eastern wine regions, New Jersey is influenced by a great body of water, in this case the Delaware River, which moderates the climate to make it more amenable to grapes. The countryside along the river is idyllic, dotted with gracious old stone farmhouses, elegant horse farms, rolling hills, and country retreats. Quaint villages that range from tourist meccas to remote and genuinely charming country hamlets fill the region. New Jersey's Hunterdon and Warren Counties lie on the east side of the river (on the opposite shore is Pennsylvania). This bucolic landscape comes as a pleasant surprise to those who think that the state is a holding tank for industry and pollution. Instead, what one sees driving along the road are contentedly grazing horses in spacious green pastures enclosed by white fences, driveways curving up to handsome country estates, and vineyards undulating across the hills.

At the other end of the state, Southern Atlantic County is largely flat, with sandy soils and a maritime climate. Set in the Pine Barrens, the strange landscape features mile after mile of short, stiff pine trees carpeting the countryside like bristles on a giant hairbrush. There isn't a whole lot to distract one in terms of sight-seeing or shopping along Routes 30 and 40, where most of the wineries are located, and there are few hotels or restaurants. That this region is so undeveloped is surprising, considering how close it is to major urban centers. Cape May, by contrast, is a bustling, alluring seaside resort area, especially in the summer months. With climate and growing conditions similar to Long Island's, this could potentially be one of New Jersey's best viticultural areas, but for now, there is only a single winery in Cape May.

Northern New Jersey

ALBA VINEYARD
908-995-7800;
    fax 908-995-7155.
www.albavineyards.com.
albavineyard@center.net.
269 Rte. 627, Village of
    Finesville, Milford, NJ
    08848.
Directions: Take Rte. 78
    west to exit 7 (Blooms-
    bury). Follow Rte. 173
    west for 2.3 miles to Rte.
    639 west. Drive 2.8 miles
    to Rte. 627 south, then 2
    miles to winery on right.
Owners: Tom Sharko &
    Rudy Marchesi.

Rudi Marchesi founded Alba Vineyard in 1983. Subsequent problems forced the winery to close for awhile until 1997, when Rudy and Tom Sharko formed a partnership. With 26 acres under vine, Alba is now up and running at full speed, producing about 10,000 cases a year. After major renovations, the beautiful 1805 stone barn has been recast as an up-to-date winery and hospitable tasting room. With panoramic views of rolling hills and vineyards, the Warren County winery is located two miles east of the Delaware River and historic Bucks County. Alba's "Raspberry" wine wins prizes across the country and is served in prestigious restaurants, such as Manhattan's

Open: Wed.–Thurs.
9am–5pm, Fri.
12noon–7pm, Sat.
11am–6pm, Sun.
12noon–5pm.
Price Range of Wines:
$6.99–$20.
Special Events: Music
festival, concert series,
fireworks, art exhibitions.

• Maréchal Foch

**AMWELL VALLEY
VINEYARD**
908-788-5852;
fax 908-788-1030.
www.amwellvalleyvine
yard.com.
80 Old York Rd. (Rte. 514),
Ringoes, NJ 08551.
Directions: From
Flemington Circle, take
Rte. 202 south. Take the
Reaville exit onto Rte.
514 east. Winery is 1.1
miles farther.
Owners: Dr. Michael Fisher,
Jeffrey & Debra Fisher.
Open: Sat.–Sun. 1pm–5pm;
and by appt.
Price Range of Wines:
$7–$20.

• Landot Noir

Gramercy Tavern. "Heritage Red" (a blend of grapes predominated by Maréchal Foch) has a popular following. The Vintage Port, a fortified wine made by traditional Port methods, is so popular that Alba has doubled the production each year — and still sells out!

Amwell Valley Vineyard is noteworthy in many respects. Founded in 1978 by Dr. Michael Fisher, a London-born scientist at Merck Sharp and Dohme Research Laboratories, this is the oldest winery in this part of New Jersey. One of Dr. Fisher's important contributions to the industry was his successful campaign to improve New Jersey's archaic winery laws. His efforts resulted in the passage of the Farm Winery Act in 1981. This act helps regulate the quality of wine produced in New Jersey and encourages the preservation of farmland. It has also opened the door to entrepreneurial winemaking. Until the passage of the act, only seven winemaking licenses had been issued in New Jersey since Prohibition.

Dr. Fisher became interested in vineyards after reading an article in *Scientific American* about the various grape-growing regions in the world. He contacted one of the contributing authors, Philip Wagner of Boordy Vineyards in Maryland, who guided the Fishers in their first planting of hybrid grapes. After the initial harvest, they began experimenting with other grapes, and today, they raise both vinifera and hybrid grapes on 11 acres of their 30-acre farm. They produce about 2,500 cases of wine, ranging from a pleasant Maréchal Foch (a hybrid) to Gewürztraminer (a vinifera). One of their most popular wines is Landot Noir, a beautifully colored fruity, Beaujolais-style wine.

"Grapes aren't as hard to grow as I had thought, as long as you select the right kind," says Michael Fisher. "Riesling, for example, is reasonably easy to grow here." But, he adds, there are other factors that help, too: "We have better fungicides and pesticides now than we used to, which makes it all possible. Also, the weather is warmer these days."

Amwell Valley's wines are mostly on the lean side and make nice picnic wines. Enjoy them either inside the large new tasting room that opened in the summer of 1996 or on picnic benches on the deck, overlooking the vineyards and a sweep of unspoiled land that stretches to the scenic Sourland Mountains in the distance.

**UNIONVILLE
VINEYARDS**
908-788-0400;
    fax 908-806-4692.
www.unionvillevineyards
    .com.
uvineyard@aol.com.
9 Rocktown Rd., Ringoes,
    NJ 08551.
Directions: From Rte. 202/31
    about 6 miles south of
    Flemington Circle, turn
    east onto Wertsville Rd.
    At the 2nd crossroads,
    turn right onto Rocktown
    Rd. Winery is first drive
    on left.
Owners: Patricia Galloway
    & Kris Nielson.

The land occupied by Unionville Vineyards had been a productive peach orchard since at least the mid-19th century. "New Jersey was one of the great peach producers in the 1800s," explains Unionville owner Pat Galloway. "Then the peach blight hit and that's when the industry moved to Georgia." In its next incarnation, this property became a dairy farm.

Established as a vineyard and winery in 1988 by Pat and her husband, Kris Nielson, Unionville released its first wines in 1992. The owners, who also jointly own an engineering firm, have recently hired Australian winemaker Keith Brown. Along with general manager Darren Hesington, who has been on the scene since the beginning, this group

Open: Thurs.–Sun.
11am–4pm.
Price Range of Wines:
$7–$24.99.

• Chardonnay
• Riesling
• Cabernet Sauvignon

has come an impressively long way with their winery. The vineyard has expanded from the original 11 acres of hybrid and vinifera grapes planted on the 90-acre property to a total of 34 acres of vineyards.

Unionville, clearly one of the best wineries in New Jersey, consistently wins prizes and awards for its wines. The semidry Riesling is a perennial favorite. Other traditional vinifera-based wines include Chardonnay, Cabernet Sauvignon, and "Hunter's Red Reserve," a Meritage-style blend of Cabernet Sauvignon, Cabernet Franc, and Merlot.

Unionville's eye-catching labels depict hunting scenes with foxes and horses, reflecting one of the popular pastimes in this region. The tasting room and winery facilities are located in a former dairy barn, which was handsomely rebuilt by a local Mennonite contractor who used fieldstones from the original foundation in the structure. Unionville is situated amid rolling farmland and vineyards, with the Sourland Mountains as a scenic backdrop.

Southern New Jersey

BELLVIEW WINERY
856-697-7172;
   fax 856-697-7183.
www.bellviewwinery.com.
bellview@aol.com.
150 Atlantic St., Landisville,
NJ 08326.
Directions: From the
   Delaware Mem. Bridge,
   follow signs for Rte.
   40/Atlantic City. Take Rte.
   40 east to intersection of
   690 (Weymouth Rd.) and
   Central Ave. Make sharp
   left onto Central and drive
   about 0.3 miles to Atlantic
   St. Turn right onto
   Atlantic to winery on left.
Owners: Jim & Nancy
   Quarella.
Open: Fri. 1pm–7pm, Sat.
   11am–5pm, Sun. 11am–
   3pm; or by appt.
Price Range of Wines:
   $7.99–$14.99.

• Red table wine
• Viognier

New Jersey's newest winery, Bellview, opened in the spring of 2001. Jim Quarella is a fourth generation farmer, who got interested in home winemaking as a young man. "Home winemaking has always been a big thing around here," Nancy Quarella explains. "A lot of the Italian immigrants, like Jim's great-grandfather, who settled here in the early 1900s made their own wine." In fact, the Quarellas still use the wine cellar built by Jim's great-grandfather.

As his interest in winemaking grew, Jim began planting vines on his 150-acre farm. To date, he has 10 acres of vines under cultivation, and he plans to gradually expand this as he experiments with different grape varieties. So far Chardonnay, Pinot Grigio, Cabernet, Merlot, and Viognier all seem to be thriving, and young Lemberger and Syrah are coming along. Jim also makes wine from a variety of hybrid and native grapes that go into his toothsome red table wine (it's already picked up a couple of medals in wine competitions, as has Bellview Viognier). The wonderfully aromatic sparkling Muscat brings to mind good Italian bubbly. Bellview is definitely an exciting addition to the New Jersey wine scene.

CAPE MAY WINERY & VINEYARD
609-884-1169;
  fax 609-884-5131.
709 Townbank Rd., Cape May, NJ 08204.
Directions: At south end of Garden State Pkwy., follow Rte. 9 south. At 4th traffic light, turn right onto Rte. 644. At next light, turn right onto Rte. 648. Drive half block to winery on left. From Cape May Ferry, take Rte. 9 north to 2nd traffic light. Turn left onto Rte. 644 and proceed as above.
Owners: Joan & Bill Hayes.
Open: Call for hours.
Price Range of Wines: $12–$25.

• Chardonnay
• Cabernet Sauvignon

New Jersey's southernmost winery, Cape May Winery opened July 1, 1994, and now produces about 900 cases of very attractive Chardonnay, Cabernet Sauvignon, Cabernet Franc, Merlot, and an understandably popular Blush wine. Owners Joan and Bill Hayes (he's an engineer recently retired from the Coast Guard) have been crafting wines that are garnering gold medals and critical praise — not just in the local press, but even from the likes of *Forbes* magazine. Among the winning wines is a delightfully weighty Cabernet Sauvignon that leaves a trail of black cherries and currants on the palate. There's hope that the high quality of these wines, along with the attractive Cape May region, will encourage other vintners to move into this area.

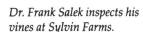
Dr. Frank Salek inspects his vines at Sylvin Farms.

Marguerite Thomas

SYLVIN FARMS
609-965-1548;
  fax 609-965-1548.
24 N. Vienna Ave., Germania, NJ 08215.
Directions: From Garden State Pkwy., take exit 44. Bear right onto Moss

This is still the most remarkable winery in New Jersey. Frank Salek is a civil engineer who retired as a college professor in the northern part of the state. After 20 years of commuting to his modest winery and vineyard on weekends, Frank now spends most of his time in the vineyard and the wine cellar. Year after year, Frank continues to turn

Mill Rd. (alt. 561) and drive 4.2 miles to Vienna Ave. Turn right in 800 ft. at winery entrance.
Owner: Franklin Salek.
Open: By appt.
Price Range of Wines: $6–$18.75.

- Chardonnay
- Sauvignon Blanc
- Merlot
- Cabernet Sauvignon
- Cabernet Franc
- Sparkling wine

out some of the best wines in the East. What's his secret? Maybe it's the vineyard's location. "Could be," Frank nods. "After all, we're on the highest point around."

Standing with him in his fields, I stare incredulously across the flat vista of the Chardonnay section of the vineyard. Well, okay, maybe the land does sort of swell up into a little mound toward the center.

"Even the slightest rise makes a difference," Frank assures me. "And in this location, the steady southwest winds permit the vines to dry off in the summer, so we have less of a problem with fungal diseases." Both the Atlantic Ocean and the Mullica River moderate the temperature, Frank explains, and he has learned, usually by hard experience, which grape varieties and clones will do well here. On the other hand, he continues to experiment with new varieties. He has recently put in several rows of Viognier and Syrah, as well as a new clone of Sauvignon Blanc. All of these, he reports, seem to be doing well. He is also excited about recent experiments with Pinot Grigio.

Despite this flurry of activity with white wine grapes, however, Frank maintains that his primary focus will always be on red wines, and in particular, on Cabernet Sauvignon, which he has described as "the nearest and dearest thing to my heart." Cabernet, he recently said, does so well here that he is about to expand the Cabernet plantings. This is good news for loyal fans who worry that there is never quite enough of Frank Salek's Cabernet around.

The wine cellar at Sylvin Farms is not one of those quaint cellars full of neatly stacked oak barrels and high-tech computerized gizmos. It's an unprepossessing basement crammed full of stainless steel containers and a few wooden barrels. Nevertheless, the Chardonnay made in this modest cellar is distinguished and golden; the Pinot Noir is redolent of fresh berries; the Cabernet Sauvignon and Cabernet Franc have great flavor intensity; and the Merlot is juicy and ripe. Frank Salek also makes some of this country's classiest sparkling Blanc de Noirs, and his sparkling Muscat draws consistent rave reviews and awards. "Wine is made in the vineyard," Frank says modestly. "I decided a long time ago that you had to have good grapes to make good wine. When I couldn't find ones I liked, I decided to grow my own. Everyone thought I was really crazy."

Nobody thinks he's crazy now. Frank Salek is the guru for most New Jersey commercial winemakers, who admire his wines, respect what he's doing in his vineyard, and frequently turn to him for advice. Charlie Tomasello (Tomasello Winery) has even teamed up with Frank to make a sparkling Rkatziteli, a regular award winner. Rkatziteli, the most common wine grape in Russia, is grown throughout Eastern Europe and appears to thrive in New Jersey. A recent joint project was a sparkling wine made from Pinot Noir, the classic Champagne grape along with Chardonnay. Frank frequently threatens to quit making sparkling wine because, he says, it is too hard to sell. Happily, he likes it as much as we do. "On the other hand, I guess I'll keep on making it since I drink most of it myself," he says wryly.

About a quarter of Sylvin Farms 40 acres of land is planted in vines. The annual output ranges from 750-1,000 cases, depending mostly on how the crops have fared in any given year. Located in a rural, pine-filled section of New Jersey, the winery has a small tasting room. Frank talks of some day expanding the small space, but for now, his attention is right where it should be — on the vineyards and the wines.

Frank Salek

Part philosopher, part scientist, and entirely devoted to vineyards and winemaking, Frank Salek is an inspiration to anyone who has even the slightest affection for wine. His wisdom and sly humor have entertained as well as enlightened many of us over the years. I recently spent several hours with Frank, sampling wines in his tasting room and directly out of barrels in the cellar, asking questions as we made our way through the vintages of the past decade, Here is some of our conversation:

Q: Your Merlot has such unusually soft tannins and long-lasting flavors. How do you achieve this great style?

A: I guess it's due to the fact that I don't have the sophisticated equipment other winemakers have. I mostly just let the wine alone without tampering with it too much. If I do anything special to this wine, it's that I give it an extended maceration [the length of time the freshly pressed juice rests on its skins]. And good bottle aging is important, too, especially for Burgundy/Bordeaux-style wines. They've just got to have enough time in the bottle.

Q: Your Cabernet Franc tastes so ripe and round. This seems to be an especially good grape in Eastern regions, which more and more vintners are beginning to embrace.

A: Yeah, it's a nice wine. I've been growing Cabernet Franc for 20 years. Why in the hell hasn't everyone else gotten onto it before now?

Q: To me, many of your wines taste very European. They have the elegance, subtlety, and complexity that one associates with fine European wines.

A: In a way, I am European in outlook, in my feelings about crops and land. My family was from Poland and other Eastern European countries. An uncle of mine had a little place up in Wallington, Bergen County, New Jersey, where he grew everything. I have vivid memories of the vegetables, of the peach trees, and other things that grew there. I remember how neatly he dispatched a rabbit for dinner. Even though I was only four or five, I remember the black hen who laid more eggs than any of the others. I don't know, maybe this kind of thing is where I get some of my ideas.

While we were talking, Frank was heating up some Italian bread stuffed with sausage, and we devoured it as we continued making our way through the wines.

Q: The Cabernet Sauvignon was delicious on its own, but I can't believe how the flavors just sing once you put them together with this sausage.

A: It's because the tannins in the wine form a loose chemical bond in the mouth with the proteins in the sausage. I agree with you, this is a very good combination. If you ask me, there's nothing like Cabernet Sauvignon. It's the nearest and dearest thing to my heart.

Q: Speaking of tannins, even your very young red wines — the ones we've just tasted right out of the barrel — have surprisingly soft and pleasant tannins. So many wines have a harsh tannic grip in their extreme youth. What do you do to get that softness?

A: I leave the wine on its skins for 21 days. Other than that, I don't do anything special, I don't add anything back in.

Q: Some of your barrels look pretty old and funky. What kinds of barrels do you mostly use?

A: I have both French and a couple of American oak barrels. But the ones you're referring to are old whiskey barrels. I decharred them and cleaned them, so they have virtually no flavor. They're just neutral storage containers.

Q: To my mind, one of the problems with a lot of wines for many years now has been an overbearing presence of flavor from oak. . . .

A: It depends on what you want to taste. It's a question of whether you want to taste the oak or want to taste the fruit and what it will evolve into over time.

Q: Well, if you aren't looking to flavor the wine with oak, what's the point of spending all that money on barrels?

A: Barrel aging is important because it does add certain characteristics to wine besides flavor. Barrels permit wine to soften and lose a certain amount of their boisterous youth. Wines are like children, who, as they grow through adolescence and enter adulthood, become more viable human beings. Of course, their basic character stays the same. Chances are that if the damn wine tastes lousy now, it will taste lousy five years from now.

Q: How exactly does the barrel-aging process work? Does the wine evaporate through the wood?

A: Yes. The molecules for alcohol are long, while water molecules are short. The short chain leaves the barrel through the porous wood. The wine becomes concentrated, and the dissolved gases dissipate as a result of fermentation.

Q: When it comes to winemaking, do you ever make mistakes?

A: Oh sure, from time to time you do screw up. I once had to dump about 500 bottles of Chardonnay from the 1991 vintage — a really terrific year, too. But I screwed it up and couldn't find any way to save it, so I ended up just pouring it down the drain.

Q: That must have hurt!

A: It did, but it would have hurt more if I'd tried to sell it to people.

Q: I honestly think your Blanc de Noirs (a Brut made from Pinot Noir) is one of the most elegant and complex sparkling wines I've ever had outside the Champagne region itself.

A: I think so, too, but I'm going to stop making it.

Q: What! Why?

A: It's too hard to sell. There just doesn't seem to be much of a market for good sparkling wine. You know, it isn't just the money. The way I make wine and the prices I can ask for it — well, let's put it this way, I'm never going to make much money on this. But there's not much point in making a wine like the Blanc de Noirs and not be able to sell it.

Q: The sparkling Muscat Ottonel must be a success, however, since it just won the New Jersey Governor's Cup Award. [This was, in fact, the Fifth Governor's Cup that Sylvin Farms had won.] Actually, I can't think of a better way to end an evening than with this wonderful glass of wine.

A: The Muscat pleases me, too. You don't need a whole lot of adjectives to describe it. In the final analysis, the question is simply: Do you enjoy it?

Q: I guess that would be the question about making wine, too. Despite all the frustrations and difficulties, do you enjoy it?

A: Look, this is an endeavor that requires a great deal of personal interest. When you get right down to it, it's madness. But it's a hell of a lot of fun.

TOMASELLO WINERY
609-561-0567,
800-MMM-WINE;
fax 609-561-8617.
www.tomasellowinery.com.
jack@tomasellowinery.com.
225 White Horse Pike,
Hammonton, NJ 08037.
Directions: From Atlantic City, take Rte. 30 west for 18 miles. White Horse Pike is just past mile marker #29. Follow signs to winery.
Owners: Charles & John Tomasello.
Open: Mon.–Sat. 9am–8pm, Sun. 11am–6pm.
Price Range of Wines: $5.24–$24.
Special Events: Opera Galas.

Frank Tomasello, a local farmer, established Tomasello Winery in 1933. Today, it is run by Frank's grandsons, Charles and John ("Jack"), whose empire is expanding at an astonishing rate. With 86 acres of vines, Tomasello is New Jersey's most important grape grower, as well as its largest winery, producing 52 percent of the state's wines (about 45,000 cases). An enormous assortment of wine (40 different selections!) comes from Tomasello. Among the most popular is an excellent Chambourcin — a light, flavorful red that reminds some people of a fruity Beaujolais. Tomasello's rich and spicy Villard Noir is another favorite that flies out the door as soon as it's released; "I wish I had a couple hundred more cases of it to sell," says Jack. Recent Cabernet Sauvignon has been particularly impressive, with a good balance between fruit flavors, complex hints of oak, and restrained tannins. Partisans of American hybrids celebrate the fact that

- Cabernet Sauvignon
- Chambourcin
- Villard Noir
- Rkatziteli

Tomasello is one of the few wineries in the region to produce well-made Concord and Catawba wines.

Tomasello is housed in a modern Mediterranean-style complex built around a courtyard. It includes a banquet room, a pleasant tasting room, and picnic facilities in addition to the winery operation.

PENNSYLVANIA

Pennsylvania ranks fifth nationally in grape production, including juice grapes. It now boasts 68 wineries spread across the land — in valleys, on mountaintops, in every corner of the state from Lake Erie down to the Delaware Bay. It is possibly the only state that includes a winery built atop a reclaimed abandoned strip mine. Many Pennsylvania wineries are located in beautifully pastoral farm country, where time seems to have slowed down, where Amish horse and buggies clip-clop along the road, where spotless white houses seem a symbol of simpler, almost forgotten values. Lancaster County, for example, is distinguished by pristine farms maintained by Mennonite and Amish farmers, who still use horses to plow the land. The striking absence of billboards, malls, and fast food outlets along the roads fills one with nostalgia for less blatantly commercial times.

Along the Delaware River, wineries are set against a backdrop that is picturesque enough to lure sight-seers from all over the world. Scenic River Road (Route 32) offers one of the prettiest drives in the entire country, hugging the river as it meanders through Bucks County. At the southern end of this road, on Christmas Day 1776, George Washington and the Continental Army crossed the icy Delaware to deal a crushing blow to the British.

In addition to winery tours in this area, there are many other recreational attractions. Among these are historic mansions, such as Pennsbury Manor, William Penn's 17th-century country estate on the banks of the river, and Andalusia, one of the finest examples of Greek Revival domestic architecture in the nation (both are open to the public). Art galleries, antique stores, and shopping outlets all beckon as well.

Pennsylvania's southern border offers a wealth of stunning routes. Travel through the Brandywine Valley, for example, stopping to visit Longwood Gardens (with more than 11,000 species of plants) or Winterthur Museum, the former Du Pont mansion that now contains an unrivaled collection of American decorative arts and antiques. Savor the peaceful country around Chadds Ford, immortalized in paintings by three generations of Wyeths; many of their paintings are displayed at the Brandywine River Museum.

Like many states in the East, this one has quirky laws regulating the ways in which wine may be sold. In Pennsylvania, consumers can buy wine at individual wineries or at winery-owned retail shops, otherwise all wine and liquor must be purchased from state-owned stores.

ALLEGRO VINEYARDS
717-927-9148.
R.D. 2, Box 64, Sechrist Rd., Brogue, PA 17309.
Directions: From I-83, take exit 6 onto Rte. 74 and drive about 7 miles beyond town of Red Lion to Brogue. Turn right at post office onto Muddy Creek Rd. Drive 2 miles and look for winery sign on left.
Owners: Carl Helrich & Kris Miller.
Open: Fri.–Sun. 12noon–5pm; or by appt.
Price Range of Wines: $7.59–$32.95.
Special Events: Chef series, musical events, an annual festival, spotlight weekends.

• Chardonnay
• Traminette
• Vidal
• Seyval
• Cabernet Sauvignon
• Cabernet Franc

Allegro wines have been among the best in the East for at least the past decade and a half. Although there are new owners now, all signs indicate that this outstanding winery will continue to delight its devoted fans and to reward stalwart explorers who are willing to trek out to this somewhat remote corner of rural southern Pennsylvania.

Allegro was founded by two former classical musicians, brothers Tim and John Crouch, who planted their vineyard in 1973 and opened the winery in 1980. After Tim's untimely death in 2001, John sold the operation to Carl Helrich and his wife Kris Miller. Happily, Carl does not plan to tamper with the stylistic standards set by the Crouch brothers, for he and John Crouch share the same winemaking philosophy. "John and I agree that what we want is to grow the best grapes possible in the phenomenal site we've got, then once they get into the winery, we don't do too much to them but babysit the wine," Carl explains. Continuing the Crouch's enlightened vinyeard practices and noninterventionist winemaking approach should mean that the Premium White (Seyval plus a touch of Vidal) will continue to taste fresh and crisp, the Traminette light and saucy, and the Chardonnay sprightly and beautifully balanced.

"You aren't planning to make any changes to Cadenza, are you?" I ask Carl nervously. The many ardent followers of this splendid limited-production Cabernet Sauvignon/Cabernet Franc blend would be dismayed if this wine's rich, supple character was altered in any way.

Carl looks astonished. "Change Cadenza? I'd never do that. The moment I first tasted that wine I fell in love. Cadenza is the reason I wanted to buy the winery in the first place."

Positive changes in future vintages include the addition of Pinot Gris to Allegro's roster of wines. These grapes are sourced from one of Pennsylvania's most respected grape growers, who will also supply Carl with Cabernet Franc. Both of these additions seem promising. With 15 acres of its own under cultivation, Allegro produces around 2,000 cases of wine. The new owners are determined to follow Tim and John Crouch's credo "of making excellent European-style table wines that are reasonably priced."

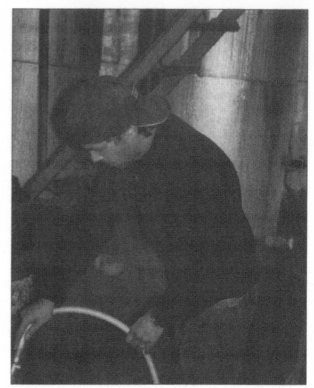

Eric Miller, Jr., new member of the winemaking team at Chaddsford Winery.

CHADDSFORD WINERY
610-388-6221;
    fax 610-388-0360.
www.chaddsford.com.
cfwine@chaddsford.com.
632 Baltimore Pike
    (Rte. 1), Chadds Ford,
    PA 19317.
Directions: From
    Philadelphia, take I-95
    south to Rte. 322 west.
    Turn left onto Rte. 1
    and drive 6 miles to
    winery.
Owners: Eric & Lee Miller.
Open: Daily 12noon–6pm;
    Jan.–Apr.: closed Mon.
Price Range of Wines:
    $8.99–$32.99.
Special Events: Labor Day
    Bash (jazz) and Mem.
    Day Bash (blues), wine

Chaddsford Winery proves that the old dictum "location, location, location" applies to wineries as well as to real estate. Situated on Hwy. 1 in the beautiful Brandywine Valley, Chaddsford each year receives thousands of drop-in visitors who cruise the gift shop, take advantage of the winery's self-guided tour, taste the wines, and stock up on their favorites. Of course, to succeed, wineries, unlike real estate, also need long-range goals, marketing skills, and a talented winemaker.

Chaddsford has been blessed with all of the above. Owners Eric and Lee Miller opened the winery in 1982, in what Eric describes as their big old Yankee barn. Eric's palate was trained in Burgundy, where he lived when he was growing up, and his winemaking abilities were honed in the Hudson River Valley region of upstate New York at Benmarl, a winery owned by his father.

classes, December
Candlelight Christmas
in Chaddsford.

• Cabernet Franc
• Cabernet Sauvignon
• Chambourcin
• Chardonnay
• Pinot Noir
• Riesling

"The soils in the Brandywine Valley are similar to those in Burgundy," says Eric, who is particularly partial to that region's wines. "And the two regions have almost the same number of growing days — there are 195 here compared to 190 in Burgundy." Chaddsford's rolling hills, with lots of southern exposure, also remind him of Burgundy's terrain.

Eric has no illusions about replicating Burgundy here — "I'm not going to be making Montrachet," he smiles — but the wines he turns out are distinctive, characterized by a bracing thread of acidity and a strength of character that make them among the best in the East. By Eastern standards, this is a large winery, producing about 75,000 cases a year. Chaddsford owns about 28 vineyard acres, where Eric has planted several new grape varieties, including Syrah and Pinot Noir. I tasted a couple of the first Pinots, which were light, lively, and fruity. Chaddsford's regular Chardonnay is clean and bright, while the Philip Roth Vineyard Chardonnay is lush and full. "Merican" — a Bordeaux/Meritage-style red blend dominated by Cabernet Sauvignon — has complex aromas, robust and long-lasting flavors, and well-balanced tannins. In a great year, it can be a stunning wine. The 2000 vintage will undoubtedly evolve into just such a wine, for as Eric says, "The year 2000 will be the Cabernet vintage that we'll talk about for a long time."

The Millers' son, Eric, Jr., has recently joined the winemaking team. It is heartening to see the third generation of eastern vintners coming on board.

FRENCH CREEK RIDGE VINEYARDS
610-286-7754.
www.FrenchCreekRidge.com.
200 Grove Rd., Elverson, PA 19520.
Directions: From the west, follow PA Turnpike and take exit 22 onto Rte. 23 east. Drive 6 miles and turn right onto Grove Rd. to winery on left. From the east, take exit 23 off PA Turnpike onto Rte. 100 north. Take 23 west and drive approx. 6 miles, then turn left onto Grove Rd. to winery.
Owners: Fred & Janet Maki.

Fred and Janet Maki bought their property, an abandoned dairy farm, in 1991 and immediately planted vineyards (with 13 acres total, seven are already under vine). The lovely tasting room, designed to reflect the traditional stone barns of the region, opened in December 2000. French Creek Ridge shot into prominence in 2001 when its 1997 Blanc de Blancs Brut won a gold medal at an international wine competition held in Paris. In addition to the sparkling wine, a nice Viognier with floral aromas and hints of tropical fruit flavors is produced here. The light-bodied Cabernet Sauvignon can start out oakey on the palate, but finishes on a note of fruit. Vidal ice wine is a classic of its type — sweet and succulent without getting too clunky on the finish. Production is currently between 2,000 and 3,000 cases, and growing. While

The attractive stone tasting room at French Creek Ridge Vineyards.

Open: Thurs.–Sun.
  12noon–5pm.
Price Range of Wines:
  $11–$50.

• Sparkling wine
• Vidal ice wine

STARGAZERS VINEYARD
610-486-0422;
  fax 610-486-0422.
www.Stargazers@kennett
  .net.
1024 Wheatland Dr.,
  Coatesville, PA 19320.
Directions: From West
  Chester or Unionville, follow Rte. 162. Turn onto
  Stargazers Rd., then turn
  left at the T curve onto
  Youngs. Turn right onto
  Laurel, then right again

the wines still seem a little unfocused, the future looks good for French Creek Ridge as its vineyards mature, and Janet Maki's winemaking skills continue to expand.

The Stargazers 15-acre vineyard was planted in 1979, and for the next couple of decades, the Weygandts sold their premium grapes to other Pennsylvania wineries, including Chaddsford (one of Chaddsford's most notable Chardonnays was made from their fruit). In 1996, Alice and John Weygandt opened their own winery. Along with neighboring French Creek Ridge Vineyards, the Weygandts' dream for the future is to establish this unique region as a fine producer of sparkling wine. The current bubbly from this relatively young winery is very delicate, but has a surprisingly firm fin-

onto Wheatland. Winery is at top of hill.

Owners: Alice & John Weygandt.

Open: Sun. 10am–6pm; or by appt.

Price Range of Wines: $7–$14.

• Chardonnay
• Sparkling wine

ish. Stargazers Chardonnay is a shy charmer, with a whisper of apricot peeking out from under a finely woven network of mineral and honey flavors.

The lyric name comes from the vineyard's location near the stone known as the "Stargazers Stone," which marks the location of the observatory used by Mason and Dixon in surveying the border between Pennsylvania and Maryland. Mason and Dixon were called "the stargazers" because they relied on celestial navigation to correct their measurements over the ground.

MARYLAND

In the earliest days of the state's history, its political leaders were eager to develop a potentially lucrative wine industry. In 1648, Lord Baltimore prompted Maryland's governor Charles Calvert to plant 200 acres of vines on the east bank of St. Marys River. The project, unfortunately, was doomed to fail as the European vines were entirely destroyed by native insects and diseases.

Maryland's first successful winery was Boordy Vineyards, first bonded in 1945. Had the state picked up the ball and been as eager as Lord Baltimore to push forward with what was clearly a promising endeavor, the history of wine in Maryland might have been very different. With a variety of grape-friendly growing sites scattered from the eastern shore to the hilly west, Maryland could now be a serious player in the East's developing wine world had it received even a fraction of the backing and support that neighboring Virginia gets from its legislature. As it is, while almost all 10 of Maryland's wineries are small, friendly, family-run operations, most of them appear to be undercapitalized, lacking leadership, and isolated from each other, as well as from the larger world of wine. Only in the past few years have various winegrowers begun uniting into a modicum of cohesiveness. With any luck, competitive wines will soon emerge. For the moment, only three wineries are truly distinguished.

BASIGNANI WINERY
410-472-4718.
15722 Falls Rd., Sparks, MD 21152.
www.basignaniwinery.com.
Bert@basignani.com.
Directions: Take I-83 north

Although his winery became bonded in 1986, Maryland native Bert Basignani left the construction business only relatively recently to head full-time into winemaking. This is good news for wine lovers. Bert currently makes 2,000 cases of wine, which he hopes to expand in the near future.

to Shawan Rd. west (exit 20B). Drive 3 miles to Falls Rd. Turn right and drive about 6 miles north to winery on left.
Owners: Bert & Lynn Basignani.
Open: Wed.–Sat. 11:30am–5:30pm, Sun. 12noon–6pm.
Price Range of Wines: $9–$21.

- Cabernet Sauvignon
- Chardonnay
- Riesling
- Seyval
- Vidal

He owns 10 acres of vines next to the winery and leases other local vineyards. The winery and tasting room are located on a pretty, wooded slope. Generally considered Maryland's premier winery, Basignani produces wines that are featured in many local restaurants and retail wineshops. The Chardonnay is lush and long-lasting on the palate, and the Seyval is unusually complex. "Elena," a white blend, is crisp and dry. The outstanding Cabernet Sauvignon tastes of spice and ripe fruit. "Lorenzo," a Bordeaux-inspired red blend, has appealing aromas, a graceful body, and robust flavors. The wines keep getting better and better, especially with a couple of recent superlative vintages (notably 1997 and 1998). On the other hand, 2000 was pretty much a disaster, while 2001 shows great promise.

BOORDY VINEYARDS
410-592-5015;
fax 410-592-5385.
www.boordy.com.
wine-info@boordy.com.

Philip Wagner, the founder of Boordy Vineyards, is one of the most important figures in the winemaking history of the Eastern United States. He was the London correspondent for the *Baltimore Evening Sun* in the 1930s when he was introduced

12820 Long Green Pike,
  Hydes, MD 21082.
Directions: From Baltimore
  Beltway, take exit 29
  (Cromwell Bridge Rd.)
  east to Glen Arm Rd.
  Turn left and drive 3
  miles to Long Green
  Pike. Turn left and drive
  2 miles to winery.
Owner: Rob Deford.
Open: Mon.–Sat.
  10am–5pm, Sun.
  11am–5pm.
Price Range of Wines:
  $7.75–$25.
Special Events: A range of
  year-round events, from
  summer concert/dancing
  series to winter Soup-In-
  The-Cellar evenings.

- Chardonnay
- Seyval
- Cabernet Franc
- Cabernet Sauvignon
- Sparkling wine

to hardy French hybrid grapes, which he was convinced produced more appealing wine than the fruit from native American vines. A home winemaker, Wagner was intrigued enough by these hybrids to bring a few vines along with him when he came back from Europe so that he could start a vineyard at his home in Maryland. He was soon certain that French hybrids were the solution to the problems American vintners faced in trying to grow European vinifera grapes; there was no way for Wagner to foresee that in a few decades, technology would make such an endeavor possible.

Philip and his wife, Jocelyn Wagner, tirelessly promoted the establishment of an American wine industry in the East. They provided fledgling vintners with everything from vines to advice. In 1943, the Wagners founded Boordy Vineyards (the name, they always insisted, has no meaning). Today, Boordy is the oldest and largest winery in Maryland.

In 1980, Rob Deford, a friend of the Wagners and one of Boordy's grape suppliers, bought the winery and moved the whole operation to his bucolic 250-acre beef and grain farm a few miles away from the original site. Located in the scenic Long Green Valley, an area listed in the National Register of Historic Places, the winery is housed in a charming 19th-century stone and wood barn.

Three recent shifts in philosophy have led to vastly improved wines and to the reemergence of Boordy as a leader in the Mid-Atlantic viticultural region. Most significantly, the decision to concentrate on vinifera — moving away from the hybrid vines that first put Boordy on the map — is proof that the wines from this historic producer now reflect contemporary consumer tastes. Stylistic advances include backing off on an overload of oak in the white wines, resulting in clearer, fruitier flavors. Recent vineyard policies are also affecting overall quality, as red wine grapes have been ripped out of the heavy limestone soils that surround the winery and replaced by white grapes better suited to these conditions. The reds, meanwhile, have been replanted in newly leased vineyards in Burkittsville, in the western section of the state, where the soils and climate are friendlier to Cabernet and Merlot.

Boordy produces about 14,000 cases a year. Tom Burns, who has been the winemaker for a dozen or so years, has recently turned out some bright, perky Chardonnays with overtones of pineapple and citrus unfettered by any overabundance of oak. The Blanc de Blancs has picked up a hint of color and a smidgen of texture from the addition of some Pinot Noir. The clean, soft Riesling was designed to be a good match for Maryland's traditional, spicy seasoning-infused seafood. Boordy's flagship Seyval — the one hybrid this winery insists that it will never give up — shows a goodly amount of depth and character. Among the red wines, Cabernet Franc from the Burkittsville Vineyard shows off black pepper and mineral elements along with a healthy ratio of tannins. Cabernet Sauvignon also tends toward an endnote of fairly firm tannins, with ripe dark berries in the foreground.

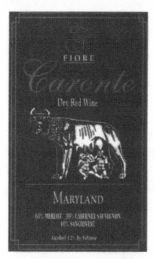

FIORE WINERY AND LA FELICETTA VINEYARD
410-836-7605, 410-879-4007.
www.fiorewinery.com.
Fiore@bellatlantic.net.
3026 Whiteford Rd.,
  Pylesville, MD 21132.
Directions: From I-95, take
  exit 77B to Rte. 24 north.
  Drive 22 miles to Rte.
  136. Drive east 1 mile to
  winery.
Owners: Mike & Rose
  Fiore.
Open: Wed.–Sat.
  10am–5pm, Sun.
  12noon–5pm; or by appt.
Price Range of Wines:
  $6–$17.50.
Special Events: August
  Wine Festival, Jazz and
  Art Festival.

Fiore and La Felicetta remind one of the small, family-run wineries in Italy. As I approach the place, I spot Mike Fiore heading off to the vineyards on a tractor. On the path to the winery, bees buzz in the roses, and the trees are filled with birds whistling Verdi. One almost expects the smell of espresso to perfume the air. But Rose Fiore isn't in the kitchen brewing coffee. She's been out since dawn pruning vines. She zips up now on a golf cart, wearing shorts, a T-shirt, blue eye shadow, and a film of vineyard dust.

We make our way to the tasting room, and as we sample a few wines, Rose tells me the vineyard was named in honor of the La Felicetta Vineyard in the Calabria region of Italy, where the Fiore family has been making wine since the 16th century. Mike grew up in Italy, working in a vineyard planted by a Fiore whose ancestor came to America 200 years ago to help Thomas Jefferson grow grapes. At the

- Chambourcin
- Chardonnay
- Vignoles

age of 17, Mike was the youngest cellar master in Italy.

The Fiores planted their first grapes here in 1982 and opened the winery in 1986. In 1998, Mike left his day job to work full-time at the winery. Fiore now has 14 acres of vines and leases an additional 10 acres at Swan Harbor, on the Chesapeake Bay. About 10,000 cases of wine are produced annually. The Fiores believe the attractive Seyval and Vidal Blanc wines owe their distinctively dry and fruity flavor to the influence of the nearby Susquehanna River and the Chesapeake Bay. The soil composition here, where marble and slate quarries abound, also adds a distinctive, mineral flavor reminiscent of rain-dampened pebbles. As good as the white wines are, Mike's passion is for red. "White wines are okay when you don't have red," he shrugs.

Luckily, the local soils seem ideal for red wine grapes. Fiore Chambourcin, fermented on Cabernet stems to give it sturdier tannins and length of flavor, has the rich aroma of cedar and licorice. The Fiores are convinced that Chambourcin does better in the Mid-Atlantic region than elsewhere in the East. "It's too cold in upstate New York and too hot in Virginia," says Rose. "L'Ombra," a Seyval/Vidal blend that spends two months in French oak is semidry and very tasty. "Caronte," a blend of Merlot, Cabernet Sauvignon, and Sangiovese delivers hints of ripe cherries and plums to the palate. Fiore's big, new tasting room has beautiful views of the vineyards and the surrounding pastoral countryside.

TOURING THE MID-ATLANTIC STATES

PENNSYLVANIA

Pennsylvania's Brandywine region includes scenic drives, pastoral countryside, excellent museums, and noteworthy gardens, as well as a handful of good wineries, including Chaddsford, French Creek Ridge, and Stargazers. Don't miss the famed Longwood Gardens and the Winterthur Museum (a superb collection of American decorative arts and antiques housed in the former Du Pont mansion). The Brandywine River Museum emphasizes American landscape and still life paintings created by some of the country's best-loved artists, including Maxfield Parrish and three generations of the Wyeth family. The museum is housed in a handsomely refurbished 19th-century gristmill. Enjoy lunch in the museum's glass-towered restaurant, overlooking the Brandywine River (608-388-2700).

For a taste of rural Pennsylvania Dutch life, spend the night at the Hickory Bridge Inn, a quaint farmhouse with five rooms (some with Jacuzzis) and four private cottages on the property. Their restaurant, which specializes in hearty, regional country fare is housed in an antiques-filled barn (800-642-1766).

CHAPTER FIVE
Virginia
COASTAL VIRGINIA,
NORTHERN & CENTRAL VIRGINIA,
& THE VIRGINIA MOUNTAINS

Courtesy Oakencroft Vineyard & Winery

The picturesque buildings at Oakencroft Vineyard & Winery, Charlottesville, Virginia.

A long the Virginia coast, winemaking remained an unfulfilled dream for many centuries despite the sandy soils and relatively mild climate that seemed well suited to viticulture. Two years after they landed in the New World, the settlers of Jamestown harvested, crushed, and fermented wild native grapes to produce America's first grape wine. While the results left much to be desired, the yearning for palatable wine and for an economically viable industry with which to slake the thirst of this large new market was strong enough to lead to years of frustrating and futile endeavors.

European grapes were imported into the colonies, and all householders were required by law to plant grape vines. French grape growers were sent by the London headquarters of the Virginia Colony to assist in the development of a wine industry. As late as 1769, despite mounting tensions with England, the colonists were still trying, without success, to make a drinkable wine in Virginia. It wasn't until the late 20th century that science and technology advanced to the point where wine, at last, was successfully produced here.

In the northern part of the state, it's an abrupt transition from bustling, cosmopolitan Washington, D.C., to the nearby graceful farmlands of Northern Virginia. This is steeplechase and fox-hunting country, and the beautiful horse farms, peaceful country roads, and alluring villages provide one set of compelling reasons to visit the area. Another is the state's wealth of Civil War and Revolutionary War era sites. American history lives in this bucolic land snuggled between the coastal plain and the Blue Ridge Mountains, a region known locally as the Piedmont. Manassas National Battlefield Park, where the Civil War battles of the First and Second Manassas (better known as Bull Run) were fought, lies only a few miles from peaceful vineyards. It was in the hills around Manassas that Stonewall Jackson got his name, when Bernard Bee, the Confederate general, rallied his men by calling out, "There is Jackson standing like a stone wall. Let us determine to die here, and we will conquer."

The town of Culpeper (where George Washington received his surveyor's license) was the place from which minutemen marched to battle carrying flags inscribed "Don't Tread On Me" and "Liberty or Death." Almost 100 years after the Revolutionary War, the town became the headquarters for the Union Army.

The countryside near Charlottesville is graced by many historic estates, including Monticello, Thomas Jefferson's famed home. James Madison's residence, Montpelier, is a few miles down the road. This is Virginia's heartland and also the center of her wine industry. One common thread that links the entire Monticello appellation, from the Piedmont all the way up to the mountains is the fact that at some point, Thomas Jefferson traversed it all on horseback.

Like the rest of the state, Virginia's mountainous country is rich in history. Bob Harper, owner of Naked Mountain Vineyard and Winery in Markham, is a walking encyclopedia of geological, culinary, and historical facts about the area that he shares with visitors in inspired moments. Among the things one might learn from Bob is that Route 688, where his winery is located, is the same road that Robert E. Lee took on his way to Gettysburg. Lee caught influenza along the way and had to spend a few days recuperating in Markham. More lore from Bob Harper: Sweet Georgia Brown is buried in the local cemetery; Revolutionary War hero Daniel Morgan was painted only in profile because one of his ears was bitten off in a barroom brawl; the town of Pumpkinville, where George Washington lived, changed its name to Paris after Lafayette came to visit in the 1790s; the Shenandoah Valley is one of the largest lamb-producing regions in the U.S.; Flint Hill, Virginia, still has the original white post set by George Washington when he surveyed the area.

The Blue Ridge, Shenandoah, Allegheny, and Cumberland Mountains frame Virginia's western border. Except for a few isolated areas, the weather in the mountainous regions is too extreme for grapes to grow. In certain places, however, specific microclimates offer vines a more hospitable environment. These tiny pockets may be at relatively high altitudes, but the right combination of proper soil and degrees of sunlight, coupled with warm days and cool nights, provides conditions in which grapes can thrive. Furthermore, the mountain air tends to be drier than in the muggier lowlands, which discourages fungus and molds from proliferating in the vineyards. Because the growing season in the mountains is long and relatively cool, grapes ripen slowly and develop intense color and flavors that are imparted to the wine.

Parts of Virginia's mountainous highland region still convey the sense of isolation and wild beauty for which this nation is noted. Hundreds of lakes, thousands of forested acres, and miles and miles of hiking trails charm nature lovers from all over the world. The 105-mile Blue Ridge Parkway and its continuation as Skyline Drive offer some of the finest scenery in America. These mountain roads are devoid of buildings, billboards, villages, restaurants, or motels, allowing travelers to savor uninterrupted natural splendor. Late spring is a fine time to travel here, when the white dogwood, the orange- and lemon-colored rhododendron, and the delicate pink wild azalea have burst into bloom, and the clouds are casting shadows that settle like giant pancakes on the Shenandoah Valley below. Indeed, every season presents its own charms along this ribbon of road, from summer's lush greenness to the vivid display of autumnal colors and even the starker beauty of the winter landscape.

Interspersed throughout Virginia's glorious scenery are some 75 wineries — a remarkable number considering that the first successful vinifera grape wines were made here a little more than a quarter of a century ago. Many of today's wineries are small, family-run operations, and to be honest, the quality of their wine is sometimes less than sterling. Unlike fully developed wine regions, such as Napa or Sonoma, where truly bad wine is a rarity these days, Virginia is still very much an emerging wine region, where the quality ranges from indifferent to good to outstanding. In the top tier, most of the best veteran producers (Barboursville, Breaux, Horton, Jefferson, Oakencroft, Prince Michel, and Rockbridge) are turning out better and better wine each year. Meanwhile, a new generation hit the ground running, winning awards and kudos with their very first vintages (Chrysalis and White Hall come to mind). In the middle ground are several smallish wineries struggling to keep up. In this latter group, quality is apt to be uneven, and there is a tendency to try to satisfy too many different palates — an understandable temptation in marginally financed operations where profit depends on quick sales; only well capitalized wineries can afford to concentrate exclusively on high-end, mature wines. Wine buffs traveling through the Virginia countryside should not pass up the opportunity to stop in for a visit at wineries that may not be included in this book, for the welcome will surely be warm, the views over the surrounding countryside magnificent, and the dedication to the often perilous business of winemaking heartwarming.

For all its current ups and downs, Virginia is potentially the most promising Eastern wine-producing state. Lying between the cold weather extreme of the Northeast and the intense heat and humidity of the South (where Pierce's Disease, a deadly vine ailment, thrives), this region is proving that its success is due to more than just unusually grape-friendly soils and weather. Another critical factor contributing to Virginia's success in the competitive wine market is the remarkably supportive state legislation that encourages both grape growers and wineries. Virginia has one of the most liberal farm winery laws in the nation. Unlike many other states in the East, wine can even be sold in Virginia's food stores. Another bonus to the wine industry is an affluent and educated population in the Washington, D.C. area, which is beginning to show an interest in local wines. Now, if only more of the top restaurants in the capital city were to start featuring Virginia wines — the way Manhattan eateries have embraced New York vintages — the picture would look very rosy indeed.

COASTAL VIRGINIA

INGLESIDE PLANTATION VINEYARDS
804-224-8687,
800-SIP-INGLESIDE;
fax 804-224-8573.

A peninsula formed by the Rappahannock and Potomac Rivers as they empty into Chesapeake Bay, the Northern Neck of Virginia is a region filled with history. Both George Washington and Robert E. Lee were born here.

www.ipwine.com.
mail@ipwine.com.
5872 Leedstown Rd., Oak
  Grove, VA 22443.
Directions: 2.5 miles south of
  Oak Grove on Leedstown
  Rd.
Owners: The Flemmer
  family.
Open: Mon.–Sat. 10am–5pm,
  Sun. 12noon–5pm.
Price Range of Wines:
  $9–$21.
Special Events: Jazz
  concerts in the courtyard,
  Fall Barrel Tasting,
  Holiday Open House.

• Chardonnay
• Cabernet Franc
• Cabernet Sauvignon
• Dessert wine
• Merlot
• Viognier

Ingleside Plantation Vineyards belongs to the Flemmer family, whose ancestor purchased the plantation in the late 1800s. The first vines were planted in 1960, and the winery began operation in 1980. Ingleside has 75 acres planted in vines and produces up to 14,000 cases of wine annually. The Chardonnay has nice rich flavors, and the Viognier is bursting with tropical fruit aromas. "Blue Crab Blanc" is a semidry white that makes a great aperitif. Cabernet Franc has nice spice and smoke characteristics, but the Merlot, with hints of mint and black cherry, is what everybody wants — it sells out quickly, leaving devotees begging for more. "Chesapeake Claret" (Cabernet Sauvignon, Cabernet Franc, Merlot, and Chambourcin) is soft but not shy, filling the mouth with flavor. The red blend "1894" is in classic Bordeaux style. "Colonial Rose" has an interesting historical twist: Inspired by the wine used for communion in Washington's day, today, it is the sacramental wine of choice for local Episcopal churches. Consumers also love this rich, sweet wine, especially around holiday time as a base for mulled wine.

**WILLIAMSBURG
  WINERY**
757-229-0999; fax
  757-229-0911.
www.williamsburgwinery
  ltd.com.
wine@wmbgwine.com.
5800 Wessex Hundred Rd.,
  Williamsburg, VA 23183.
Directions: From Colonial
  Williamsburg, take Rte. 31
  toward Jamestown. Turn
  left onto Rte. 199 east,
  right onto Brookwood Ln.,
  and left onto Lake Powell
  Rd. Winery entrance is on
  left.
Owner: Patrick Doffeler.
Open: Mon.–Sat. 11am–
  5:30pm, Sun. 12noon–
  5:30pm.

Belgian-born Patrick Doffeler was a business executive in France and New York, working for Eastman Kodak and Phillip Morris. "After I'd lived as a corporate mercenary for 20 years, my wife, Peggy, said, 'Now do something intelligent,'" recalls Patrick. His answer was to buy a farm in Williamsburg in 1983, which he converted into a vineyard and winery. Why wine? "Because it's the last consumer product that isn't standardized," Patrick explains. "There are too many variables in winemaking for it to ever become standardized." Patrick first came to Williamsburg in 1951, when he was a high-school student. "The place stands for our history, for a century of enlightenment, for grace of architecture," he says. "It stands for searching for a way of doing things differently."

Price Range of Wines:
  $7–$28.
Special Features: Colonial
  wine bottles on display.
Special Events: Candlelight
  Open House in
  conjunction with
  Colonial Williamsburg
  (Dec.).

• Cabernet Sauvignon
• Chardonnay
• Merlot

By nature, Patrick loves a challenge (one of his great passions is to race vintage automobiles), and so embarking on a winemaking project in an area where others had floundered for 300 years was just the sort of thing that interested him. It was also intelligent, as it turns out, for Williamsburg Winery has achieved surprising success. Financially, the winery has enjoyed small but solid sales growth, and critically, it has received numerous awards and national attention, including praise from such respected writers as Robert Parker.

Williamsburg has 60 acres under vine. It is the largest producer of wines in Virginia (more than 50,000 cases annually), and it has the state's largest barrel cellar, with a capacity for 1,200 barrels. It is also Virginia's most aggressive marketer, having succeeded in placing its wines in restaurants from Vermont to Atlanta.

Williamsburg produces some terrific wines, all from vinifera grapes. Steve Warner, the winemaker, graduated from Fresno State University in California. Most of his wines have layers of complex flavors under full fruit tones. This leaves a pleasing, long aftertaste at the back of the palate. The whites include "Governor's White," Williamsburg's most popular wine, a good sipper made from Riesling and Vidal. John Adlum Chardonnay honors the foremost Virginia winemaker in Thomas Jefferson's day. Act 12 of Sixteen-Nineteen Chardonnay is named after the law passed by the Virginia House of Burgesses in 1619, requiring every householder to plant and maintain 10 vines.

The full-bodied Merlot has rich flavors of spice and fruit. The "Gabriel Archer Reserve," named for the co-captain of the *Godspeed*, which brought the first settlers to Jamestown in 1607, is a Bordeaux-style blend of Cabernet Sauvignon, Cabernet Franc, and Merlot. This wine is produced only in years when the fruit achieves an exceptional degree of ripeness.

NORTHERN & CENTRAL VIRGINIA

**BARBOURSVILLE
VINEYARDS**
540-832-3824; fax
  540-832-7572.

Barboursville is a Virginia winery with an Italian accent. It is owned by the Zonin family, Italy's largest wine producer (the Zonins own 10 wineries in Italy). Barboursville is guided by an

Luca Paschina, winemaker at Barboursville Vineyards.

Marguerite Thomas

www.barboursvillewine
.com.
bvvy@barboursvillewine
.com.
17655 Winery Rd.,
  Barboursville, VA 22923.
Mail: P.O. Box 136, R.R. 777,
  Barboursville, VA 22923.
Directions: At junction of
  Rtes. 20 & 33, take Rte. 20
  south for 200 yds. Turn
  left on Rte. 678 and drive
  0.5 mile. Turn right onto
  Rte. 777 (Winery Rd.),
  then turn right at 1st
  driveway and follow
  signs.
Owners: The Zonin family.
Open: Mon.–Sat.
  10am–5pm, Sun.
  11am–5pm.
Price Range of Wines:
  $8–$50.

Italian winemaker, Luca Paschina, a graduate in viticulture and enology from the Institute Umberto Primo in Alba. Luca arrived at Barboursville in 1990.

One of the pioneering Virginia wineries, Barboursville was founded in 1976 by Gianni Zonin. In addition to establishing an outstanding winery, Zonin's great contribution to the Virginia wine industry was to bring a gifted young agronomist named Gabriele Rausse from Italy to manage the Barboursville property. Despite the skepticism of just about everyone around, Gabriele was the first to show that vinifera grapes could be raised successfully in Virginia.

Turning a deaf ear on the prevailing opinion that vinifera grapes couldn't survive in Virginia, Gabriele followed his own logic. If grapes could grow in the region northwest of Venice that was

Special Features: A restaurant specializing in Northern Italian fare, guest houses.

Special Events: Shakespeare in the Ruins, Autumn Explosion & Barrel Tasting, Old-World Christmas Celebration, Guest Chef Dinner Series, Virginia Opera.

- Barbera
- Cabernet Sauvignon
- Cabernet Franc
- Chardonnay
- Dessert wine
- Gewürztraminer
- Merlot
- Pinot Grigio
- Pinot Noir

his home, he reasoned, they ought to be adaptable to Virginia's climate as well. By applying the latest advances in viticultural management and by concentrating on grape varieties that would be most appropriate to Barboursville's specific growing conditions, Gabriele's theories were put to the test. The success of Barboursville's 1979 vintage proved him right. Until that point, no one else was interested in the "experimental" vines being raised by the Italians at Barboursville, but opinion changed radically. "By 1980, we had sold 100,000 vines to other people." Gabriele recalls with a smile. "They bought everything we had. It was a very exciting time."

When Gabriele went on to become the Assistant Director of Monticello's gardens and grounds, he was succeeded at Barboursville by Luca Paschina, who has consistently produced some of Virginia's most cutting-edge wines. Daringly adhering to the firm's heritage, Italian classics, such as Pinot Grigio, Sangiovese, and Barbera are emphasized. In addition to the Italian varietals, Barboursville also turns out Chardonnay, Cabernet Franc, Pinot Noir, and Cabernet Sauvignon. All the red wines are characterized by deep color, complex and inviting flavors, and a long aftertaste that lingers satisfyingly in the mouth. Malvaxia Reserve, a dessert wine produced from late-harvest Malvasia grapes, explodes in the mouth like a comet of sweet golden fruit (the Malvaxia bottle is a reproduction of an antique olive oil bottle discovered in the ruins of the plantation house). "Philéo" is a sweet and wonderfully fragrant blend of Muscat, Gewürztraminer, and Malvasia grapes. Annual production of all wines is 35,000 cases.

Barboursville's Tuscan-style tasting room includes a large brick fireplace, an Italian terra-cotta floor, and a long tasting bar. A handsome restaurant specializing in Northern Italian fare opened in 1999.

The winery is part of a lovely 900-acre estate (120 acres of vines) that also includes the picturesque ruins of a plantation house that once belonged to James Barbour. In addition to serving as Governor of Virginia from 1812-1814, Barbour was a U.S. Senator and a Secretary of State. His good friend Thomas Jefferson designed the house.

Marguerite Thomas

Winemaker David Collins with his award-winning wines from Breaux Vineyards.

BREAUX VINEYARDS
540-668-6299; fax
540-668-6283.
www.breauxvineyards
.com.
breauxvin@aol.com.
36888 Breaux Vineyards
Ln., Purcellville, VA
20132.
Directions: From Rte. 9,
drive through Hillsboro
and drive 2 more miles to
Harpers Ferry Rd. Bear
right to winery, 1 mile on
right.
Owners: Paul & Alexis
Breaux.
Open: Thurs.–Mon.
11am–5pm.
Price Range of Wines:
$10–$18.
Special Features: Informal
café, outdoor patio
seating.

The first vintage of this new and already very exciting winery was in 1997. Winemaker David Collins helped the original owners plant the vines in 1985, several years before the Breauxs bought the property. David then went on to Willowcroft Vineyards, where he honed his skills in the art and science of winemaking. When Alexis and Paul bought the vineyard and nurtured it back to health after it had been neglected for several years, they hired David to come back as winemaker. Perhaps he feels a sense of parental connection to the grapes, or maybe this site is particularly suitable for vines. Having the unconditional and enthusiastic support of the owners surely inspires him ("Paul poured his heart and pocketbook into this venture," he says). Whatever the reasons, David's evident passion for this vineyard and winery translates into some mighty superior wines. I

Special Events: Spring Cajun Festival, with live music and Louisiana cuisine.

• Chardonnay
• Cabernet Franc
• Cabernet Sauvignon
• Sauvignon Blanc
• Riesling
• Vidal

wouldn't hesitate to recommend all of Breaux's wines, from the spicy, ripe Seyval to the rich Barrel-Fermented Chardonnay, whose flavors linger hauntingly in the mouth. Madeleine's Chardonnay is as charming as the owners' young daughter, after whom the wine was named. The light, bright Lafayette Cabernet Franc — whose crawfish label is a reminder of the Breaux's Cajun origins — delivers a jolt of fruity aftertaste.

Breaux produced about 8,500 cases in 2001, but the targeted goal of about 10,000 cases is not far off. The more of these fine wines the better, as far as I'm concerned.

The winery is located near historic Harpers Ferry and is only a couple of miles from Hillsboro, a picturesque village of stone houses.

Government & Grapes

That Virginia wineries are the healthiest and fastest growing among the Eastern states is probably due more to the political climate than to weather patterns and soil types. "Virginia's wine industry is becoming widely recognized as one of the best in the nation," Governor Jim Gilmore remarked in 1999. "Its success is due in no small measure to the commitment by the state government to foster a climate in which it has been able to thrive."

"A couple of progressive governors started the ball rolling," recalls state enologist Bruce Zoecklein. "They saw that it wasn't just beverage alcohol they were looking at, but value-added products that impact on the state in the form of agricultural production, marketing, tourism, and tax revenues."

People who may have been initially hesitant — from government to higher education — got on board. "When I first arrived here in 1985, it would have taken an Act of Congress to get a local restaurant to pour Virginia wines," says Bruce. "Now we have people who are genuinely interested in the industry, including restaurateurs, retailers, and customers."

Without vigorous state support, Virginia's wine industry would be nowhere near as strong as it is. "We provide tax advantages to our wineries and fund research and marketing for the industry," Governor Gilmore explained. Bruce Zoecklein's contributions through Virginia Tech are among the most striking examples of what forward-thinking support can achieve. A large part of Bruce's job is to identify and address problems of climate, fruit chemistry, technical deficiencies, and the economics of growing grapes and making wines. His strategies are fivefold:

- To conduct a wide-ranging program for grape growers and winemakers, including short courses, seminars, and symposia that bring in producers and researchers from all over the world.
- To organize winery roundtables targeted to local vintners. "How many of them actually come to these?" I asked Bruce. "Why, all of them," he replied. "Virtually every commercial vintner in Virginia has attended." Wines of particular regions and styles are tasted and evaluated sensorially and blindly, then discussed. "This has had a major impact on creating a sense of community," says Bruce. It has also upped the winemaking ante by exposing vintners to styles of wine they might otherwise never encounter — if you aren't intimately familiar with fine wines, you'll never be able to make them yourself.
- To oversee a laboratory that provides free analytical support of chemical, physical, microbiological, and sensorial grape components.
- To conduct on-site visits to wineries. "It's harder to do that now because we have so many wineries," Bruce acknowledges, "but it allows me to keep my finger on the pace of development."
- To publish a bimonthly journal, providing news and information to vintners.

Working with his counterpart, Virginia Tech viticulturist Tony Wolf, Bruce explains that a nice synergism is at work: "The state realized that if the industry is going to be competitive, it needs to have help. We get more support commensurate to our size than our California counterpart with U.C. Davis." The results of this support are clear, in quantity and quality. When Bruce arrived in 1995, Virginia produced 30,000 cases of wine a year. Today, with 70 wineries operating and more in the wings, 300,000 cases are produced.

"I am very proud of our wine industry and enthusiastically support its success," Governor Gilmore declared. Would that all state leaders felt this way.

BURNLEY VINEYARDS
540-832-2828;
 fax 540-832-2280.
www.burnleywines.com.
burnleywiens@rlc.net.
4500 Winery Ln.,
 Barboursville, VA 22923.
Directions: From
 Charlottesville, drive
 north 15 miles on Rte. 20
 to Rte. 641. Turn left and
 drive 3 miles to winery.
 From intersection of Rtes.
 33 & 20, take Rte. 20
 south 2 miles. Turn right
 on Rte. 64 and drive 3
 miles to winery.
Owners: The Reeder family.

Burnley is a small family winery (about 5,000 cases), with a big selection of wines: at least 11 different choices. The Reeder family began planting vines in 1977, making this one of the oldest vineyards in the Monticello viticultural area (30 acres in all). Lee Reeder studied wine technology at Virginia Tech, graduating in 1983. He began making wine at Burnley shortly afterwards, and in 1985, the Reeders opened their own tasting room. The rustic barnlike space affords lovely views of the countryside (in cool weather, a wood-burning stove provides a cozy ambience). "Rivanna White" is a pleasant Vidal, and "Rivanna Red" is an unusual blend of Cham-

Open: Apr.–Dec.: daily
  11am–5pm; Jan.–Mar.:
  Fri.–Mon. 11am–5pm;
  or by appt.
Price Range of Wines:
  $8–$18.
Special Features: Rental
  house.
Special Events: Holiday
  Open House, Spring
  Cabernet Tasting,
  Summer Fest.

• Cabernet Sauvignon

bourcin, Maréchal Foch, and Cabernet Franc. The
unfined and unfiltered Cabernet Sauvignon is
full-bodied and full of personality.

A variety of wine from Chrysalis Vineyards.

Marguerite Thomas

CHRYSALIS VINEYARDS
540-687-8222, 800-235-8804;
  fax 540-687-8666.
www.chrysaliswine.com.
23876 Champe Ford Rd.,
  Middleburg, VA 20117.

Chrysalis is nestled deep in the Mosby Heritage Area; John S. Mosby was the Confederate colonel who led the only unit that never surrendered during the Civil War. This is one of the
youngest wineries in Loudoun County, a popular

Directions: From Washington, D.C., take Rte. 50 west to Champe Ford Rd. Drive left on Champe Ford about 1.3 miles to winery on left.
Owner: Jennifer McCloud.
Open: Daily 10am–5pm.
Price Range of Wines: $12–$25.50.
Special Events: Concerts, barrel tastings, and much more.

• Chardonnay
• Norton
• Viognier

winegrowing district only an hour or so from Washington, D.C. Chrysalis was founded in 1997 by a tall, energetic woman named Jennifer McCloud. Before she turned her attention to vines, the entrepreneurial Jennifer had been involved with the start-up of 13 different businesses. After selling off her interests in her last venture (a computer software business), she was ready for a complete change. A self-confessed, type-A personality, Jenny had developed an abiding interest in wine. Combine all this with a passion for growing things — in Miami she had once raised tropical fruits — and, well, launching a winery seemed like the next logical step, at least to Jennifer McCloud.

But why Virginia rather than a place where the wine industry was already established, as in, say, Napa? "I wanted to be a little bit bigger fish in a small pond," Jenny explains candidly. "More importantly, I wanted to play a role in the movement to establish a new wine region."

The 209-acre horse farm that Jenny purchased and turned into Chrysalis — a name that she says reflects the metamorphosis of grapes into wine — includes 24 acres of vines (27 additional acres are located on other properties). A 2,500-square-foot tasting room and gift shop that opened in July 2001, plus a separate 10,000-square-foot winery, are impressive structures, but they are merely temporary facilities filling in while a showcase winery capable of producing 75,000 cases is built.

Despite their youth, Chrysalis wines already show considerable merit. The Chardonnay is nicely balanced, with good fruit flavors. A proprietary red dubbed "Rubiana" (a spicy blend of Tempranillo, Graciano, Cabernet Sauvigon, and Tannat) made its debut in 1999. It's an enticing mouthful of wine. But it is the flagship Viognier — bursting with the flavors of ultraripe melons — that is most exciting, at least for now. But who knows what other treasures may emerge from Chrysalis? Jenny is experimenting in the vineyard with a variety of unusual grapes, including Albariño, Petit Verdot, Verdejo, and Petit Manseng (a dessert wine grape from Southwestern France). Her greatest passion, however, is a dark-skinned grape called Norton.

"I am really excited about Norton," Jenny exclaims. Norton is arguably the only American vine species capable of producing premium wine free of the "foxy" flavors so often associated with nonvinifera grapes. It is also, says Jenny, highly disease resistant, a definite plus in Virginia's often dauntng climate. Furthermore, Norton is loaded with resveratrol, a naturally occurring antioxidant compound that is said to promote health for the heart. "I am a Norton evangelist," laughs Jenny. "I dream of seeing the rolling Virginia countryside carpeted with Norton."

The first Norton had yet to be bottled when I last visited Chrysalis, but I went down to the cellar with Jenny where we tasted wines straight from the barrel. Norton has a wonderful aroma, but it is characteristically high in acid and tends to be very short in the mouth once the initial burst of flavor disappears. But Jenny's samples demonstrate that if a small amount of Petit Verdot and Tannat are blended in with the Norton, the wine becomes softer, rounder, and longer lasting, while still maintaining its good, fruity aroma and soft tannins. "Isn't Norton great?" Jenny purred, her eyes dancing with pleasure.

GRAY GHOST VINEYARDS
540-937-4869;
   fax 540-937-4869.
14706 Lee Hwy., Amissville, VA 20106.
Directions: From Warrenton, take Hwy. 211 west for 11 miles to winery on left.
Owners: Al & Cheryl Kellert.
Open: Fri.–Sun. (Mon. federal holidays) 11am–5pm; other days by appt.
Price Range of Wines: $9.50–$30.

• Cabernet Franc
• Chardonnay
• Merlot
• Vidal

This winery is named for John Mosby, the Confederate colonel who gained a place in history for having never surrendered during the Civil War. Mosby's other claim to fame was his ability to persistently avoid capture by seeming to vanish into thin air, earning him the sobriquet of the Gray Ghost. Colonel Mosby was also a wine drinker.

Al and Cheryl Kellert, the owners and winemakers at Gray Ghost Vineyards, share both an interest in the Civil War events that unfolded near their property and a passion for wine. Al began making wine when he was a college student. Later, he and Cheryl planted vines in their suburban garden near Washington, D.C. In 1986, they bought this farm, which had earlier been an apple orchard and a horse farm, and they moved their vines here. They now have 11 acres of vineyards, planted mostly with vinifera grapes, supplemented by small amounts of Vidal and Seyval.

Al recently retired from the U.S. Postal Service in Washington and has joined Cheryl (who trained at several Virginia wineries) in running Gray Ghost full time. The 3,400 cases of wine produced annually include a gentle Chardonnay that is fermented in new French oak barrels and an unfiltered, nicely balanced Cabernet Franc.

Gray Ghost reds have a distinctive, pleasantly smoky aroma. "We've noticed that, too," Al nods. "We suspect it might be something in the soil." Hmmm, I wonder if John Mosby smoked. . . .

Dennis Horton, co-owner of award-winning Horton Cellars.

Marguerite Thomas

HORTON CELLARS
540-832-7440, 800-829-4633; fax 540-832-7187.
www.hvwine.com.
vawinee@aol.com.
6399 Spottswood Tr. (Rte. 33), Gordonsville, VA 22942.
Directions: From Rte. 29, take Rte. 33 east for 8 miles to winery entrance on left. From Gordonsville, take Rte. 33 west for 4 miles to winery entrance on right.

Like many winery proprietors in the East, Dennis Horton started in 1983 by planting a small vineyard at his home. As his interest and knowledge grew, he began to realize that the humid conditions in the East favored grapes with thick skins and loose clusters. In his search for the ideal grape, he gravitated to the Rhône Valley in southern France, where he was impressed by the refined wines produced despite hot summer weather that rivaled Virginia.

Viognier, a thick-skinned, loose-clustered, heat-loving grape, used most notably in the wines of Condrieu, particularly struck his fancy. When

Winery is 0.5 mile from Barboursville.
Owners: Dennis & Sharon Horton & Joan Bieda.
Open: Daily 10am–5pm; closed Thanksgiving, Christmas, New Year's Day.
Price Range of Wines: $7–$25.
Special Events: Annual Pig Roast in June.

• Grenache
• Malbec
• Marsanne
• Mourvèdre
• Norton
• Syrah
• Viognier

Dennis and his business partner Joan Bieda began planning their vineyard, they concentrated on Viognier and other Rhône varieties, such as Marsanne, Mourvèdre, Syrah, Grenache, and Malbec. The vineyard was planted in 1988 under the supervision of Dennis's wife, Sharon.

But the Rhône was not Dennis Horton's only fixation. He also had a crush (so to speak) on Norton, a true Virginia grape propagated in 1835 in Richmond, Virginia, by D. N. Norton, who wanted to develop a grape suitable for Virginia's climate. The Norton was so successful that it became the backbone of the Monticello Wine Company in Charlottesville, and as early as the late 1800s, the Monticello Company made Virginia the capital of the Eastern Wine Belt. It retained its position until the state's entire wine industry collapsed under the pressure of Prohibition. Dennis, who had found a few Norton survivors in his home state of Missouri, became interested in reviving this historic grape. The wine has an astonishingly dark, inky color and a pronounced aroma reminiscent of cherries and plums. Horton Viognier also has an intense aroma — putting nose to glass is like burying your face in a hedge of honeysuckle. It has the dryness and depth that one associates with fine Viognier and a satisfying long finish. Robert Parker wrote about the 1993 vintage, "While it will not replace a great Condrieu from the likes of Marcel Guigal or André Parret, it represents a major breakthrough in what can be achieved in specific microclimates in the Mid-Atlantic region . . . Bravo!" Horton's newest wine is a sparkling Viognier. The winery's total production is about 30,000 cases.

Viognier

Redolent of peaches, apricots, and honeysuckle, Viognier is one of the most deliciously fragrant and distinctive white wines in the world. It is traditionally associated with France's Northern Rhône region, and specifically with the village of Condrieu, where relatively miniscule quantities of this wine are produced. Viognier has been cultivated in Condrieu — at the bend in the river just below the Côte Rôtie red wine district — for at least 2,000 years. At one time, Condrieu wines were sweet, but today, almost all Viognier wine is vinified dry. Château-Grillet, one of France's smallest wine appellations (and one of the few with a single owner) is a narrow enclave nestled within Condrieu. Thomas Jefferson was a great admirer of Château-Grillet. About 2,000 or so cases of wine are squeezed out of the tiny Château-Grillet vineyard (under 10 acres in all), and because of its rarity, the wine is, understandably, very expensive.

In the 1970s, Condrieu's fame (and price) started to rise after a slump in the 1960s. Viognier plantings began to spread outside of Condrieu into the Ardèche and Languedoc and by the 1980s, into California. At about this time, Dennis Horton had begun planting his vineyard in Central Virginia. While he was interested in Rhône vine varieties in general, Viognier was the grape that most excited him. His faith in this grape has been richly rewarded as he is recognized today as one of the best producers of Viognier in the country (his 1993 vintage is arguably the best Viognier yet produced in America). A handful of other Virginia vintners have since heeded the call and are turning out some astoundingly good Viognier, among them Barboursville, Breaux, Chrysalis, and Ingleside.

One reason Viognier adapts well to conditions in Virginia is that it thrives in a warm climate. Its thick skin helps protect it from various vine diseases and pests, and its loose clusters allow good air circulation. Because Viognier is susceptible to powdery mildew, a constant threat in the damp East, good vineyard management is essential to keep the fruit healthy. "Viognier gets 50 percent less rot," says Dennis Horton. "Furthermore, it holds its acid better than Chardonnay, and it sugars up a lot better." Dennis recalls the disastrous 2000 vintage when it rained four weeks during harvest time. "Viognier was the only fruit I picked that was clean and had nice sugars. All the other grapes — forget it!"

Viognier grapes are deep yellow, which results in richly colored, golden wine. California Viognier has a tendency to be over-the-top high in alcohol and monstrously full-bodied and full-flavored. Good Virginia vintages, by contrast, exhibit more subtlety and delicacy, while still showing off the floral and fruity aromas and flavors that give Viognier its particular charm.

JEFFERSON VINEYARDS
434-977-3042, 800-272-3042; fax 434-977-5459.
www.jeffersonvineyards.com.
info@jeffersonvineyards.com.
1353 Thomas Jefferson Pkwy. (Rte. 9), P.O. Box 293, Charlottesville, VA 22902.
Directions: On Hwy. 53 bet. Monticello and Ashlawn-Highland just southeast of Charlottesville.
Owner: Stanley Woodward, Jr.

In 1774, Filippo Mazzei, an Italian viticulturist and a friend of Thomas Jefferson, planted vinifera wine grapes on this site. Mazzei's efforts to grow grapes and to make wine were ultimately unsuccessful, but today, 17 acres of vines that were planted in the same spot in 1981 have fared well. "This is one of the best vineyard sites in the state," Michael Shaps, the winemaker, who, in the late 1990s, helped position Jefferson among the top ranks of the state's wineries, once told me: "It's on a southeast-facing slope. It's hot, but it gets a good breeze coming down the mountain so we don't have much of a problem

Open: Daily 11am–5pm;
  closed Thanksgiving,
  Christmas, New Year's
  Day.
Price Range of Wines:
  $11.95–$32.95.
Special Events: Autumn
  Harvest Party and Pig
  Roast.

• Cabernet Franc
• Cabernet Sauvignon
• Chardonnay
• Pinot Gris
• Rosé
• Late Harvest Vidal

with humidity and mildew. Because of the heat, the fruit ripens very fast."

Under Michael's stewardship, Jefferson sales doubled in just a handful of years, and production also doubled, from 4,000 to 8,000 cases. Frantz Ventre, who took over from Michael in 2001, seized the momentum, and he will clearly propel Jefferson to new heights. A native of St. Émilion and a graduate of the University of Bordeaux, Frantz brings to the job a French sensibility that Thomas Jefferson would have appreciated.

Jefferson's tasting room and deck are packed on weekends. People come here both for the winery's proximity to Monticello and, increasingly, for the excellence of the wines. Pinot Gris is soft and mouth filling. "Fantaisie Sauvage," a delectable Chardonnay made from native yeasts, is creamy and aromatic; it is also hard to come by as fewer than 500 cases are produced each year. "Clairet," a lively Merlot/Cabernet-based Rosé, is more full-bodied than most pink wines. The first vintage of a flavorful Viognier and a Viognier/Chardonnay blend was released in 2001. Red wines (the fine Meritage and the Estate Reserve, for example) tend to be huge, deep, and intense with ripe fruit and earthy tones. Late Harvest Vidal (made from grapes that have been frozen to concentrate the juice) is a sweet delicacy that has picked up a fair amount of complexity in the past couple of vintages. It is gratifying to find these terrific wines coming from vineyards set in the countryside that Thomas Jefferson so loved.

OASIS VINEYARDS
540-635-7656, 800-304-7656.
www.oasiswine.com.
oasiswine@aol.com.
14141 Hume Rd., Hume,
  VA 22639.
Directions: Driving west on
  I-66, take exit 27 at
  Marshall and follow Rte.
  647 south for 4 miles to
  Rte. 635. Turn right and
  drive 10 miles to winery.
Owners: Dirgham &
  Corinne Salahi.
Open: Daily 10am–5pm;
  closed Thanksgiving,

Oasis Vineyards claims to own the oldest plantings of Chardonnay and Cabernet Sauvignon grapes in Virginia. It was also the first in the state to focus exclusively on vinifera grapes and the first to make a sparkling wine.

From its initial vintage in 1980, when 186 cases of wine were produced, Oasis is now up to about 20,000 cases and still growing. The winery owns 80 acres of vineyards at the winery site, plus 20 additional acres. The proprietors are Jerusalem-born Dirgham Salahi and his Belgian wife, Corinne. Many of the winery responsibilities are

Tareq Salahi, winemaker at Oasis Vineyards.

Marguerite Thomas

Christmas, New Year's Day.
Price Range of Wines: $10–$89.
Special Features: Indoor or outdoor café-style seating, heated pavilion seating 2,500.
Special Events: Spring Open House with hors d'oeuvres and live music, Polo Wine and Twilight Dine, Murder & Winemaker Dinner, August Blessing of the Vines.

• Chardonnay
• Gewürztraminer
• Merlot
• Cabernet Sauvignon
• Sparkling wine

now in the hands of the Salahi's son Tareq, who received a degree in enology from U.C. Davis. Tareq's first job after graduation was at Domaine Carneros, the Napa winery known for its sparkling wines. This training shows in the high quality of Oasis Vineyards sparkling wines, which are among the best in the state. The Brut tends to be delicate, the Cuvée D'Or is somewhat more full-bodied, and both finish on a clean, dry note.

Oasis Chardonnay is usually bright and lively, the Riesling leaves a crisp impression even though it is somewhat sweet, and the Gewürztraminer has a characteristic spicy quality. The red wines — Merlot, Cabernet Sauvignon, and the Meritage blend — are apt to be soft and discreet in style.

Oasis has a small café that offers Virginia

cheeses, smoked trout, and other informal lunch fare, which can be enjoyed outside on the sunny terrace where there are splendid views of the surrounding mountains.

Marguerite Thomas

John Fitter, veteran winemaker at Piedmont Vineyards & Winery.

PIEDMONT VINEYARDS & WINERY
540-687-5528; fax 540-687-5777.
www.piedmontwines.com.
info@piedmontwines.com.
Rte. 626, P.O. Box 286, Middleburg, VA 20118.
Directions: From Washington, D.C., take I-66 to Rte. 50 west and follow to Rte. 626 south. From Middleburg, it's 3 miles south on Rte. 626.
Owner: Gerhard von Finck.
Open: Daily 11am–5pm, except major holidays.

Piedmont Winery was started in 1973 by a 75-year-old woman named Elizabeth Furness, who converted her former dairy farm to a winery when she realized grapes could be more profitable than milk. Today, Piedmont is owned by German investor Gerhard von Finck. The winemaker, John Fitter, is heading into his second decade at Piedmont. Twenty-eight acres are under cultivation, and 3,500 cases are produced annually. One must commend this winery for focusing on only two grape varieties — Chardonnay and Cabernet Sauvignon. Too many wineries try to capture the market with a bewilderingly diverse selection that inevitably includes at least

Price Range of Wines:
$13–$25.

• Chardonnay
• Cabernet Sauvignon

a couple of off-putting wines, and these, unfortunately, are often the very wines that visitors remember.

Piedmont's trio of different Chardonnays is crowned by the glorious Native Yeast Chardonnay, made from fruit that comes from vines planted in 1973 — possibly the oldest vinifera vines in Virginia. This wine (made only in superior years) could hold its own against fine Chardonnay from Napa or Burgundy. The best vintages of Piedmont Cabernet Sauvignon offer pleasantly balanced ripe fruit flavors. While white wines represent 80-85 percent of Piedmont's production, red wine is beginning to play a bigger role here and can be expected to grow in importance. The recent planting of 2,000 new Cabernet vines is indicative of the move in this direction.

Richard Robinson

The wines of Prince Michel Vineyards.

**PRINCE MICHEL
VINEYARDS**
540-547-3707, 800-869-8242;
fax 540-547-3088.

Prince Michel, established in 1983, and its affiliate, Rapidan River Vineyards, are owned by French businessman Jean Leducq. The

www.princemichel.com.
info@prince michel.com.
Rte. 29, Leon, VA 22725.
Mail: HCR Box 77, Leon,
   VA 22725.
Directions: 10 miles south
   of Culpeper on Rte. 29.
Owner: Jean Leducq.
Open: Daily 10am–5pm.
Price Range of Wines:
   Rapidan River
   $12.95–$30.
Special Features: Wine
   museum, gift shop,
   restaurant, guest suites.

• Cabernet Sauvignon
• Chardonnay
• Merlot
• Merlot/Cabernet

winemaker is Tom Payette. The combined acreage at both wineries includes 100 acres at Prince Michel and 115 acres at Rapidan, making this one of the largest vineyard holdings in Virginia. Furthermore, Prince Michel's 45,000-case annual production is one of the largest in the state; one oddity at Prince Michel is that it is one of the few Virginia vineyards to machine-harvest its grapes.

Jacques Boissenot, a noted wine consultant from Bordeaux, is often called upon to share his expertise at Prince Michel. Among Boissenot's other clients are some of France's most illustrious châteaux, including Pichon-Longueville, Léoville-Barton, and Château-Margaux, as well as the Lafite-Rothchild's operations in Chile. Boissenot is one of the "flying winemakers" who have exerted a considerable influence on the quality and style of wine around the world.

Bruno Prats, of France's prestigious Cos d'Estournel Winery and who also consults at Millbrook Winery in New York's Hudson River Valley, is another of the influential global winemaking consultants. The most renowned of them all is Michel Rolland, who in addition to crafting wine at his own Château Bon Pasteur in Bordeaux, jets around the world helping to shape the destiny of winemaking at some of the most prestigious establishments in France, Australia, Chile, California, Long Island, and even India.

Prince Michel's Barrel Select Chardonnay is brimful of fresh, yeasty overtones. The Merlot/Cabernet, with Bordeaux as its model, delivers delicate hints of tobacco and black pepper (only 1,000 cases or so of this wine are produced annually). Wayside Merlot is made exclusively from the grapes harvested from the Wayside Vineyard, a two-acre plot visible on the right-hand side of the driveway as one faces the winery. The first vintage of this classy, limited, single-vineyard wine was 1999.

Prince Michel has a superior gift shop and a small but interesting wine museum. Visitors are encouraged to take an informative self-guided tour of the winery, where detailed explanations of each aspect of winemaking are clearly illustrated. Prince Michel's restaurant specializes in French haute cuisine. For overnight visitors, four comfortable, nicely furnished suites set amid the vineyards are available.

TARARA VINEYARD & WINERY
703-771-7100.
www.tarara.com.
specialevents@tarara.com.
13648 Tarara Ln., Leesburg, VA, 20176.
Directions: From Leesburg, take Rte. 15 north about 8 miles to Lucketts. Turn right onto Rte. 662 and drive 3 miles to winery sign. Driveway is on left.
Owners: Margaret & Whitie Hubert.
Open: Daily 11am–5pm.
Price Range of Wines: $12–$25.
Special Features: B&B, picnic deck overlooking the Potomac, hiking trails, softball diamond, volleyball court, horseshoe pit.
Special Events: Vintners' dinners, wine festivals, wine seminars.

• Cabernet Franc
• Cabernet Sauvignon
• Merlot
• Pinot Gris
• Viognier

Margaret and Whitie Hubert named their 475-acre farm after the Tarara River, which flooded the area in 1985, the year they bought their property. Tarara is also "Ararat" spelled backwards, which was the name of the mountain where Noah landed after the great flood (the first thing Noah then did was to plant a grape vine). It's hard to believe that this idyllic spot, overlooking the Potomac River, is only 60 minutes from the turmoil of Washington, D.C. The site offers a hospitable environment for vines as a constant breeze from the river moderates the temperatures. To provide a cool, stable climate in which his wines could age gracefully in their French barrels, Whitie (a retired contractor and developer) blasted a 6,000-square-foot cave out of the land. In the tasting room above the caves, samples are poured from bottles with colorful labels designed by the Huberts' daughter, Martha, a San Francisco artist.

Australian winemaker Daniel Alcorso arrived at Tarara in the summer of 2001, and it seems that a little touch of Down Under style is just what this winery needed to propel it into a higher realm. The unusual Pinot Gris is stylistically halfway between austere Pinot Grigio and lusher Alsace. Chardonnay is nicely balanced, and Viognier is round and plump, with flavors reminiscent of ripe melons. Tarara Cabernet Franc lends further credibility to the oft heard notion that this is Virginia's very best red wine grape. Merlot, meanwhile, is soft and well structured, and Cabernet Sauvignon has an air of refinement that surfaces after a big, bold first impression. "Terra Rouge," an easygoing blend of Chambourcin and Vidal Blanc with a touch of sweetness, has a loyal following of fans who consider it the ultimate picnic wine. The winery has 55 acres under cultivation and produces 8,000 cases annually.

THE VIRGINIA MOUNTAINS

OUR DOG BLUE

CHATEAU MORRISETTE

CHÂTEAU MORRISETTE
540-593-2865; fax
540-593-2868.
www.thedogs.com.
info@chateaumorrisette.com.
287 Winery Rd. SW, Floyd,
VA 24091.
Mail: P.O. Box 766, Meadows
of Dan, VA 24120.
Directions: From Blue
Ridge Pkwy., turn west at
mile post #171.5 onto
Black Ridge Rd. (Rte.
726). Take immediate left
on Winery Rd. to winery
on right.
Owners: The Morrisette
family.
Open: Mon.–Thurs.
10am–5pm, Fri.–Sat.
10am–6pm, Sun.
11am—5pm.
Price Range of Wines:
$9.95–$18.50.
Special Features: Restaurant.
Special Events: Winemakers'
dinners, Black Dog Jazz
Concerts, Our Dog Blues
Festival.

Château Morrisette gradually expanded from the original modest stone building into the spectacular winemaking and tasting room facility it now occupies. Built in 1998 from massive beams recycled from the St. Lawrence Seaway, the 2,400-square-foot structure houses a tasting room inside a 83-foot-tall tower and a winery that is surely one of the most impressive winemaking facilities in the East. The excellent restaurant has also expanded, and it now occupies all the space in the original stone building.

The two vineyards (32 acres in all) owned by this property tell a story of mountain grape growing. The smaller vineyard, visible from the winery, has gradually been replanted with Niagara grapes to replace the original Vidal vines, which were having difficulty surviving up here at 3,450 feet above sea level. The larger vineyard, only 10 miles away and at an elevation of 1,800 feet, seems to be a fine place to grow red grapes — Merlot, Cabernet Sauvignon, Pinot Noir, and Chambourcin — as well as the Chardonnay and Seyval that also thrive here. All the wines made

- Cabernet Franc
- Chardonnay
- Merlot

from these grapes tend to be rich, full-bodied, and satisfying.

Winemaker Dan Tallman arrived at Château Morrisette a couple of years ago from California. Dan wholeheartedly believes in the advantages of blending grapes from different climates, as well as from different vineyards. The Chardonnay, for example, is usually made by mixing several wines that have been fermented and aged separately. Grapes from different vineyards go into the blend: austere, high-acid mountain grapes, for example, may be blended with fatter, fleshier fruit from central Virginia for a more perfect balance of flavors.

"Black Dog" is an unassuming blend of red grapes that's a good bet for people who haven't developed a taste for heavy, tannic reds, while "Black Dog Blanc" is its simple white equivalent. "Black Dog Blush" is, of course, a sweetish pink wine, and "Our Dog Blue" is a fruity red in a blue bottle. "Sweet Mountain Laurel" is a very sweet wine made from Niagara.

Winemaking Migrations

Twenty years ago, no serious winemaker would have considered leaving California to work in the Eastern United States. By the 1990s, a small trickle of winemaking cross-migration was underway — at about the same time that Dan Kleck left Long Island's Palmer Vineyards to go to Kendall-Jackson in Napa, for example, John Sotello made his way from Sonoma's prestigious Iron Horse to Sakonnet Vineyards in Rhode Island. There has by no means been a groundswell of adventurous vintners rushing eastward — indeed, the momentum in this country is always toward the west — but as this region's potential becomes increasingly apparent, audacious Californians are answering the Eastern call of the wine.

One of the most recent California transplants is Dan Tallman, who arrived at Château Morrisette in Virginia's Blue Ridge Mountains in 2000. Dan was trained in California (U.C. Davis) and worked at a diverse group of critically acclaimed wineries in the Bear State, including Clos de Bois and Matanzas Creek. Because he is one of those pioneering types who ahbors complacency and refuses to become set in his ways, Dan jumped at the opportunity to sign on at Château Morrisette. "I get bored after a while and like to move on. I like to face new challenges and learn new things," he explains. "I thought it would be exciting to work in a young, emerging region. Virginia reminds me a lot of Sonoma County 20 years ago, when it was just coming out of prunes, apples, and dairy farming and going into viticulture. They didn't know how to grow grapes there at all then. It takes awhile to figure out the details."

The "details" to be figured out in Virginia include, of course, the weather. "It's definitely harder to grow grapes here," Dan acknowledges. "The weather messes with you in a way that it doesn't in California. This is a little closer to what goes on in France." Far from discouraging him, however, Virginia's climate strikes Dan as an interesting challenge to be met head on. Finding the vineyard sites best suited to the local climatic patterns is critical. "Even in Sonoma things like appropriate site selection were a major challenge," he recalls. "Now they have it pretty much figured out in California, but in Virginia, wineries are still spread out all over the state."

Wines that may be popular in Virginia but are virtually unknown in California are another challenge to confound any transplanted winemaker. "I'm intrigued by some of the unique varietals, such as Chambourcin and Vidal," says Dan. As he sees it, part of his job at Château Morrisette is to learn how to make good, dry wines from grapes that are often vinified in a sweeter style in the East. As for some of the more traditional grapes, Dan brims with enthusiasm. "Cabernet Franc, for example, is really exciting here. I'm also very excited about working with the grape growers in the region. I'd say that since 85 percent — maybe even more — of a wine's success depends on the quality of the grapes, it's important for me to work closely with the people who grow them. A lot of the growers here are also California transplants," he continues. "Like me, they were bored with what they were doing in the West and wanted more of a challenge. And Virginia certainly is a challenge, so we're all having a good time."

LINDEN VINEYARDS
540-364-1997; fax
540-364-3894.
www.lindenvineyards
.com.
linden@crosslink.net.
3708 Harrels Corner Rd.,
Linden, VA 22642.
Directions: From
Washington, D.C., take
I-66 to exit 13 in Linden.
Drive 1 mile east on Rte.
55, then turn right onto
Rte. 638 and drive 2 miles
to winery.
Owner: Jim Law.
Open: Apr.–Nov.:
Wed.–Sun. 11am–5pm;
Dec.–Mar.: Sat.–Sun.
11am–5pm.
Price Range of Wines:
$13–$28.
Special Events: Vintners'
dinners with guest chefs

Jim Law's science and agricultural background helped him determine what conditions to look for when he decided to plant a vineyard in Virginia. "We knew we wanted a mountain site," Jim says, explaining that the cooler air in the mountains helps delay the ripening of the grapes, which promotes more intense flavors. "When grapes grow in hot and humid climates, they ripen in Aug. and don't have a lot of finesse. In our area, the sunny days and cool nights allow the grapes to ripen over a longer period of time. We feel that this adds elegance and harmony to the wine."

Finally, in 1985, Jim settled on a spot at a 1,300-foot elevation in the Blue Ridge Mountains to plant his vineyard. "It's ideal for grapes," he says. "They ripen late in Oct., when the fruit has great intensity." The winery produces 6,000 cases of wine annually from its 16 acres of vines, plus

Linden Vineyards in the Blue Ridge Mountains.

Marguerite Thomas

from local fine restaurants, Winter Soup Weekends, barrel tasting (Apr.).

- Chardonnay
- Dessert wine
- Cabernet Sauvignon
- Sauvignon Blanc
- Seyval

other grapes that are purchased from two Linden staff members who got bitten by the wine bug and planted their own vineyards a few years ago (13 acres in all).

When Jim discovered how different the fruit from each of these different vineyards was, he began focusing on making single-vineyard designated wines. Since 1997, he has been turning out three separate Bordeaux-style Cabernet-based wines named for the separate vineyards. "We felt that this was the way to make the best wines we could," says Jim. "Linden Red," a simpler, less intense version of these wines, is designed for easier, earlier drinking; no bottle aging necessary — the cork can be popped as soon as the bottle leaves the winery.

Happily, white wines have not suffered from neglect despite the red wine fever that has seized everyone at Linden. Sauvignon Blanc (the first one was released in 1998) is one of the best in the East, beautifully aromatic and crisp without tartness. Reserve Chardonnay is a powerhouse of ripe fruitiness. Late Harvest is a dessert wine made from Vidal grapes that have been frozen to concentrate the flavor. Come to think of it, every Linden wine is a beauty that can compete in quality with wines from anywhere in the world.

Bob Harper, owner of Naked Mountain Vineyard and Winery, proudly stands next to his trusty van.

Marguerite Thomas

NAKED MOUNTAIN VINEYARD AND WINERY
540-364-1609; fax 540-364-4870.
www.nakedmtn.com.
nakedmountain@yahoo.com.
2747 Leeds Manor Rd., Markham, VA 22643.
Directions: From Washington, D.C., take I-66 to exit 18 in Markham. Drive 1.5 miles north on Rte. 688 to winery.
Owners: Robert & Phoebe Harper.
Open: Mar.–Dec.: Wed.–Sun., including holidays, 11am–5pm; Jan.–Feb.: Sat.–Sun. 11am–5pm.
Price Range of Wines: $12–$16.
Special Features: Light snacks.

The name provokes a lot of speculation. "More than a few people get carried away by the name Naked Mountain," admits winery owner Bob Harper, flashing a wicked grin. In fact, the name, which is found in the original 1765 deed to the property, aptly describes the mountain, whose soil composition is mostly schist and decomposed rock.

Because of a thermal inversion, the eastern slope of the Blue Ridge Mountains is relatively sheltered from winds and enjoys milder winter temperatures and cooler summers than many other areas in the state. "It is the best place in Virginia for grapes," says Bob. Of course, there are certain problems, such as the Clipper, a wind-borne cold front that sometimes whips through here. Bob seems unfazed when such topics are mentioned. "This is agriculture," he shrugs. "There are no freebies."

Naked Mountain Winery produces 6,500 cases of vinifera wine annually from its 20-acre vine-

Special Events: Chef's dinners, Lasagne Lunch Weekends, Bluegrass Bar-B-Que.

- Chardonnay
- Cabernet Franc
- Cabernet Sauvignon
- Riesling

yard, plus some additional grapes from local growers. Altogether the winery has three white and two red wines, all of them clean, pleasing, and well made.

Bob is a former lubricants engineer with Texaco. "I'm just working with another kind of lubricant now," he jokes. The winery is less than an hour from Washington, D.C., and Bob is proud to point out that Naked Mountain wine was served in the Clinton White House.

OAKENCROFT VINEYARD & WINERY
434-296-4188; fax 434-293-6631.
www.oakencroft.com.
mail@oakencroft.com.
1486 Oakencroft Ln., Charlottesville, VA 22901.
Directions: From Rte. 29, drive 3.5 miles west on

Oakencroft was part of Virginia's first generation of serious winemakers. When they first became interested in making wine, Felicia Warburg Rogan and her late husband, John Rogan, planted an experimental vineyard and made Seyval Blanc, Chardonnay, and Merlot with amateur equipment in a converted tool shed.

Barracks Rd. (Rte. 654) to Garth Rd. Winery entrance is on left.

Owner: Felicia Warburg Rogan.

Open: Apr.–Dec.: daily 11am–5pm; Jan.–Feb.: by appt.; Mar.: weekends only 11am–5pm.

Price Range of Wines: $10–$18.

Special Events: Jazz and other concerts, including Red, White, and Listen to the Blues, Spring Fiesta, Christmas Open House and Candlelight Tour.

- Cabernet Franc
- Cabernet Sauvignon
- Chardonnay
- Merlot

ROCKBRIDGE VINEYARD
540-377-6204, 888-511-WINE; fax 540-377-6204.
www.rockbridgewine.com. rockwine@cfw.com.
30 Hill View Ln., Raphine, VA 24472.

Directions: From I-81/I-64, take exit 205 and drive west on Rte. 606 for 1 mile to winery.

Owners: Shepherd & Jane Rause.

Open: May–Oct.: Wed.–Sun. 12noon–5pm; Apr. & Nov.–mid-Dec.: Sat.–Sun. 12noon–5pm; closed mid-Dec.–Mar.

Price Range of Wines: $8–$18.

Special Events: Summer Breeze Fête, End of Summer Solace, Fall Harvest Fest, Holiday Open House.

In 1982, Felicia carried the venture a step further. She hired a vineyard manager, planted a 17-acre vineyard, and began producing a variety of wines from both hybrid and vinifera grapes. The wines kept getting better and better. This was one of the first Virginia labels to travel outside the state when, in 1988, it went to Moscow with President Reagan, who presented Mikhail Gorbachev with a gift of Oakencroft Seyval Blanc.

Current production, under the care of winemaker Michael Schaps, is about 6,500 cases. Most of the Chardonnays taste fresh and lively, with an overlay of fresh green apple flavor. The plummy Merlot and smooth Cabernet Sauvignon are also highly recommended, as is the Cabernet Franc with its delicate hint of cherries.

At 2,000 feet above sea level, Rockbridge grapes tend to ripen later than the fruit in other regions. Chardonnay, for example, is about two weeks behind most other Chardonnay in Virginia. The extra ripening time gives the fruit ample opportunity to develop full, rich flavors, which is one of the reasons why Shepherd and Jane Rause share a quiet optimism about the future of their winery.

Shep, who previously worked at wineries in Germany and in California's Napa Valley (where he specialized in sparkling wines), is one of the state's leading vintners, who has done much to shape the successful character of the wine in this state. His name is inevitably at the top of the list whenever Virginia winemakers are discussed.

Visitors to the Rauses' big, restored dairy barn and 17-acre vineyard can discover Rockbridge's classy, award-winning wines for themselves. There's an intensely aromatic Moselle-style Riesling, for example, and a flavorful and harmonious Chardonnay. "Tuscarora White," a Ries-

- Chardonnay
- Cabernet Sauvignon
- Merlot
- Riesling
- Vidal
- Dessert wine

ling/Vidal blend with a touch of sweetness, is named after the Tuscarora white sandstone deposits that are prevalent in the region. Tuscarora was also the name of the Iroquois tribe that migrated south from New York to hunt in the Blue Ridge Mountains. Don't overlook Rockbridge's popular St. Mary's Blanc, a dry, spicy wine made from Vidal that has been fermented in French oak. It's named after the nearby St. Mary's Wilderness Area, which is a beautiful place to go hiking. The Rockbridge Merlot and Cabernet blend is a delicious, full-bodied red with plenty of character and a prolonged finish. Val d'Or is a sumptuous Vidal sweetie that sets the standard for Virginia dessert wines. Rockbridge currently produces about 6,500 cases of wine annually.

VALHALLA VINEYARDS
540-774-2610; fax
540-774-7858.
www.valhallawines.com.
valohallava@aol.com.
5371 Silver Fox Rd.,
Roanoke, VA 24014.
Directions: From Roanoke, take Rte. 419 west to Rte. 221 at Brambleton Ave. Turn onto Rte. 221 and drive to 2nd light. Drive right onto Roselawn Rd. for 2.3 miles to stop sign. Turn left on Chestnut Rd. and drive 0.8 miles to winery on left.
Owners: Jim & Debra Vascik.
Open: Apr.–June: Sat. 12noon–5pm, Sun. 1pm–5pm; Aug.–Oct.: Sat. 12noon–4pm, Sun. 1pm–4pm; or by appt.
Price Range of Wines: $16–$25.
Special Events: Blessing of the Vines (Aug.), "Stomp" Harvest Celebration, Holiday Open House (Nov.),

Debra and Jim Vascik were both working in the medical profession when they became seriously distracted by their passion for wine. Jim hasn't quit his day job yet, but Debra left hers in Aug. of 1998 to make wine and run Valhalla full time (the winery opened in May 1999). Their state-of-the-art winemaking facility includes a 200-foot underground cave that they blasted out of the granite mountain (the cave is 60 feet under the vineyard at its deepest point). Everything produced here is a premium dry table wine made from grapes grown in Valhalla's own 21-acre vinifera vineyard. Chardonnay surprises with its richness. Syrah gives off whiffs of cocoa and coffee, and Sangiovese delivers layers of fruit flavors. Late Harvest Viognier is thick and unctuous. One of Valhalla's most unusual (and popular) wines is made from Alicante Bouschet. Alicante is a French vinifera grape that has red flesh, as well as red skin, unlike Merlot, Cabernet, or Pinot Noir, which all have pale flesh and depend therefore on their skins to add color to the wine. Alicante yields a deep and dense ruby red wine, with pronounced aromas and flavors of cedar and berries.

Christmas in the Cave
(Dec.), Valentine's Day
Chocolate and Red Wine
Open House (Feb.).

• Alicante Bouschet
• Chardonnay
• Cabernet Sauvignon
• Syrah
• Viognier

VILLA APPALACCIA
540-593-3100.
www/villaappalaccia.
chianti@villaappalaccia.com.
762 Rock Castle Gorge,
Floyd, VA 24091.
Directions: From Charlottesville, take I-64 to I-81.
Drive south to Christians-
burg exit to Rte. 8. Follow
Rte. 8 east through Floyd
and 6 miles farther to Blue
Ridge Pkwy. Drive south
on Pkwy. for 5.2 miles
to Rte. 720 on left
(immediately after mile
post #170 sign on right).
Follow gravel road to
winery entrance.
Owners: Susanne Becker &
Stephen Haskell.
Price Range of Wines:
$12–$19.
Special Events: Frequent
food and wine pairings.

• Sangiovese
• Pinot Grigio
• Cabernet Franc
• Vidal

WHITE HALL VINEYARDS
434-823-8615; fax
434-823-4366.
www.whitehallvineyards
.com.
tastingroom@whitehall
vineyards.com.
5184 Sugar Ridge Rd., White
Hall, VA 22987.

The name Valhalla, says Debra, "refers to 'heaven on earth' in Norse mythology — it's the highest spot on earth." Gazing out at the spectacular view from the winery site, one does indeed feel that this spot truly represents a little bit of heaven on earth.

Northern Italy is the inspiration for the wines, the architecture, and the very spirit of Villa Appalaccia. Located above the Rock Castle Gorge National Forest on the Blue Ridge Parkway, the tile-roofed stone buildings set an attractive Mediterranean stage for the Italian-style wines, including "Simpàtico," a fragrant, fruity, and dry blend of various white grapes. "Lirico" is a clean, crisp, Vidal-based vino bianco. Francesco Cabernet Franc gives off a heady aroma of cherries and raspberries. "Toscanello" is a dynamite Sangiovese and Cabernet blend, with smoky overtones, a hint of raspberries, and soft, plush tannins. Owners Susanne Becker and Stephen Haskell are to be commended for their commitment to making food-friendly wines.

Considering that the vineyard was planted in 1991, that 1994 was the first vintage released, and that the winery opened only in 1996, White Hall is producing some astonishingly good wines whose stylistic maturity belies the relative youthfulness of the endeavor.

When Tony Champ took early retirement from the corporate world, he and his wife, Edie, spent

Marguerite Thomas

Tony Champ, owner of White Hall Vineyards.

Directions: From Rte. 29 in Charlottesville, drive west on Barracks Rd. to White Hall. From I-64, take Crozet exit, then Rte. 250 east. Turn left on Rte. 240 and take Rte. 810 to White Hall. In White Hall, take Rte. 810 north (Brown's Gap Turnpike). Turn left on Break Heart Rd. (Rte. 674) and continue to Sugar Ridge Rd. Winery is 1.5 miles on right.
Open: Wed.–Sun. 11am–5pm; closed Dec. 15–Mar. 1.
Owners: Antony & Edith Champ.

a year looking for an appropriate place where they could fulfill their longtime dream of growing grapes and producing wine. They finally decided on a site at an 800-foot elevation at the foot of the Blue Ridge Mountains, where they now have 25 acres planted exclusively in vinifera grapes. "We get a breeze blowing almost constantly through a gap in the mountains, so we've had nice clean fruit and little problem with frost or humidity," says Edie.

Wines produced by White Hall (6,000 cases annually) include one of the very best Chardonnays in the whole country, elegant and beautifully balanced. Pinot Gris mingles elements of apple, pear, and minerals. Cabernet Sauvignon is rich and concentrated, with traces of cassis and cherries lurking beneath the surface. The bold

Price Range of Wines:
$7.99–$22.50.
Special Events: Art Festival
in the Vineyards (Oct.),
Feast Day of St. Vincent
Ferrer, patron saint of
winemakers.

• Chardonnay
• Cabernet Franc
• Cabernet Sauvignon
• Merlot
• Gewürztraminer

**WINTERGREEN VINE-
YARDS & WINERY**
434-361-2519; fax
434-361-1510.
www.wintergreenwinery
.com.
info@wintergreenwinery
.com.
P.O. Box 648, Nellysford, VA
22958.
Directions: From Charlottesville, drive south on Rte.
151 for 14 miles to Rte.
664. Turn west and drive
0.5 mile to winery. From
Blue Ridge Pkwy., take
exit onto Rte. 664 at mile
post #13. Winery is 5 miles
on left.
Owners: Jeff & Tamara
Stone.
Open: Apr.–Oct.: daily
10am–6pm; Nov.–Mar.
10am–5pm.
Price Range of Wines:
$7–$24.

• Chardonnay
• Cabernet Sauvignon
• Cabernet Franc
• Merlot

Merlot is spicy and earthy, and the Cabernet Franc tends to be smoky and supple. "Cuvée des Champs" is a big, brooding Bordeaux-style red blend.

The winery is beautifully situated, with spectacular views of the Blue Ridge Mountains.

With its first vintage in 1992, Wintergreen Vineyards established a distinct style of big, buttery California-style Chardonnay and semidry Riesling. These wines suit the tastes of new owners Jeff and Tamara Stone, who purchased Wintergreen in 1999. Perhaps even more than for the whites, the Stones are very excited about the new red wines that they're making, especially a Bordeaux-style blend of Merlot, Cabernet Franc, and Cabernet Sauvignon. To date, the winery is turning out about 5,500 cases of wine annually.

The original owners gave full credit for the success of the wines to their vineyard site, a former apple orchard with rocky, clay loam that the vines seem to love. The Stones concur that this is a great place to grow vines. It's a nice site for visitors, too, as the winery is located next to the Wintergreen Resort, where summer hiking and golf and winter skiing attract tourists year-round.

TOURING VIRGINIA

NORTHERN & CENTRAL VIRGINIA

Northern Virginia's Loudoun County may be the state's most popular wine region. Only an hour or so from the nation's capital, it attracts scores of visitors to the scenic rolling foothills of the Blue Ridge and Bull Run Mountains, the horse farms, and the ever-increasing number of vineyards, undulating in regimented rows across slopes and valley. The region is also historically rich, especially in Civil War battle sites. Chrysalis Vineyards, nestled deep in the Mosby Heritage Area (named for the Confederate General John Mosby), is the region's newest winery and the one closest to Washington, D.C. Piedmont Vineyards & Winery is three miles to the south of Middleburg, a small, attractive, shop-filled town.

Although there are many lodging options in the region, consider treating yourself to an evening at the incomparable Goodstone Inn. Situated on 265 acres of woods and trails not far from the Stoneleigh golf course, this establishment feels both welcoming and elegant, reflecting its distinguished 250-year-old history as a private country estate. Restored and converted to a privately owned inn in 1999, this refined establishment offers 14 different accommodations, four in the old Carriage House (where suites have been converted from the former stables) and others in private stone cottages on the estate (540-687-7056).

The following morning head north toward Leesburg; originally dubbed "George Town" for the reigning monarch George III, the name was changed in 1758 to honor Virginia's prominent Lee family. On the National Register, Leesburg is described as "one of the best preserved, most picturesque communities in Virginia." Among the town's many good restaurants, two in particular stand out both for their fine food and their good representation of local wines: Tuscarora Mill (703-771-9300) and Lightfoot Restaurant (703-771-2233).

Breaux Vineyards, at the western edge of Loudoun County, is set in a narrow, peaceful valley only a few moments away from Hillsboro, a tiny village known for its 18th- and 19th-century stone houses. Willowcroft Farm Vineyards is on the other side of Mt. Gilead, nestled up against the flank of the mountain. Heading back toward Washington, D.C., stop off for the night at Tarara's bed-and-breakfast.

One good way to experience Virginia horse country is to attend one of the polo exhibitions jointly sponsored by Oasis Vineyards and Bleu Rock

Vineyards Inn and Restaurant. Bleu Rock also provides a good base for touring the local wine country, especially for horse lovers. It is situated on 80 rural acres and offers five bedrooms, each with private bath and balcony, as well as its polo ring and equestrian center (800-537-3652). Another option might be the Black Horse Inn, a restored Civil War-era estate (nine rooms, private baths, period antiques) that will arrange for horseback riding and/or fox hunting for guests (540-349-4020).

More interested in Pinot than tallyho? Head on down to Barboursville, Virginia's premier Italianate winery for a good sampling of Barbera, Chardonnay, Merlot, and Barbaresco, as well as Pinot Grigio and Pinot Noir. Make a reservation for lunch or dinner at Barboursville's acclaimed Northern Italian restaurant. Or for a taste of France, venture over to Prince Michel and splurge on a meal in this winery's upscale French restaurant. Spend the night in princely luxury in one of their guest suites situated amid the vines.

Any excursion in Central Virginia must include a visit to Horton Cellars to sample some of the best Viognier and other Rhône varietals in the East. For a contrast to this big, polished establishment, stop in at Burnley Vineyards, a small, friendly, family-run operation.

THE VIRGINIA MOUNTAINS

The Blue Ridge Parkway is one of the loveliest roads in America, uniquely suited to a leisurely wine-oriented road trip. Three wineries are located along this gentle, curvaceous road with its spectacular views of mountains and valleys. Hiking, horseback riding, golfing, and biking are among the other lures that bring visitors to this incomparable region. Villa Appalaccia and Valhalla are both good examples of dynamic new wineries eager to make their name with wines that are somewhat unusual in the East (Pinot Grigio, Syrah, and Alicante Bouschet, for example).

Château Morrisette has been around long enough to have already undergone major winery and restaurant expansions (in 1998). The restaurant at Château Morrisette is a wonderful place to stop for lunch or dinner. Among the many accommodations to choose from in the region, Harmony Farm Bed & Breakfast (three private rooms, each with its own bath) is conveniently located only a mile from Château Morrisette (540-593-2185). Or, if you want to get right into the rustic mountain spirit of the region, you might like to stay in one of the log cabins available at Beano Hills (540-728-2939).

CHAPTER SIX
Winery Restaurants & Lodging

Marguerite Thomas

While visiting the winery at Bully Hill Vineyards in the Finger Lakes, stop at their restaurant, with its indoor and open-air dining.

A developing trend in wine country is the number of wineries that feature their own dining opportunities, ranging from small snack bars to full-blown gourmet restaurants. Many wineries also have B&Bs, providing cozy and sometimes very elegant accommodations right in the heart of the vineyards.

Dining Price Codes:

$	$10–$25
$$	$25–$65
$$$	$65–$125
$$$$	$125 and up

Lodging Price Codes:

$	Up to $75 for a double
$$	$75–$150
$$$	$150–$250
$$$$	More than $250

NEW ENGLAND

WINERY RESTAURANTS & CAFÉS

Connecticut

**SHARPE HILL
VINEYARD**
860-974-3549.
108 Wade Rd., P.O. Box 1,
  Pomfret, CT 06285.
Directions: From I-395,
  take exit 93. Drive west
  on Rte. 101 (which
  becomes Rte. 44) for 7
  miles to Rte. 97 (in
  Abington district of
  Pomfret). Drive south
  on Rte. 97 exactly 4
  miles to Kimball Hill
  Rd. Turn left and drive
  1.8 miles to winery.
  From I-84, take exit 69.
  Drive east on Rte. 74 to
  end. Make a left onto
  Rte. 44 east and drive to
  Abington district of
  Pomfret. Turn right onto
  Rte. 97 south and
  proceed as above.
Open: Café: L 11am–5pm
  weekends; Tavern:
  winter: D Fri.;
  May–Oct.: D 2nd Fri.
  every month.
Price: $–$$.

The sun-dappled wine garden café is as charming, sophisticated, and unintimidating as the Sharpe Hill wines themselves. In winter months, enjoy the warm and cozy ambience of the Fireside Tavern. Catherine Vollweiler, who owns Sharpe Hill along with her husband Steven, prepares a range of appealing dishes, from salads and cheese platters to wood-grilled filet mignon or seafood.

WINERY LODGING

Rhode Island

Marguerite Thomas

The Roost, a country-style bed-and-breakfast at Sakonnet Vineyards.

THE ROOST AT SAKONNET VINE-YARDS
401-635-8486, 800-998-8486; fax 401-635-2101.
www.sakonnetwines.com.
sakonnetri@aol.com.
162 West Main Rd. (Rte. 77), P.O. Box 197, Little Compton, RI 02837.
Directions: From I-195, take Rte. 24 south and continue to Tiverton-Little Compton/Rte. 77 exit. Drive south on Rte. 77 through traffic light at Tiverton Four Corners. Sakonnet is 3 miles from this junction on left.
Open: Year-round.
Price: $$.

The original shingled farmhouse on the winery property has been turned into a country-chic bed-and-breakfast. Located close to beaches and the quaint village of Little Compton, as well as Rhode Island and Massachusetts wine country, this is a great place for families or a group of friends to take over the entire three bedrooms (each with its own bath) for a weekend or even a week.

NEW YORK STATE

WINERY RESTAURANTS & CAFÉS

The Finger Lakes

BULLY HILL RESTAURANT
607-868-3610, 607-868-3210.
8843 Greyton H. Taylor Mem. Dr., Hammondsport, NY 14840.
Directions: From Rte. 17, take exit 38 to Rte. 54. In Hammondsport, take Rte. 54A along west side of lake to County Rte. 76. Follow Rte. 76 for 1.5 miles to Greyton H. Taylor Mem. Dr. and winery.
Open: May–Oct.
Price: $–$$.

Looking out over a colorful landscape of flowers, shrubs, bushes, and trees, with Keuka Lake in the background, the large open-air dining deck is an inviting place to stop for a bowl of soup, a vegetarian pizza, a couple of crab cakes, or a hearty luncheon salad. In inclement weather, the indoor dining room, with its copper-topped tables, is a cozy alternative. The dynamic Lillian Taylor not only runs the winery, but is also the restaurant chef.

THE CAFÉ AT FOX RUN
315-536-4616, 800-636-9786.
670 Rte. 14, Penn Yan, NY 14527.
Directions: From I-90, take exit 42 to Rte. 14 south. Winery is on Rte. 14 bet. Geneva and Dresden.
Open: Daily 11am–5pm.
Price: $.

A sleek glass case holds gourmet salads, sandwiches, and other light fare.

GINNY LEE CAFÉ AT WAGNER VINEYARDS
607-582-6574.
9322 Rte. 414, Lodi, NY 14860.
Directions: From Rte. 17, take exit 32 to Rte. 14 north. In Watkins Glen, take Rte. 414 north. The winery is bet. Valois and Lodi.
Open: L, Sun. B. Contact winery for hours and days open.
Price: $.

Named for Bill Wagner's daughter, the café has a splendid view of the lake. The fare ranges from light to robust with imaginative appetizers and such items as salmon that's been smoked over barrel shavings from the winery.

The restaurant at Knapp Vineyards Winery, Romulus, New York in the Finger Lakes.

Marguerite Thomas

KNAPP VINEYARDS RESTAURANT
607-869-9271, 800-869-9271.
2770 County Rte. 128,
Romulus, NY 14541.
Open: Apr.–Dec.: L
Mon.–Sun. 11am–4pm, D
Thurs.–Sun. 5:30pm–
8:30pm; closed Jan.–Mar.
Price: $$–$$$.

An elegant dining room set amidst a lush flower garden makes this one of the region's most attractive restaurants. Whether eating inside or outdoors on the garden patio, the international menu offers something to please every palate. Light fare runs the gamut from Greek salad and Mexican burritos to artichoke pizza, as well as sandwiches and burgers. More substantial main courses include pan-seared duck breast, seafood pasta, and steak. Among the tempting desserts are pineapple-coconut pound cake and Kahlúa crème brûlée.

LOGAN RIDGE ESTATES RESTAURANT
607-546-6600, 866-546-6486.
3800 Ball Diamond Rd.,
Hector, NY 14841.
Directions: From Watkins
Glen, take Rte. 414 north.
Follow winery signs
north of Hector.
Open: Contact winery for
hours and days open.
Price: $–$$$.

The dining room is dominated by a vast stone fireplace, making this restaurant a cozy retreat in cool weather. In any season, the views of the lake are unbeatable — this is arguably the best place in the entire region to watch the sun set across the lake. The menu covers a wide range of styles, with special themes an option on designated evenings (come on Wed. for Risotto Night or Fri. for Lobster Bake). Open Grill Night is on Thurs., with grilled meats, chicken, or fish accompanied by a selection of comfort foods, such as herb-roasted red potatoes or horseradish mashed potatoes.

THE RED NEWT BISTRO
607-546-4100.
3675 Tichenor Rd., Hector,
NY 14841.
Directions: From Rte. 17,
take exit 32 to Rte. 14
north. In Watkins Glen,
take Rte. 414 north. Turn
right on Tichenor Rd. to
winery.
Open: Thurs.–Sun.: L
12noon–4pm, D 4pm–
9pm; closed end of
Dec.–Mar.
Price: $$–$$$.

The slope in front of Red Newt is planted with Concord grapes, which are there solely to welcome guests with their heady perfume, saturating the autumnal nighttime air. The bistro was designed to be both rustic and elegant: think summer camp with white tablecloths and candlelight. A bank of windows looks out over those aromatic vines to the lake. Service is cheerful and efficient. Debra Whiting's considerable culinary capabilities have grown in tandem with her husband's winemaking skills, and today her sophisticated regional American cooking has contributed to raising the gastronomic level of the entire region. Among the many menu items that stand out are the organic salads and vegetables that Deb purchases from local farmers, the wonderfully hearty soups, nicely grilled game birds, a selection of New York State cheeses, and a handful of exceptional desserts.

Marguerite Thomas

The Café at Sheldrake Point Vineyard offers gourmet dining.

SHELDRAKE POINT VINEYARD CAFE

607-532-9401.
7448 County Rd. 153, Ovid, NY 14521.
Directions: Follow Rte. 89 north from Ithaca or south from Seneca Falls. Look for signs directing you down County Rd. 139 to Sheldrake. Turn right at 4-way stop onto County Rd. 153 to winery a few hundred yards on right.
Open: L, D, Sun. B. Contact winery for hours and days open.
Price: $–$$.

Situated on an idyllic point of land on the western shore of Cayuga Lake, this handsome new restaurant reflects the growing appreciation for gourmet dining in the Finger Lakes. Light luncheon fare includes such innovative items as Caribbean scallops (served over sweet potato lattice with gingered coconut and pineapple salsa), or wild mushrooms in puff pastry. Main courses range from rack of lamb with cranberry-peach demi-glace to a grilled vegetable éclair with parsley sauce. Tough decisions for Sunday brunch: Eggs Niagara (smoked salmon and poached eggs in cider béarnaise), grilled salmon in fresh orange and red onion sauce, vegetable fritatta, or cinnamon French toast.

STANDING STONE SMOKEHOUSE WINE & CHEESE BAR

607-582-6051, 800-803-7135.
9934 Rte. 414, Hector, NY 14841.
Directions: From Rte. 17, take exit 32 to Rte. 14 north. In Watkins Glen, take Rte. 414 north. Winery is north of Valois.
Open: Contact winery for hours and days open.
Price: $.

Cheeses, pâtés, smoked and roasted salmon, and other informal, light picnic fare — perfect for enjoying with a glass of wine out on the deck with a million-dollar view of Seneca Lake.

VERAISONS AT GLENORA WINE CELLARS

607-243-5511, 800-243-5513.
5435 Rte. 14, Dundee, NY 14837.
Directions: From I-90, take exit 42 to Rte. 14 south. Winery is east of Dundee.
Open: Daily B, L, D.
Price: $–$$$.

Large glass windows afford diners a sweeping view of vineyards and Lake Seneca. The ambitious menu offers a diverse range of items from crab ravioli to steak with roasted garlic-shallot mashed potatoes to bison burger. Veraisons is open for breakfast, lunch, and dinner.

WINERY LODGING

The Finger Lakes

THE INN AT CHATEAU LAFAYETTE RENEAU
607-546-2062, 800-469-9463.
www.clrwine.com.
clrwine@aol.com.
Rte. 414, Hector, NY 14841.
Directions: From Rte. 17,
   take exit 32 to Rte. 14
   north. In Watkins Glen,
   take Rte. 414 north.
   Winery is 7.4 miles
   northeast of Watkins Glen.
Open: Year-round.
Price: $$–$$$.

A carefully restored, sparkling white farmhouse built in 1911 has been turned into Chateau LaFayette Reneau's bright and cheerful inn. The rooms have unique antique furnishings, and each boasts a view of the vineyards and lake. All the rooms have private bathrooms, and three have Jacuzzis. Even the most stressed-out urbanites slip into a relaxed state the moment they sink into a chair on the wide, wraparound porch, pour a glass of Riesling and settle back to watch the fiery evening sun slide over the hills across the lake.

Marguerite Thomas

The Inn at Glenora boasts one of the most magnificent views in the region.

INN AT GLENORA WINE CELLARS
607-243-5511, 800-243-5513;

With a backdrop of vines, the modern redwood and glass inn stretches languidly

fax 607-243-5514.
www.glenora.com.
wine@glenora.com.
5435 Rte. 14, Dundee, NY
  14837.
Directions: From I-90, take
  exit 42 to Rte. 14 south.
  Winery is east of Dundee.
Open: Year-round.
Price: $$–$$$.

**KEUKA OVERLOOK
  WINE CELLARS AND
  BED & BREAKFAST
  INN**
607-292-6877;
  fax 607-292-6820.
www.keukaoverlook.com.
tab6877@aol.com.
5777 Old Bath Rd., Dundee,
  NY 14837.
Directions: From Rte. 17,
  take exit 38 to Rte. 54
  north. Drive north 6
  miles to Hammondsport.
  Take Rte. 54 north to Rte.
  230 to winery on left.
Open: Year-round.
Price: $$.

along a bluff overlooking Seneca Lake. Each of the 30 rooms has either a private balcony or patio with a lakeside view. Many of the rooms feature fireplaces, whirlpool tubs, and king-sized beds. Attractive, cherry Mission-style furniture adds further distinction.

This restored Victorian house sits atop a high knoll, overlooking both Keuka Lake and Wanetka Lake. Four rooms, each with a private bathroom, are furnished in turn-of-the-century country style.

VIRGINIA

WINERY RESTAURANTS & CAFÉS

Northern & Central Virginia

**PALLADIO AT
  BARBOURSVILLE
  VINEYARDS**
540-832-3824.
17655 Winery Rd.,
  Barboursville, VA 22923.
Directions: At junction of
  Rtes. 20 & 33, take Rte. 20
  south for 200 yds. Turn
  left on Rte. 678 and drive
  0.5 mile. Turn right onto
  Rte. 777 (Winery Rd.),

This elegantly rustic Italian enclave in the middle of Virginia has tiles, terra-cotta, and other colorful symbols of a Tuscan villa. The menu is likewise inspired by Northern Italy. Choose from the regular menu or the special tasting menu (which offers food and wine pairings.) A typical meal at Barboursville's Palladio Restaurant might begin with prosciutto-wrapped Mission figs stuffed with Gorgonzola cheese, followed by ravioli filled with ground

Fine dining is offered at the Palladio Restaurant at Barboursville Vineyards.

Marguerite Thomas

then turn right at 1st driveway and follow signs.
Open: L Wed.–Sun. 12noon–3pm (reservation suggested); D Fri.–Sat. 7pm–9:30pm (reservation required).
Price: $$–$$$.

veal and beets with sage-butter sauce (all pastas are handmade). For the main course, braised osso buco over soft polenta is a delectable choice. If there's any room left for dessert, try the tiramisù, or for something lighter, perhaps the Philéo gelato with almond biscotti; Philéo is one of Barboursville's fragrant, sweet dessert wines.

PATIO MADELEINE AT BREAUX VINEYARDS
540-668-6299.
36888 Breaux Vineyards Ln., Purcellville, VA 20132.
Directions: From Rte. 9, drive through Hillsboro and drive 2 more miles to Harpers Ferry Rd. Bear right to winery, 1 mile on right.
Open: L Thurs.–Mon. 11am–5pm.
Price: $.

Enjoy light luncheon fare (cheeses, smoked fish, pâtés) at a café table on the Patio Madeleine. The view over the narrow valley hemmed in by mountains is unbeatable.

OASIS CAFE AT THE VINEYARDS
540-635-7656, 800-304-7656.
14141 Hume Rd., Hume, VA 22639.

Informal picnic foods to savor indoors in inclement weather, or outdoors on the stone terrace when the sun shines. A bottle of Oasis Cuvée d'Or sparkling wine, a serving of smoked

Directions: Driving west on I-66, take exit 27 at Marshall and follow Rte. 647 south for 4 miles to Rte. 635. Turn right and drive 10 miles to winery.
Open: Daily 10am–5pm, except Thanksgiving, Christmas, New Year's Day.
Price: $.

trout, and striking views toward the mountains — life could be worse.

PRINCE MICHEL DE VIRGINIA
CHARDONNAY
2000 Virginia Chardonnay
Produced and Bottled by Prince Michel Vineyards, Leon, VA • Alcohol 13.2% by Volume

PRINCE MICHEL VINEYARDS
540-547-3707, 800-869-8242.
Rte. 29, Leon, VA 22725.
Directions: 10 miles south of Culpeper on Rte. 29.
Open: Contact winery for hours and days open.
Price: $$$.

Hard not to feel a bit like royalty in Prince Michel's elegantly appointed dining room overlooking the vineyards. I was tempted to go with seafood all the way through the meal since my bottle of Prince Michel Chardonnay cried out for fish. Seared ahi tuna was therefore followed by Chilean sea bass with sweet potato crust and wasabi vinaigrette, with crème brûlée to wind things up. A meal fit for a royal (or a very fortunate commoner).

The Virginia Mountains

CHÂTEAU MORRISETTE RESTAURANT
540-593-2865.
287 Winery Rd. SW, Floyd, VA 24091.

Because it's situated along the Blue Ridge Pkwy. at 3,450 feet above sea level, the restaurant at Château Morrisette likes to say that it offers "high-altitude dining." The dining area

Directions: From Blue Ridge Pkwy., turn west at mile post #171.5 onto Black Ridge Rd. (Rte. 726). Take immediate left on Winery Rd. to winery on right.
Open: L Wed.–Sat. 12noon–2pm, Sun. 12noon–5pm; D Fri.–Sat. 6pm–9pm.
Price: $$–$$$.

is tastefully furnished but informal, with attention rightly focused on the gorgeous scenery outside the windows. For lunch, a simple sandwich might appeal, or perhaps stuffed quail salad, pan-fried cornmeal trout, or coconut-curry tofu. For heartier appetites, or at dinnertime, go for a big, flavorful dish like the lamb with sun-dried cherry and Cabernet Franc sauce, or rib eye steak oozing black olive butter. Don't pass up the berry cobbler or the chocolate "oblivion" cake (what a way to go).

WINERY LODGING

Northern & Central Virginia

BARBOURSVILLE VINEYARDS GUEST HOUSES
540-832-7572 (lodging), 540-832-3824; fax 540-832-7572.

Tucked away in the quiet countryside behind the historic ruins of Governor James Barbour's house, the original slave quarters have been restored and converted into two charming guest houses. In addition, a mansion on the

One of the guest houses at Barboursville Vineyards.

Marguerite Thomas

www.barboursvillewine
.com.
bvvy@barboursvillewine
.com.
17655 Winery Rd.,
Barboursville, VA 22923.
Mail: P.O. Box 136, R.R. 777,
Barboursville, VA 22923.
Directions: At junction of
Rtes. 20 & 33, take Rte. 20
south for 200 yds. Turn
left on Rte. 678 and drive
0.5 mile. Turn right onto
Rte. 777 (Winery Rd.),
then turn right at 1st
driveway and follow
signs.
Open: Contact winery for
hours and days open.
Price: $$$$.

property is in the process of being converted into
luxury accommodations.

**BURNLEY HOUSE AT
THE VINEYARDS**
540-832-2828, 540-832-3874;
  fax 540-832-2280.
www.burnleywines.com.
burnleywiens@rlc.net.
4500 Winery Ln.,
  Barboursville, VA 22923.
Directions: From
  Charlottesville, drive
  north 15 miles on Rte. 20
  to Rte. 641. Turn left and
  drive 3 miles to winery.
  From intersection of Rtes.
  33 & 20, take Rte. 20
  south 2 miles. Turn right
  on Rte. 64 and drive 3
  miles to winery.
Open: Year-round.
Price: $$.

Spend a night (or longer) in this fully furnished cabin in the woods, overlooking the vineyards. The house has air-conditioning, heat, and a balcony for enjoying the rural vistas. It can accommodate four guests.

**PRINCE MICHEL
VINEYARDS**
540-547-3707, 800-869-8242;
  fax 540-547-3088.
www.princemichel.com.
info@princemichel.com.
Rte. 29, Leon, VA 22725.
Mail: HCR Box 77, Leon,
  VA 227215.
Directions: 10 miles south
  of Culpeper on Rte. 29.
Open: Contact winery for
  hours and days open.
Price: $$$$.

Four separate suites, stylish French Provincial furnishings and spalike bathrooms all add up to luxurious accommodations right in the middle of the vines. The front porch is an ideal spot to sit and sip a glass of Prince Michel Gewürztraminer, while watching the sun set over the vineyards. The only sound apt to break the nighttime silence is grape leaves rustling in the breeze. Wake up in the morning to the invigorating aroma of breakfast on the tray that's delivered to your door.

**TARARA BED &
BREAKFAST**
703-771-7100, ext.4,
  Margaret Hubert.
www.tarara.com.
specialevents@tarara.com.
13648 Tarara Ln., Leesburg,
  VA, 20176.
Directions: From Leesburg,
  take Rte. 15 north about 8
  miles to Lucketts. Turn
  right onto Rte. 662 and
  drive 3 miles to winery
  sign. Driveway is on left.
Open: Year-round.
Price: $$$.

The guest rooms are located right in the winery building, but far enough away from the hubbub to be serenely quiet. This vast estate along the Potomac River offers alluring opportunities for hiking, bird-watching, or simply settling down on the terrace with a good book. Hard to believe while relaxing in this bucolic setting that Washington, D.C. is less than an hour away.

CHAPTER SEVEN
Wine Information

© Jon Reis / Photolink

Barrels such as this one can be seen throughout the Finger Lakes Region

This chapter is a compendium of information about the many facets of wine. We hope this information inhances your visits to the many East Coast wineries listed in this book.

HOW WINE IS MADE

The best way for consumers to learn about winemaking is to visit a winery. A firsthand glimpse at the various winemaking steps — from growing grapes in the vineyard all the way through bottling the wine — leads to a better understanding of the process. While the precise methods of making wine may vary from winery to winery, the fundamental techniques are the same everywhere in the world.

The basics of winemaking have not changed significantly since winemaking began 7,000 years ago. True, the equipment used in modern wineries is stupendously high tech. And it is also true that winemakers have become better at counteracting some of the adverse forces of nature. But the basics of harvesting, pressing, and fermenting grapes is immutable — as is our enjoyment of the resulting product. Around the dawn of civilization, when it was first discovered that fermented fruit juice tastes good and can have a pleasant effect on anyone who drinks it, wine was viewed as a magic potion; those of us who love wine still think of it that way.

The various steps, then and now, for converting grapes into the alcoholic beverage we call wine are outlined below and are readily understood. There is no substitute for a winery visit, however, because reading about wine is a poor proxy indeed for actually tasting it.

From budbreak to harvest: The annual cycle of grape growing begins in early spring with budbreak, when the vine's winter hibernation ends and pale green shoots begin to emerge on the bare vine. Budbreak is an exciting time in the vineyard as it signals the start of the life cycle, but it can also be an anxious time, for the delicate new shoots are extremely vulnerable to damage from late spring frosts. This is a particular concern for vineyardists in the Eastern states, where spring freezes are not unusual. Some of the largest vineyards are protected by wind machines that help dispel freezing temperatures. Vintners with particularly deep pockets may also hire helicopters to fly over the vineyards when frost danger is high.

Roughly eight months after budbreak, the vineyard is ready for harvesting. Grapes are picked either by hand or by machine. Mechanical harvesting first began to be seen in the 1960s. Most modern mechanical grape harvesters work by driving through the vineyards a machine that strikes the top of the vines, knocking off the grapes and catching them on horizontal conveyor belts. From the winegrower's perspective, the advantages of harvesting by machine are obvious as the workforce can be reduced from dozens and dozens of pickers in a vineyard to one driver and an assistant or two. Furthermore, the whole process can be accomplished in a fraction of the time that it takes human workers to pick the grapes. As seasonal laborers become increasingly difficult to find in most winegrowing countries, it is easy to see why machine harvesting has been adopted in almost every wine region in the world.

The disadvantages of mechanical harvesting is that the machines can operate only where the vines are spaced widely enough for the harvester to fit between the rows. Additionally, machines cannot navigate in hilly terrain where the pitch of the slopes is too extreme. But even in places where mechanical harvesters could be used, many of the world's most prestigious wineries continue the tradition of harvesting by hand. The primary reason for relying on manual picking is to avoid having the grapes bruised and punctured by the machines and to avoid the inclusion of stray leaves and branches that are inevitably mixed in with grapes harvested by machine. The gentler touch of hand harvesting, along with the option of selectively picking only fully ripe, undamaged fruit, are among the reasons cited by many vintners for their refusal to harvest by machine.

Manual harvesting is accomplished by laborers moving up and down the rows of vines, usually armed with a short knife with a hooked tip for clipping off bunches of grapes. The grapes are placed in small baskets, formerly made of wood or wicker, but today almost universally of easier-to-clean plastic. When the baskets are full, they are dumped into a large container (often called a "gondola") that is transferred to the winery as soon as it's filled.

Grape ripeness: Ideally, the grapes have reached a desirable degree of ripeness by the time they are harvested. The process of ripening begins early in the season when the hard, green grapes begin to soften and to take on color. This stage in the vine's development is known as *veraison* (vuh-**ray**-shun). If you've ever tasted one of the grapes that hang on vines in early summer like tiny green beebees, its tartness surely puckered your lips. There is no sugar in this fruit yet, but within less than a week, the first berries on a bunch will already have accumulated enough glucose and other sugars to taste dramatically sweeter. In addition to sugar, the other part of the flavor equation in mature grapes is acid. While sugar builds up as the grapes ripen, the acid levels decline. Because this process is regulated by temperature, the acid level in cool-climate grapes tends to be higher than grapes grown in places where the weather is hot. Ideally, the proper balance of sugars and acids will have been reached by the time the grapes are picked; low sugar means tart wines, low acid can result in flaccid wine.

The length of time between veraison and harvest varies from region to region and grape variety to grape variety. Cabernet Franc, for example,

Richard Robinson

The extensive vineyards at Prince Michel in Virginia.

matures at least a week earlier than Cabernet Sauvignon, making it a safer bet in the unpredictable weather of the Eastern states.

Vintners can tell how ripe the grapes are and what their sugar content is by using a portable instrument called a refractometer, which measures the amount of dissolved compounds in grape juice in "Brix" degrees; grapes for fine wines are usually harvested when the Brix degrees reach into the low to mid-20s. While almost all modern vintners use refractometers or similar devices, many of them rely perhaps even more on the time-tested method of walking through the vineyard and simply tasting the grapes to assess their ripeness.

Why so much emphasis on ripeness? First of all, there must be enough sugar in the grapes for fermentation to take place. Furthermore, underripe fruit yields wine that may be thin-flavored, vegetal, and/or overly acidic. By contrast, overripe fruit often lacks the touch of acidity that gives a wine backbone, it can taste excessively raisiny, or it may even have acquired off-flavors because of mold or rotting.

The ripeness of the grapes, however, is far from being an exact science or an absolute ideal. Not only does the perception of ripeness tend to be subjective, but it is also, to some extent, influenced by fashion. Grapes that taste ripe to one winemaker may taste underripe or overripe to another. Contemporary palates tend to favor big, lush wines — both red and white — that are redolent of rich, ripe fruit. But there will always be a market for lean, refined, and delicate wines, which many gastronomes consider to be better partners for food.

Crushing: Once the harvested fruit is transferred to the winery, weight is applied to it via some device — originally human feet, today most likely mechanical crushers. Crushing splits the grape skins, thereby releasing the juice so that it is available for fermentation. Modern crushers are designed to crush the grapes gently without breaking the seeds, which would release bitter tannins into the juice. Usually called crusher-destemmers, these machines separate out the bitter stems. The crushed grapes are now ready to have the juice pressed out of them.

Pressing: Pressing squeezes the liquid from the solid part of the grapes or grape bunches. Because it is easier and faster to extract juice from smashed grapes, they usually have been crushed before pressing begins. In the case of white wines, a press is used to gently squeeze the juice away from the skins and seeds before beginning fermentation. Red wines are generally fermented for a time along with their skins after they've been pressed, which lends both flavor and color to the wine (most grapes, even those with red skins, are white inside). Some whites also rest on their skins for a brief time.

Fermenting: After pressing, the juice, which is called "must" at this point, is transferred for fermentation to large, open, wood, concrete, or fiberglass vats, or, more commonly today, large cylindrical stainless steel tanks. Certain premium wines, both red and white, may be fermented in small oak barrels. Barrel fermentation is trickier than fermenting in stainless steel tanks, and it requires more attention from the winemaker, but complex and pleasing flavors picked up from the wood can be transmitted to the wine.

Fermentation occurs when yeasts (either commercially produced or natural yeasts clinging to the fruit) feed on the sugars in the grape juice. As the sugar is consumed, it is converted to alcohol (ethanol) and carbon dioxide. Ever wonder where the word "fermentation" comes from? It's derived from the Latin *fermentum,* which means "boil." Anyone who's seen the carbon dioxide bubbles "boiling" up from fermenting wine can understand how this word came into usage.

One of the most significant advances in modern winemaking is the vintner's ability to control the temperature of fermenting must. For white wines, particularly, going through a cooler fermentation has resulted in fruitier, fresher wines.

The skins are left in the tank with fermenting red wine until the desired color has been extracted from them, then the must is "racked," or transferred away from the skins into another tank.

Good Rosé wine, incidentally, is usually made by leaving the skins in the fermentation tank just long enough to create a rosy color; some Rosés are simply a mixture of red and white wine, though the end result of this method usually yields a less interesting wine.

The length of time required for fermentation to be completed varies considerably and is dependent primarily on the temperature maintained in the fermenting mass. White wines, which are almost always fermented at cool temperatures, take several weeks, or sometimes even months, to finish fermenting. Reds, by contrast, usually complete fermentation within about a week.

Some wines undergo a second fermentation, called "malolactic fermentation." This procedure converts the wine's harsh and astringent malic acid (the kind found in apples) into supple, softer lactic acid (the kind found in milk). Wines that have gone through "malo" generally have a creamier texture, a faint buttery aroma, and, ideally, more complex flavors. Some grapes, most notably Chardonnay, seem to be better suited to malolactic fermentation than others; white wines, meant to be drunk young, for example, and light red wines tend to lose their character if they undergo malolactic fermentation.

After fermentation: Fermentation stops when all, or at least most, of the sugar molecules have been converted to alcohol. The resulting alcoholic content of the wine varies from an average of seven to nine percent (especially when grapes are grown in very cool regions such as Germany) to 10 to 14 percent (most of the table wines we drink fall in this latter range). When all the sugar in the wine has been used up, we say it is a "dry" wine. In actuality, it is almost impossible for all of the different types of sugar in grape juice to be converted to alcohol. The few remaining sugar cells are called "residual sugar," or RS. The amount of RS in wine can vary from one gram per liter to 2.5 grams or more, but most wine that contains less than two grams of residual sugar will be perceived as dry. Obviously, the higher the amount of residual sugar, the sweeter the wine will taste.

There are many different ways to make sweet wines. One popular way is to pick the grapes very late in the season when their juice has become rich and concentrated; these are known as late-harvest wines. Another common technique is to use frozen grapes. The eiswein of Austria and Germany and Canada's ice wine are the standard bearers of this method, in which the grapes are allowed to freeze on the vine. They are then picked and crushed before thawing so that the water in the fruit can be removed in the form of ice, leaving behind highly concentrated, sweet fruit juice. While most of the vineyard regions in the Eastern United States don't have dependably freezing weather, a technique has been developed to replicate this style of wine by freezing the grapes as soon as they are picked.

Aging and barrels: Wine that has just finished fermenting may look cloudy and smell gassy or yeasty. Red wine in its infancy usually leaves a rough, abrasive feel in the mouth from the tannins that have been extracted from the skins and seeds. All wine needs a period of "aging" to allow these unpleasant side effects of fermentation to dissipate or at least to have their rough edges smoothed over. Most wines, both red and white, are meant to be consumed young and therefore need only a brief period of aging at the winery. A few of the finest wines, however, develop more complex flavors and more appealing texture when they are aged for many months, and sometimes years, in cellars at the winery. Many of these wines mature first in barrels, then in bottles.

At the winery, white wine is frequently aged for a few months in stainless steel tanks before it is bottled. The resulting wine will, ideally, taste as crisp and bright as a fresh apple or pear. Some fine white wines, especially those made from Chardonnay, are matured in small oak barrels. The oak can add complex and appealing nuances, often likened to the flavor of vanilla, as well as a weightier body. Too much oak, on the other hand, can completely dominate the flavor of the fruit; among the disparaging terms for overoaked wine are "oak tea," "splinter soup," and "plonk de plank."

Premium wines, both white and red, are often left to age for a brief period "sur lie," or on the lees. Lees are sediments, including dead yeast cells and fragments of seed, pulp, or skin, that settle on the bottom of the fermentation barrel or tank. Aging on the lees also adds richness and depth of taste to the wine. When the wine has been removed from the lees, the solid matter left behind is sometimes returned to the vineyard to add organic substances to the soil.

Red wine may be aged from a few weeks to three years or more before bottling. Longer maturing usually takes place in oak barrels, also called "barriques." The barriques favored by the majority of winemakers today hold about 225 liters, or 60 gallons. This follows the example set in Burgundy and Bordeaux. Aging in oak helps to soften and round out the harsh tannins in red wine. The oak also imparts certain desirable flavors to wine that remind people of vanilla, various spices, or toasted bread. Since contact with oak barrels also improves a wine's ability to age, most of the fine wines that are kept in a cellar for several years to mellow and to mature have usually spent some time in oak barrels.

Some winemakers like to use new oak barrels, which impart a stronger "oakey" flavor. After three or four years, they may sell their barrels to other vintners, who prefer the subtler flavors imparted by older, seasoned oak and who also may prefer to buy less expensive used barrels — pricey new oak barrels add a tremendous amount to a winery's overall budget.

Owner Jennifer McCloud in the barrel room at Chrysalis Vineyards in Virginia.

Marguerite Thomas

Classic barriques are usually made from French oak, but many wine-makers are turning to American oak. There are various arguments on each side of the issue, ranging from "American oak is better for American wine" to "American oak is too tannic" or "too sappy." American oak, incidentally, is widely used in the viticultural regions of South America, Australia, and Spain, where its somewhat more aggressive flavor may be counteracted by the potent wines from these warm countries. One of the principal virtues of American oak is that it is much less expensive than French oak barrels, costing half as much on average. In the past few years, the quality of the best American oak barrels has greatly improved thanks to several factors, such as air versus kiln drying.

An alternative to expensive oak barrels is the use of oak chips — little nuggets of wood that are usually added to wine during fermentation to impart some of the desirable characteristics provided by oak barrels. While oak chips may be useful in inexpensive wines, they will never convey the same subtlety and complexity as oak barrels and are more likely to add a klunky, rather than refined, note to the wine.

First-time visitors to the cellar where barrels are stored are sometimes surprised to hear people talking about toast — light toast, medium toast, heavy toast. No, these folks aren't describing breakfast, they're referring to the process in barrel making when the cooper places a barrel over a source of heat that chars the wood inside to a lesser or greater degree. In addition to adding important flavor components to the finished wine, the toasting forms a barrier between the liquid and the wood that helps protect the wine from the oak's tannins.

Clarifying the wine: Because wine is usually left with a certain amount of sediment after maturing, various methods have been employed over the ages to remove it. This is known as "clarifying" or "fining" the wine. One of the oldest techniques, and one still commonly used, is the application of beaten egg whites, which attracts particles suspended in the wine. Other methods for fining wine include the addition of gelatin or various kinds of clay, such as bentonite.

Filtering: Before bottling, most wines are passed through a filter to remove any remaining particles. But many winemakers, and consumers as well, object to rigorous clarification and filtration of wine, claiming that these procedures can strip wine of some of its character and complexity. American consumers have been accused of demanding a squeaky-clean product — a beautifully transparent wine, but one perhaps lacking some of its personality. The trend today at many high-end wineries is to move away from fining and filtration.

Sulfites: Unless it has been pasteurized, wine continues to evolve even after it has been bottled as tannins, pigments, alcohols, and certain microscopic elements act, react, combine, and interact with the wine itself. Sulfur-based compounds have been used in winemaking since antiquity to protect and to preserve the wine. Sulfite, which includes various compounds of sulfur, notably sulfur dioxide (SO_2), is the chemical traditionally used to keep wine stable. It is a sterilizing agent, usually added during the bottling process, to protect wine against harmful bacteria and spoilage. Although regulations permit adding up to 220 parts per million of sulfite to wine, most wineries today rely on only 40 to 60 parts per million, and sometimes much less. It is virtually impossible to make drinkable wine on a commercial scale without adding sulfites (because sulfur is considered a "natural" product, wines labeled "organic" may have been treated with sulfur). For that matter, since SO_2 is one of the natural by-products of fermenting grapes, wine, like bread dough, contains certain sulfites inherently.

Bottles and bottle stoppers: Many wineries have their own automated bottling line, while others usually rely on mobile bottling lines set up in a truck that drives to different wine regions during bottling season. Once the wine is in a bottle, it must be sealed with a stopper of some sort, then a foil placed over that. Today, the "foil" is just as apt to be made of plastic as metal. Alternatively, some wine producers seal their corks with wax rather than with a foil.

Cork, the most commonly used wine bottle closure, is a very touchy topic in wineries these days because of a cork taint that damages wine. Though not harmful to humans, corkiness, as the problem is known, gives the wine an extremely off-putting aroma often compared to the smell of wet cardboard. Corked wines appear randomly, affecting anywhere from one to five percent of all bottles of wine, though seldom turning up in more that one bottle at a time. It is rare, for example, to find more than a single corked bottle in a case, but because that bottle of wine is rendered virtually useless, complaints from consumers and restaurateurs have motivated vintners to seek alternative closures for their wine bottles. Ersatz corks made of plastic compounds have gained considerable favor, though there is still some controversy about their ability over the long haul to fully protect the wine. Screw caps, believe it or not, are becoming more widely accepted among winemakers, who seem to think they are a cheap and efficient way to protect wine from outside air. New Zealand vintners, in particular, have been leading the charge in this direction. It remains to be seen, however, how readily consumers will accept this unorthodox method of stoppering a bottle of wine.

WHEN IS A WINE READY TO DRINK?

Numerous factors determine when a wine is ready to drink: the type of wine, the year the grapes were grown, the vintner's skills, and even the storage conditions. Most white wines and Rosés are ready to drink as soon as they are purchased. A year or two after they have been released from the winery, they may become oxidized, acquiring a brownish tint and a tired flavor vaguely resembling sherry. A few of the best made, oak-aged white wines (especially Chardonnay and Riesling) may gain richness and intensity of flavor over a period of a few years. Some of the greatest whites are still good after 10 years or more, but these are exceptions.

Red wines vary even more in their ability to improve with age. Most Eastern American reds are best consumed as soon as the winery releases them, or at least within a couple of years of their release, for they are unlikely to improve significantly (if at all) over the years. But a few wines, like certain people, get better as they get older, improving in complexity and depth of character after 10 or even 20 years. Merlot, Cabernet Sauvignon, and Bordeaux-style blends are most apt to mature well and, indeed, to improve with age.

In the Eastern states more than in temperate California, the climate of any given year will affect the outcome of the wine to a greater or lesser degree. Frost-kill during budbreak, for example, can significantly decrease grape production, while cool, rainy days around harvest time can limit the fruit's sugar production. Long stretches of warm summer days and cool evenings promote grapes with a good sugar/acid ratio, while too much rain at the wrong time can lead to watered down, flabby flavors.

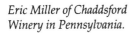
Eric Miller of Chaddsford Winery in Pennsylvania.

Courtesy Chaddsford Vineyards

In the Northeastern viticultural regions particularly, summers are sometimes too cool and short for many grape varieties to ripen properly. Pinot Noir, for example, may perform beautifully in good years, but fail to ripen when conditions are unfavorable. This is where winemaking skills are important. In bad years, vintners must decide whether to produce the wine, perhaps under a second, less expensive label; to sell the crop to another, less demanding, winery; or simply to write it off as a loss. "Vintage conditions put the house to the test," observes Chaddsford Winery's Eric Miller. "In trying times, a house should never relinquish responsibility to excellence."

TASTING WINE IN A WINERY

Most wineries have a tasting room, where visitors are invited to sample the wines. There is usually no fee for tasting, although a few wineries have begun to charge a modest amount, usually a couple of dollars, for this age-old tradition. By contrast, in California's Napa Valley, it is rare, if not impossible, to find a tasting room that does not charge a fee, and the price for wine tasting is creeping ever-upward. Tasting room fees have come into play for two principal reasons: the first is to cut the winery's losses, which becomes a more compelling incentive for wineries as increasing numbers of thirsty visitors flood into the tasting rooms; the second is to discourage visitors from drinking too much before getting back into their cars. But even when visitors have to pay a nominal fee, visiting a winery's tasting room enables them to try the wines of a given region without making a heavy capital investment.

Courtesy Barboursville Vineyards

Barboursville Vineyards, one of Virginia's pioneering wineries, is part of a 900-acre estate.

While every vintner entertains the fond hope that tasters will become buyers, there is little pressure to buy in the tasting room. After all, it is in a winery owner's best interest to acquaint as many people as possible with the product he or she is selling. In actuality, most visitors do end up buying at least a bottle or two if they like what they've sampled. All things considered, it makes good business sense for a winery to introduce people, especially those who are unfamiliar with wine, to the pleasures of drinking it. Sampling a variety of selections at different wineries is one way for consumers to learn more about wine, while at the same time allowing the vintner to discover the kind of wine their customers like best.

Tasting at a winery used to involve standing around a chilly wine cellar that was undecorated, except for the barrels of wine, a dim light bulb, and the winemaker, who would dribble wine into glasses that might or might not have been rinsed out that day. A few châteaux in France and Italy are still like this, but in America, winery owners sometimes invest in a glitzy tasting room as soon as they plant their vines.

Winery and tasting room architecture has come a long way in the past couple of decades. On Long Island, for example, the first wineries were most often remodeled potato sheds. Today, new owners, with more money, are either revamping original wineries (Bedell Cellars) or establishing palatial new structures (Raphael and Macari).

Souvenir T-shirt from Chaddsford Winery.

Marguerite Thomas

Some tasting rooms still consist of not much more than a simple counter in a corner of the winery, while others are stylish enough to grace the pages of architectural magazines. One thing that almost all tasting rooms have in common, however, is a gift shop. Even the most modest winery today is bound to have a few corkscrews and T-shirts for sale, while the more ambitious ones will offer an astonishing array of preserves, crackers, grape seed oil, and other food products, as well as jewelry, posters, books, glassware, banners, caps, and sweatshirts. While much of this merchandise is fairly mundane, some gift shops have made a concerted effort to stock crafts and artwork that are truly out of the ordinary. ("Do you know how much money I make off of this cash cow?" one winery owner asked me, gazing around his well-stocked gift shop as he rubbed his hands in glee. I won't even repeat the astounding figure he whispered in my ear, for you'd never believe it.)

Behind the bar in the tasting room stands a person who knows something about the wines being poured. The best thing that can happen is that the winemaker will be on duty pouring, although as wineries become bigger and more successful, this is increasingly less apt to occur. In some of the larger wineries, there may be a young "intern" pouring for you who can rattle off a series of memorized facts, but who won't necessarily be able to help much with detailed questions. But never mind — you're here to taste the wine. Here's how to do it.

Selecting the wines to taste: Tasting wine and drinking wine are two different activities — the former is a somewhat unnatural imitation of the latter. One thing that differentiates the two is that in most wine-drinking situations, such as a dinner party, one generally consumes only one, or perhaps a couple of different wines. In an average tasting room, the selection may range from six to 12, or even more wines.

For those interested in sampling an entire range of wine, the general rule of thumb is to start dry and finish sweet. In other words, begin with the simplest, driest white wine, moving on to more complex whites that have, perhaps, been aged in oak. Then it's on to light- and medium-bodied reds, finishing with the fullest, most complex red wines. If the winery makes dessert wines, try these at the very end of the tasting.

Another difference between tasting and drinking is that wine is meant to go with food. In a tasting room, there is rarely any food, except perhaps a dish of bread chunks or crackers. (Please note: These are not intended as hors d'oeuvres — they're for cleansing the palate between wines.) Food consumed with wine inevitably changes the flavor of the wine — almost always for the better — and by the same token, food usually tastes better with wine. For this reason, when I'm tasting wines, I like to try to imagine what food might taste good with each individual wine.

Looking at the wine: Several character traits can be revealed by taking a moment to study the wine in the glass. For example, one of the first things people may notice is a film of clear liquid on the glass just above the wine, forming droplets that trickle down the sides of the glass back into the wine. One explanation I've been given to explain this occurrence, known as "tears," or "legs," is not related to viscosity or to glycerol as is commonly assumed; rather, it is a complicated phenomenon having to do with tensions between liquid and glass and with the evaporation of alcohol from water. I confess that this concept is too technical for me to truly grasp, but one thing I do know is that the presence of "legs" indicates that the wine has a fairly high level of alcohol — at least 12 percent.

To really see the color of a wine, it helps to look at it against a white or light-colored surface (holding it up to a window or other source of direct light actually makes it more difficult to "read" the color). Tipping the glass at a slight angle reveals a concentration of color around the edge. Certain grape varieties produce lighter or darker colored wines. Pinot Noir, for example, is usually a much lighter colored wine than, say, Cabernet Sauvignon.

Color indicates something about a wine's age. Young white wines, for example, are usually pale yellow, often deepening in color as they age. Full-bodied whites, especially those that have been aged in oak, tend to take on a rich, golden color. A brownish tinge in white wine is a warning sign: Just as oxidation turns a cut apple brown, it will also cause white wine to discolor, indicating that the wine is too old.

Unlike white wines, reds *lose* color intensity as they age. A young red wine is usually a masterpiece of dense, purplish colors that evolve into translucent hues of ruby or garnet over time. With further aging, the density of color fades in red wine. Older wines are often a transparent brick red. They may have brownish tones around the edges, which isn't necessarily a sign of trouble, but may indicate instead that the wine has matured into a fine, mellow vintage that is ready to be savored.

Sniff and swirl, winemaker Eric Fry of Lenz Winery, Long Island, New York, tastes his wine.

Marguerite Thomas

Smelling the wine: Experienced wine tasters swirl their glass and sniff, swirl again and sniff, sniff and swirl. This may strike the uninitiated as obsessive behavior, but aroma can reveal far more than taste alone. Swirling air through the wine by rotating the glass in gentle circles coats the edges of the glass with wine and fans the perfumes up toward the top (to prevent wine from sloshing over the side, glasses should never be filled more than half way). After swirling the wine, some tasters plunge their entire nose over the rim of the glass to inhale the released scents; others dip one nostril at a time over the glass, or pass the glass back and forth under their nose. Whatever technique is used, the goal is to get a good sense of the wine's aroma.

Most of what we call "taste" is really smell, which is why food tastes so bland when we have a cold. Taste buds can actually perceive only four or five different sensations, notably sweet, bitter, salty, and sour. The nose, on the other hand, is a magnificent organ capable of detecting at least 10,000 different aromas. One of the body's most important receivers of pleasurable sensations, the nose can tell us, among other things, whether the wine is young or old; young wines tend to have a simple fruity smell, while mature vintages will develop more complex aromas.

Experienced wine drinkers recognize and describe the nuances of aroma in a wine by using terms used to describe similar odors. White wines, for example, may exude aromas that resemble those of pineapple, mango, melon, and other tropical fruits, or even butterscotch and caramel. The typical odor of Sauvignon Blanc is said to be "herbaceous" or "grassy." Some white wines, particularly Riesling, may smell like flowers, and a fine Riesling sometimes also has a distinctive, oily odor described as "petrol." When a wine gives off only a very faint aroma, or none at all, it is said to be "closed," or going through a "dumb" phase. Sometimes a closed wine will open up and exude an aroma after a few moments in the glass.

Red wine may resemble any number of red fruits aromatically, including cherries and various berries. It may smell like roses, violets, or certain trees, such as cedar or eucalyptus. An earthy odor, resembling mushrooms or wet leaves, might also be detected. A whiff of black pepper can often be picked up in red wine, also licorice, mint, smoke, or tobacco aromas. Certain vegetable smells are often associated with red wine — green peppers or beets, for example. Many tasters claim that fine red wines give off hints of cheese rinds or the oft-cited "barnyard smell." While many of these descriptions may not sound appealing — and overbearing doses of any one of them would be considered a flaw — they are part of the overall subtle, evocative appeal of wine.

A myriad of aromas are found in the best wines, released by a swirl of the glass the way a gust of wind sends forth the full fragrance of an apple tree in blossom. The better the wine, the more layers of half-hidden perfume are there awaiting discovery. Beginning tasters usually wonder what the fuss is all about. "It just smells like wine," they'll shrug. But those who persist soon discover that although it takes both experience and concentration before one begins to recognize and to identify a variety of aromas in wine, this is all part of the fun and the challenge of wine tasting.

Of course, we shouldn't overlook the fact that sometimes one encounters an unpleasant or "off" smell in the wineglass. Two of the most easily recognizable of these are "corkiness" — the problem discussed above where the wine smells like wet cardboard, indicating a cork has been contaminated — and sulfur. The presence of sulfur is readily identifiable as the wine smells like hard-boiled eggs, or like burnt matches. Hints of sulfur often dissipate after a few moments, while a "corked" wine never recovers and will inevitably get worse the longer the wine is exposed to air.

Tasting: Having gained an impression of the wine through its appearance and aroma, the time has finally come to taste it. The standard procedure is to take a sip, allowing the wine to sit a moment or two on the tongue while the taste buds do their job of sorting out sweetness, acidity, astringency, bitterness, and tannin. The mouth evaluates whether the wine feels thin, or if it has viscosity or "body." There may be the sensation of a slight spritziness (an indication that a little carbon dioxide still remains in the wine). The sum of these impressions is known as "mouth feel."

At this point, some tasters swish the wine around in their mouth vigorously. They may "chew" the wine or aerate it by carefully (sometimes noisily) inhaling air through their mouth to stimulate the interaction of taste buds and wine. These activities send aromas to the brain via the olfactory receivers, and perceptions from both the mouth and nose are synthesized into the sensation we call "taste."

Most experienced wine tasters spit each wine out after "mouthing" it. While novices find this a bizarre and unappetizing practice, its advantage for the professional wine taster, or for anyone else who plans to taste many different wines in one day, is obvious. And remember, especially if you're driving: All those little sips do add up. It has become common practice in wine regions where many wineries are clustered together — the Finger Lakes, for example, and Long Island — for wine tasters to hire a car or limo to transport them from tasting room to tasting room. The presence of these vehicles has become an accepted part of the wine country landscape.

What are some of the impressions one might expect to get from all the sniffing, swirling, and sipping? While each winery produces wine with its own distinctive characteristics, certain generalizations might be made in identifying wines from the Eastern states. First, it is important to remember that this is mostly a cool-weather growing region. The wines, therefore, will be typically crisp and lively rather than rich and opulent, except, perhaps, when they come from some of the warmer areas, such as Virginia, or from an unusually warm-weather vintage.

Eastern wine tends to be delicate and subtle, rather than bold and overbearing. It may not be as intensely colored as wine made from warmweather grapes. Because of the cool weather and shorter growing season, Eastern wines may be relatively high in acidity, which when balanced with other flavor components, such as fruitiness or tannins, makes them a good match for food. Thanks to this hint of acidity, many of the slightly sweeter wines are clean tasting rather than cloying, which also makes for an appealing accompaniment to food. The best Eastern late-harvest wines and eiswein-style wines — those made from grapes that have a high concentration of sugar either because they have been picked after fully ripening or because they have been frozen — can be nice after-dinner sipping wines. These are excellent whether on their own or with dessert.

The attentive consumer will soon discover that wine from the Eastern states, like all good wine, can be as mysterious, elusive, and multifaceted as fine poetry.

WHERE TO BUY EASTERN WINES

Almost half of the wine produced in the East is still purchased right at the individual winery. As I travel around the various wine regions in the East, I am sometimes reminded of France, where Parisian, Italian, German, and English customers make annual pilgrimages to Bordeaux or Burgundy or to Alsace or Provence, with the specific goal of buying wine. Some of these customers visit a variety of wineries every year to taste and to compare the new vintages, while others head straight for their favorite winery, whether it is a renowned château or an obscure country wine cellar. The goal, for all, is the same: to load up the back of the car with enough cases of wine to last until they return again the following year.

In the Eastern United States, similar rituals occur. Some loyal consumers come to stock up at their local winery because they like driving out into the countryside, tasting a variety of wines right where they were made, and chatting with the winemaker about that particular vintage. In short, they like the personal contact. Many folks travel to wineries simply because a particular wine that has captured their fancy is available only at the winery, or because they live in a state that prohibits the shipping of wine.

Evidence that East Coast wines have reached maturity is that many of the wines have finally become available in select retail stores, both locally but also in major metropolitan centers, such as Boston, New York, and Washington, D.C. Call the individual wineries to find out where their wines might be available in your locale, or find out if you live in a state where wine can be shipped directly to you from the winery.

BIBLIOGRAPHY

Adams, Leon D. *The Wines of America*. NY: McGraw-Hill, 1985.

Beltrami, Edward J., and Philip F. Palmedo. *The Wines of Long Island — Birth of a Region*. Great Falls, VA: Waterline Books, 1993.

Borello, Joe. *Wineries of the Great Lakes*. Lapeer, MI: Raptor Press, 1995.

Brenner, Leslie. *Fear of Wine: An Introductory Guide to the Grape*. New York, Toronto, and London: Bantam Books, 1995.

Lee, Hilde Gabriel, and Allan E. Lee. *Virginia Wine Country Revisited*. Charlottesville, VA: Hildesigns Press, 1994.

Lukacs, Paul. *American Vintage: The Rise of American Wine*. Boston & New York: Houghton Mifflin Co., 2000.

Martell, Alan R., and Alton Long. *The Wines and Wineries of the Hudson River Valley*. Woodstock, VT: Countryman Press, 1995.

McCarthy, Edward, and Mary Ewing Mulligan. *Wine for Dummies*. Boston: IDG Books, Worldwide, Inc., 1995.

Robinson, Jancis. *The Oxford Companion to Wine*. New York: Oxford University Press, 1999.

Wiener, Susan. *Finger Lakes Wineries*. Ithaca, NY: McBooks Press, 1992.

Index

Treleaven Wines, 84–85

U
Unionville Vineyards, 99–100
Uplands region, xxi

V
Valhalla Vineyards, 147–48
veraison, 169–70
Veraisons at Glenora Wine Cellars, 159
Vidal Blanc, 7
Villa Appalaccia, 148
vinifera (grapes), 5–10
Viognier, 132–33
Virginia: coastal wineries, 120–22;
    mountain wineries, 140–50;
    northern & central wineries,
    122–40; restaurants and lodging,
    161–66; state support for wine
    industry, 126–27; touring, 151–52;
    wines, wine regions, xviii, xxi,
    117–20; winemakers and
    winemaking, 141–42
viticulture. *See* winemaking
Vitis varieties, 5–10

W
Wagner Vineyards, 75–76; Ginny Lee
    Café at, 156

Westport Rivers Vineyard & Winery,
    18–20
White Hall Vineyards, 148–50
Wiemer, Hermann J., 76–77
Williamsburg Winery, 121–22
wine regions, overview, xvii–xxi
wine: making of, 1–5, 168–76; marketing
    of, 10–11; readiness to drink,
    176–77; shipping, direct, 9–10;
    tasting, xxi–xxii, 178–85; where to
    buy, 285
wineries: Connecticut, Coastal, 14–18;
    Finger Lakes Region (NY), 61–89;
    Hudson River Valley (NY), 90–92;
    Long Island (NY), 31–56; Maryland,
    xvii–xviii, 111–15; Massachusetts,
    18–20; New Jersey, xvii, 97–106;
    Pennsylvania, xvii, 107–11; Rhode
    Island, 21–24; tasting rooms,
    178–80; Virginia, xviii, 120–50
Wintergreen Vineyards & Winery, 150
Wolf, Tony, 127
Wölffer Estate, 54–56

Z
Zoecklein, Bruce, 126–27

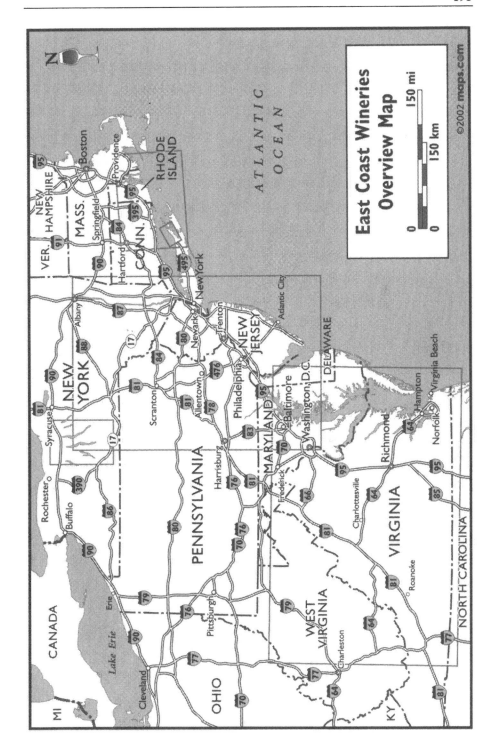

East Coast Wineries
Overview Map

©2002 maps.com

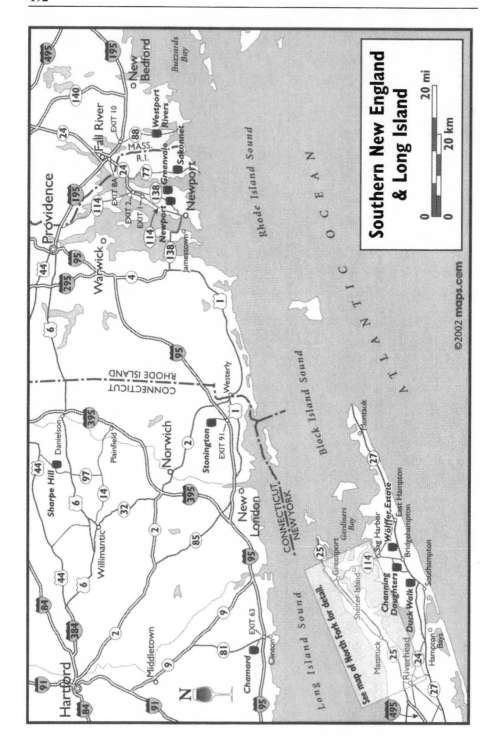

Southern New England
& Long Island

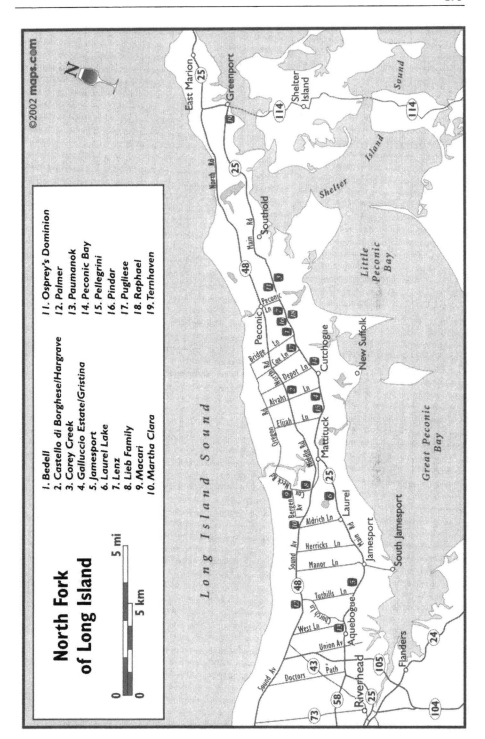

©2002 maps.com

N

**North Fork
of Long Island**

0 ——————— 5 mi

0 ——————— 5 km

1. Bedell
2. Castello di Borghese/Hargrave
3. Corey Creek
4. Galluccio Estate/Gristina
5. Jamesport
6. Laurel Lake
7. Lenz
8. Lieb Family
9. Macari
10. Martha Clara

11. Osprey's Dominion
12. Palmer
13. Paumanok
14. Peconic Bay
15. Pellegrini
16. Pindar
17. Pugliese
18. Raphael
19. Ternhaven

East Marion
25
Greenport
73
114
Shelter Island
114
Sound
North Rd
25
Southold
Main Rd
Shelter Island
48
Peconic
Peconic Ln
Little Peconic Bay
Bridge Rd
North Rd
Cox Ln
Cutchogue
Depot Ln
New Suffolk
Alvahs Ln
Elijah Ln
Mattituck
Oregon Rd
Wick Rd
Middle Rd
Great Peconic Bay
25
Laurel
6
Bergen Av
Aldrich Ln
Long Island Sound
Herricks Ln
Main Rd
Jamesport
Manor Ln
Sound Av
South Jamesport
48
Tuthills Ln
Church Ln
Aquebogue
West Ln
Union Av
Flanders
24
Sound Av
43
Path
Doctors
105
Riverhead
58
25
104
73

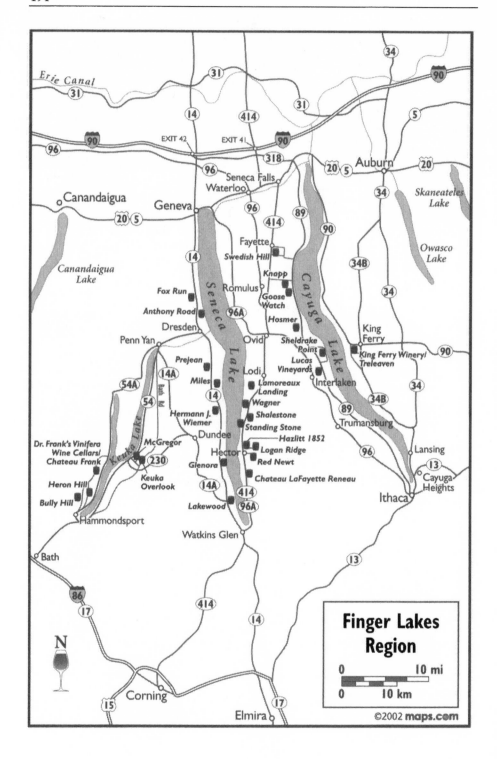

Finger Lakes
Region

0 _____ 10 mi

0 _____ 10 km

©2002 **maps.com**

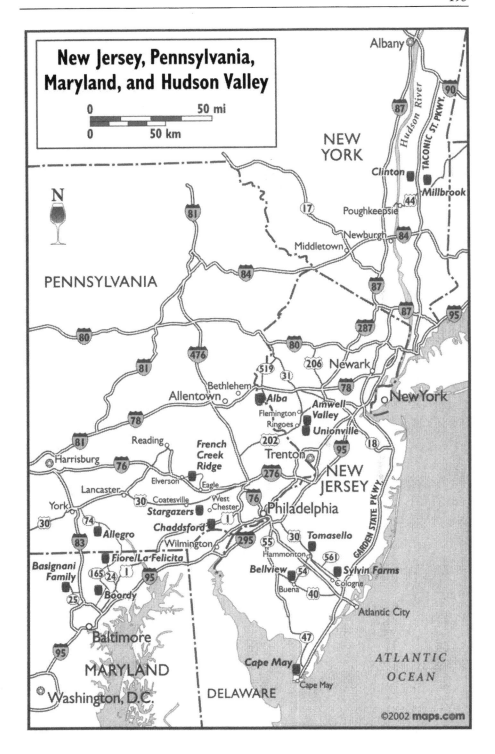

New Jersey, Pennsylvania, Maryland, and Hudson Valley

0   50 mi
0   50 km

N

NEW YORK

Albany

Hudson River

TACONIC ST. PKWY.

90

87

Clinton

44   Millbrook

17   Poughkeepsie

Newburgh   84

Middletown

81

PENNSYLVANIA

84

87

87

95

287

80

80

476

519   31   206   Newark

81

Bethlehem

Allentown   Alba

Flemington   Amwell Valley

78

Ringoes

Unionville

Reading

French Creek Ridge

202

Trenton

95

18

NEW YORK

78

Harrisburg

76

Elverson   Eagle

Lancaster

York

30   Coatesville

Stargazers

West Chester

276

76

NEW JERSEY

Philadelphia

GARDEN STATE PKWY.

30

74

Allegro

Chaddsford

Wilmington

295   55

30   Tomasello

83

Basignani Family

165   24

Fiore/La Felicita

95

Hammonton

561

Bellview   54

Sylvin Farms

Boordy

Buena   40   Cologne

25

Atlantic City

95

Baltimore

47

MARYLAND

Cape May

ATLANTIC OCEAN

Washington, D.C.

DELAWARE

Cape May

©2002 maps.com

196

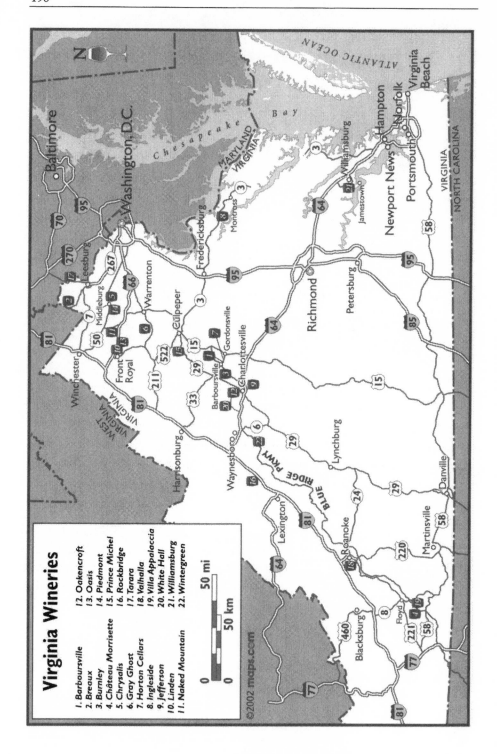

Virginia Wineries

1. Barboursville
2. Breaux
3. Burnley
4. Château Morrisette
5. Chrysalis
6. Gray Ghost
7. Horton Cellars
8. Ingleside
9. Jefferson
10. Linden
11. Naked Mountain
12. Oakencroft
13. Oasis
14. Piedmont
15. Prince Michel
16. Rockbridge
17. Tarara
18. Valhalla
19. Villa Appalaccia
20. White Hall
21. Williamsburg
22. Wintergreen

50 mi

50 km

©2002 maps.com

About the Author

Jeanne Milligan

Born in California and raised in France, *Wine News* travel editor Marguerite Thomas began her research on Eastern wines with great skepticism. *If this wine is so good, why haven't we heard of it before?* Berkshire House was so pleased with her research that we devoted an entire **Great Destinations**' title to her findings! And, we are pleased to report, Thomas's enthusiasm for these wines keeps growing.

In addition to her work with *Wine News*, Thomas regularly contributes to the *Los Angeles Times* syndicate and *Saveur* and *Santé* magazines. In addition, she writes about food, wine, travel, and people for a variety of publications, including *National Geographic Traveler* and *Travel Holiday*. Thomas also is the author of an acclaimed cookbook, *The Elegant Peasant*. She now makes her home in Baltimore and New York City.

Made in the USA
Columbia, SC
01 December 2018